RECAPTURING MARXISM

RECAPTURING MARXISM
An Appraisal of Recent Trends in Sociological Theory

Edited by
Rhonda F. Levine and Jerry Lembcke

PRAEGER

New York
Westport, Connecticut
London

Library of Congress Cataloging-in-Publication Data

Recapturing Marxism.
    1. Sociology—Methodology. 2. Marxian school of
sociology. I. Levine, Rhonda F. II. Lembcke, Jerry,
1943-
HM24.R39   1987   301'.1   87-11589
ISBN 0-275-92576-5 (alk. paper)
ISBN 0-275-92638-9 (pbk. : alk. paper)

Library of Congress Catalog Card Number: 87-11589
ISBN: 0-275-92576-5
ISBN: 0-275-92638-9 (paperback)

First published in 1987

Praeger Publishers, 1 Madison Avenue, New York, NY 10010
A division of Greenwood Press, Inc.

Printed in the United States of America

The paper used in this book complies with the Permanent
Paper Standard issued by the National Information Standards
Organization (Z39.48-1984).

10   9   8   7   6   5   4   3   2   1

Contents

Preface

In an unpublished paper written shortly before his death, Al Szymanski wrote, "The future prospects for a rebirth of . . . imaginative Marxist theory are thus great. . . . As difficult as it might be in the absence of significant mass movements when we are facing strong counter currents wherever we turn . . . we must keep the seed grain from rotting." Al Szymanski's persistence in the attempt not only to keep Marxism alive, but to further the Marxian project within U.S. social science, was an inspiration to many of us.

The present book was originally envisioned by Al Szymanski and is intended to provide a general critique of the state of sociology in the 1980s. Szymanski's untimely death left the manuscript unfinished. The selection of essays presented in this volume reflects the spirit of Szymanski's concern for the direction of Marxist sociology in the 1980s and his commitment, shared by the editors, to advance the application of Marxist theory to contemporary concerns. More likely than not, Szymanski would have had some disagreements with issues raised in the essays that follow. But no doubt he would have welcomed the arena for continued debate in areas such as class analysis, liberation movements, race and class, and large-scale social change—specifically the transition to socialism.

As a teacher, colleague, friend, and comrade, Al Szymanski left a legacy of commitment and dedication to applying Marxist theory to concrete circumstances. Through his prolific writings, his role in the creation and continued production of *The Insurgent Sociologist*, his teaching efforts—both in the classroom and at the *Insurgent* table at ASA meetings—Al Szymanski played a central role in radicalizing U.S. sociology. His professional and academic work, however, did not take Szymanski away from political activism. Al Szymanski never faltered in combining a Marxist theoretical framework with political action. No one could ever accuse Szymanski of being an armchair Marxist. It is to this memory of Al Szymanski that we dedicate this book.

Acknowledgments

Jerry Lembcke wishes to thank Patricia Bauer, Chris Gamsky, June Woods, and the Lawrence University faculty research grant program for supporting the preparation of material in this volume.

Rhonda Levine wishes to thank Thelma Mayer and Margaret Abbot for help in the preparation of material in this volume.

Introduction: Marxism, Neo-Marxism, and U.S. Sociology

Rhonda F. Levine and Jerry Lembcke

In the lead article of this volume, Al Szymanski argues that Marxist theoretical work goes through cycles. Marxism is energized by the growth of revolutionary movements when theorists are integrated with the practical work of social change. These periods of revitalization in Marxist theory are followed by periods of crisis. As the gains of the movements for social change are consolidated, theorists become separated from these movements. Although their "verbal discourse" continues for a time to be "one of orthodox Marxism, the substance of that discourse, as reflected in the real meaning of words and theories, undergoes a fundamental transformation in the direction of idealism, eclecticism, voluntarism, subjectivism, democracy, reformism, and evolutionary politics."

This collection of essays is offered with the recognition that Marxist theory in the United States is now on the down-side of the cycle described by Szymanski. While the discourse of radical sociology has become increasingly "Marxian," the content of that discourse has moved away from a Marxism that is primarily concerned with analyzing vehicles for large-scale social change. This appropriation of Marxist categories has been the means by which a new cohort of sociologists has been able to ride the crest of theoretical insurgency generated during the early 1970s into the establishment ranks of professional sociology.

Marxist analysis has been more prevalent within U.S. sociology than any other social science discipline. The American Sociological

1

Association (ASA) is the only academic professional organization that has a formally established Marxist section. Moreover, articles published in professional journals, such as *The American Sociological Review*, *The American Journal of Sociology*, and the special issue of *The American Journal of Sociology* devoted to recent works in Marxist sociology, illustrate the flourishing of Marxist analysis within the profession. The fact that Marxist sociology has developed despite the absence in the United States of a Marxist intellectual tradition makes the phenomenon interesting in and of itself. Yet it is the direction taken by Marxist sociology during the 1980s that proves most interesting.

FROM SOCIOLOGY LIBERATION MOVEMENT
TO MARXIST SECTION

The formation of the Sociology Liberation Movement at the 1968 annual meetings of the ASA signified the growing presence of radical sociologists within the U.S. sociological enterprise. Young sociologists who were involved in the campus activities at Berkeley and Columbia and the larger struggles encapsulated within the student movement and the anti-war movement formed the Sociology Liberation Movement. The formation of the movement signaled the independence of a radical sociology from the mainstream, widely-held structural-functionalist analyses represented in the professional journals of the time. The Sociology Liberation Movement was organized on the assumption that a radical sociology was needed to address the social and political issues of the day. This radical sociology was to be built on a class analysis and develop theoretical guidance for political practice. In 1968 the Sociology Liberation Movement provided the forum to develop a sociology that would not be prone to what was thought to be the "trivial and obscure undertakings upon which professional sociology was built . . . " (*Insurgent Sociologist* 1977, p. 2). In essence the Sociology Liberation Movement was a separatist movement and, as such, developed outside of the American Sociological Association.

In 1969 the Sociology Liberation Movement became the Union of Radical Sociologists. The movement for a radical sociology established counter meetings to the official ASA format, established its own journal, *The Insurgent Sociologist*, and formed organizations such as the Union of Marxist Social Scientists and the East Coast Conference of Socialist Sociologists. *The Insurgent Sociologist* began as a newsletter and was printed at Washington University, St. Louis. The purges at St. Louis compelled *The Insurgent Sociologist* to relocate at Rutgers in 1971. In the same year at the ASA annual meetings, the Union of Radical Sociologists disbanded and the Radical Caucus within the ASA was formed on an ad hoc basis. In 1972 *The Insurgent Sociologist* began publishing as a journal and was housed at the University of Oregon in Eugene.

The period between 1972 and 1976 witnessed an intellectual growth of radical sociology that was developing a theoretical identity with Marxism. *The Insurgent Sociologist* mirrored this development by publishing Marxist scholarly work in a variety of substantive areas. In its early stages, radical sociology was represented within only a few sociology graduate programs throughout the United States. However, as a Marxist sociology began to develop, Marxist scholars became more legitimate and acceptable within the U.S. sociological profession and few sociology departments were without their Marxist, however token he or she might have been. In March 1975 the Council of the American Sociological Association verified receipt of sufficient signatures on a petition calling for the establishment of a section of Marxist sociology. In 1976 Marxist sociology became part of the ASA. By September 1986 the Marxist section of the ASA had about 406 dues-paying members (a decline from 561 members in November 1979) and was the 13th largest of 25 sections (a change from being the seventh largest section in 1979).

Thus, Marxist sociology re-entered the mainstream of the profession and so began the process of professionalization of Marxist analysis. The Vietnam War, and the social and political struggles associated with the time, ended and a separatist sociology was no longer necessary or desirable. Young sociologists who were so central to the formation of a radical sociology and the formation of a distinctly Marxist perspective within the U.S. sociological profession were soon to approach the critical tenure stage of their careers. With the tenuring of Marxist sociologists throughout U.S. universities and the teaching of Marxism in graduate and undergraduate sociology programs, Marxism has become one of many legitimate perspectives within the discipline.

But legitimation, as we know, often comes at a high price. The claim that Marxism has become legitimized is also a claim that there is a new, Marxian establishment in sociology. A network analysis of Marxist sociology might link a core group of individuals whose work is widely acclaimed as Marxist through editorial power over professional journals, positions within the established professional organizations, affiliations with sociology departments that dominate the profession, and an informal social network that merges professional and radical identities. Such intellectual cross-dressing could lead one to suppose that professional sociology and Marxism have become one, but a closer look at the actual content of the work leads us to consider the likelihood that Marxism has been co-opted by the profession and is doing as much to revitalize the mainstream of the discipline as it is to inform movements for social change.

FROM MARXISM TO NEO-MARXISM

The growth and legitimacy of Marxism within the U.S. sociological profession has developed along with a growing differentiation within U.S. Marxist sociology. This differentiation follows along the lines of substantive areas within sociology as well as theoretical and methodological divisions. Sociologists, for example, have provided Marxist analyses of education, criminology, social psychology, urbanization, medical sociology, the family, sex and gender roles, race and ethnicity, work, social stratification, social movements, politics, and the like, grounding theoretical assumptions on a wide variety of Marx's insights (ranging from the concept of alienation found in the early Marx to the concept of exploitation found in the late Marx) and employing a variety of methodological approaches and techniques (ranging from qualitative, to historical, to quantitative methods of social research). Application of Marxist analysis to the various sociological problems led to a reinterpretation of Marx, and to the recognition of the lacuna in Marx's own theoretical scheme for examining certain areas of social life. Just as the New Left distinguished itself from the Old Left, a growing number of sociologists wanted to distinguish their work from the overly economic deterministic tendencies of the work of previous generations of Marxist intellectuals. It was only a matter of time before Marxism within U.S. sociology would be known as neo-Marxism, and not only distinguishable from orthodox Marxism, but from a Marxism that has strategic relevance for social transformations. In the process, the holistic and dialectical properties of Marxist methodology were lost, and basic Marxist concepts like class and exploitation were either discarded or reinterpreted (see Chapters 1 and 9 by Szymanski, and Chapter 2 by Meiksins). Such analyses began building on increasingly reductionist models borrowed from Weberian sociology having little strategic relevance not only for understanding the mechanisms of capitalism and all its exploitative and oppressive aspects, but perhaps more importantly, for unraveling and discovering the mechanisms for social transformation from capitalism to socialism. The trajectories of world systems analysis, state theory, and domestic urban and labor studies are but a few examples of the transformation of Marxism into a U.S. version of neo-Marxism.

The formative years of Marxist sociology within the U.S. sociological profession were dominated by scholarly work in areas of the sociology of development and imperialism. The intellectual interest in these substantive areas arose from the political involvement of young Marxist sociologists of the time. The field of sociology of development clearly was advanced by the work of Marxists, and the analysis of underdevelopment and Third World liberation movements matured through the careful analysis based on a Marxist critique of capitalist development. In time, the sociology of development and imperialism was theoretically advanced by Marxist analysis of production relations on a world scale and class formation in the peripheral zones of the world economy. However, as Marxist class analysis based on production relations began to have an impact on the sociology of development, Weberian sociological analysis began to have its impact on the sociology of development. And so developed world systems analysis. Whereas classical Marxist approaches to the study of the Third World were based on class relations, world systems analysis began to focus on exchange relations and market relations. When criticized for ignoring accumulation, world systems analysis developed to include an analysis of accumulation, but the framework became further and further removed from the basic tenets of historical materialism. The defining characteristic of capitalism as a world system is not, as Marxists have argued, a system based on relations of exploitation, but rather is a system based on ceaseless accumulation. This ceaseless accumulation is made possible by the rational decisions made by accumulators (entrepreneurs) and corresponding household structures that ensure the reproduction of the divisions between accumulators and direct producers. On a world scale, then, the drive for ceaseless accumulation results in an unequal distribution of consumption. Political struggles arise over the issue of distribution. Accumulators are able to overcome obstacles in one zone of the world economy because accumulation may continue in other zones that have a cheaper supply of direct producers. The cheaper supply of direct producers available to accumulators is a direct result of the creation and reproduction of certain household structures that are either more or less dependent on the wage of the direct producers for their well-being (Wallerstein 1982, pp. 7–54).

In brief, the refinement of world systems analysis has moved further away from a Marxist vantage point and closer and closer to a Weberian notion of "economy" and "society." Often identified as neo-Marxist because of the language of the concepts as opposed to the conceptual content, world systems analysis leaves us with a problematic conclusion concerning the mechanisms for change (see Chapter 5). Whereas Marxism has identified the historical agency for change within the working class, world systems analysis not only does not identify the agency for change, save for passing references to "anti-systemic" movements, but makes no attempt to arrive at a strategy for change. Rather, in a way similar to the Weberian problematic, according to this analysis social action will occur in the social/cultural sphere, but in whose interest and toward what end is uncertain.

The growth of Marxist sociology in the United States also coincided with a renewed intellectual interest in the study of the state apparatus in the advanced capitalist world. Internationally, debates on the state have focused on the relationship between the state apparatus and the process of capitalist development. While the literature on this debate has been substantial, U.S. contributions to it have not. In his excellent review of postwar Marxist analyses of the state, Bob Jessop (1982) states,

> I deliberately ignore American contributions to the analysis of the state. Most of these [U.S.] theories are heavily imbued with instrumentalism and/or adopt crude forms of reductionism and thus merit no more inclusion than their European counterparts. Those few analyses that escape this criticism generally owe so much to other European approaches considered here and/or bear such marked similarities to them that a separate review is not required. More generally it would be an interesting exercise to consider how far the absence of a well-developed 'state tradition' in Britain and the USA and the corresponding dominance of liberal, pluralist conceptions of government and citizenship has led to the extraordinary weakness of Marxist theories of the state in these countries.

Theda Skocpol's review essay on neo-Marxist theories of the state and her critique of the various theories as applied to the New Deal provides probably the best example of the Weberianization of Marxist analysis within U.S. sociology. Although it is unclear that one can situate Skocpol within the Marxist tradition, her work does point to the problems of those sociologists who distance themselves from a specifically class analysis of politics and the state in the United States

(Skocpol 1980). To begin with, Skocpol criticizes Marxist structuralists for reducing state activity to class relations and class struggles. Correctly criticizing many Marxists and neo-Marxists for failing to consider the specificity of U.S. party and state structures, Skocpol centers her analysis on the structural organization of the state. As such, she conceptualizes the state as independent from the social relations of production and proceeds to analyze the specificity of the structure of the state without theoretically deriving the state in the first place. By calling for a more complete analysis of particular state structures and party organizations, Skocpol's state-centered theory proceeds to reduce the state to an independent organization with its own interests and an internal structure that is independent from the mode of production. Skocpol seems to suggest that "independent" refers to unimpeded voluntary activity engaged in by state officials. However, just as capitalists at the point of production, for example, cannot impose with impunity their class program on the working class, state officials and politicians cannot impose their policies independent of ongoing processes of social reproduction and transformation. When viewed in this light, state-centered theory dissolves into a form of macro-pluralism. Moreover, such a theoretical analysis of the state and party organizations as "organizations of specifically political domination, organizations with their own structures, their own histories, and their own patterns of conflict and impact upon class relations and economic development" (Skocpol 1980, p. 199) leads to a mistaken interpretation of the New Deal period and presents problems for understanding the present conjuncture (see Chapter 4 for an extended critique of state-centered theory).

The influence of Weberian sociology is also evident in recent studies of labor and urban social change. Labor studies during the last decade have been dominated by two developments: the influence of social history and the concern with control of the labor process. Heavily influenced by the British Marxist historians, U.S. historians Herbert Gutman, David Montgomery, and a group of younger New Left historians centered around the journal *Radical America* launched an attack in the early 1970s on the dominant historiographical paradigm of institutionalism. The attack was made at two levels. First was the preoccupation of the institutionalists with trade unions as a focus for working-class historical experience. This focus, argued the new social historians, had made organizations the object of study while writing rank-and-file workers out of history.

Second, the attack on institutionalism served, euphemistically, to revive the tradition of anarcho-syndicalism within the U.S. left and to restore a mode of analysis consistent with Weberian sociology. The New Left historians argued that institutions, such as unions and political parties, were per se prone to conservatism and that organizations like the Communist party, which had emphasized the building of union and party organizations, had retarded the development of the U.S. working class. The new social historians drew upon the work of critical theorists, social psychologists, and anthropologists to focus analyses on the problems of class consciousness, mass movements, spontaneous worker rebellions, and the anarcho-syndicalist traditions in U.S. labor history.

The limitations of the new radical history all but disqualified its proponents from studying the period most relevant to contemporary activists—the 1930s and 1940s. By the mid-1930s the locus of class struggle had shifted away from consciousness formation at the experiential, shop-floor level. The *decisive* struggles of the period took place on a plane where organizational mediations held sway and physical compulsion was the ultimate arbiter; the struggle for leadership and control in organizations such as unions and political parties was the key to the resolutions of the period's struggles. Moreover, the most important and progressive activists of the period were Communist party members, a fact very difficult for the New Left historians to treat objectively. As a result, the new social history has remained in relatively safe water and has been of little use to activists.

The second influence on labor studies came from the labor process literature that followed in the wake of Harry Braverman's *Labor and Monopoly Capital*. The labor process analysts argued that with the erosion of individual craftspersons' control of the production process, the capacity for resistance of the working *class* was also eroded. Thus, proletarianization, which Marx and Engels saw as a contradictory process that enhanced class capacity while diminishing individual autonomy over production, is a one-way street that has no dialectical properties. As Lembcke argues in Chapter 3, a methodological implication of the theory is that class capacity becomes an aggregate of individual capacities rather than something *sui generis* with a dialectical relation to the autonomy of individual members of the class. The focus of analysis in these studies consequently shifts from the level of *class* properties to levels of individual power in the work place and to studies of consciousness. The political implication of the labor process trend has been to supplant the working class as the agent of social change in advanced capitalism with the petty bourgeois and middle class. Consistent with the Weberian tradition and pluralist sociology, intellectuals, union bureaucrats, politicians, urban planners, technicians, and even managers are more likely than workers to reform, if not transform, capitalism.

Urban theory has gone through similar cycles. After a revival of the Marxist tradition during the 1970s, erstwhile Marxists now declare the death of Marxist urbanology (Szelenyi 1986) and present themselves as what Richard Peet in Chapter 7 calls a "neo-Marxist-Social Democratic-neo-Liberal 'left'." Marching under the banner of "economic democracy," this group has produced what Peet calls "a stream of post-Marxists, each more abstruse than the last." The group theorizes not about the problem of transforming capitalist social relations but about moderating and managing capitalism's excesses. By combining models of mixed economies (borrowed from social democratic traditions) with models of producer co-ops and worker-owned factories (borrowed from the syndicalist tradition), the economic democracy group seeks a more perfect world without breaking with the basic logic of a market economy. The social base of the economic democracy strategy is an amalgamation of elected officials, policy planners, and co-op activists; in class terms, it is purely middle-class–based with unions and especially union members playing an ancillary role.

CONCLUSION

Unlike Europe, where a Marxist intellectual tradition developed as part of the communist and socialist movements, Marxism in the United States developed primarily within the academic discipline of sociology. Sociology, maturing after the bourgeois revolutions in Europe and before the proletarian revolution in Russia, took as its primary concern the conditions of the lower classes and strata. Sociologists, however, did not develop their theories of capitalist society and strategies for socialist movements from experiences with working-class struggles as Marx and Engels did. Rather,

> classical sociologists worked out their theory of the social determination of human behavior from their own quite different experiences of capitalist society and its problems and contradictions. This too was largely a critical experience of capitalism, and experience of crisis—but one undergone by intellectuals who were not related to the working class. On the contrary, they looked at the working class and the problems posed by it from the point of view of bourgeois society [Therborn 1976, p. 241].

The decline of a Marxist analysis that has strategic relevance within sociology can only be understood in relationship to the current political climate. It can be argued safely that in the United States no great breakthrough has been made in Marxist theory since the mid-1970s, to say nothing at all of the lack of any new strategy for social transformation. The social movements of the late 1960s and 1970s had produced a generation of sociologists in the United States who did have an impact on the discipline (see, for example, Chapter 6) and began what appeared to be the development of a distinctly Marxist sociology. However, those sociologists who remained active in political work soon found great difficulty in maintaining academic posts (see Chapter 8) since Marxist analysis generally had not been evaluated favorably by those in positions to grant contract renewals and tenure. With the development of a more professionally acceptable neo-Marxism, moreover, the support of even supposed fellow travelers has become problematic.

Without linkages to the working class and concrete political struggles to focus their work, radical intellectuals were "free" to develop their critique within the generalized bourgeois world view and also "free" to develop theory that had little relevance to political strategy. Instead of speaking to the concrete needs of liberation struggles, neo-Marxist work tends to fall into the purview of national politics, as traditionally defined by mainstream academics. In short, the Marxist sociology that we know today has developed primarily out of graduate departments; since the late 1970s it has not been political experience that led sociologists to their theoretical positions, but rather it is their theoretical positions that have led them to certain political conclusions.

Interventions into a wide range of social change situations during the 1980s have been informed mainly by theory coming out of a neo-Marxist/neo-Weberian trend, and those interventions have been on the most part failures. But as Lembcke (1984) wrote in his critique of the Youngstown, Ohio plant closure movement, the real tragedy is the failure to learn from past mistakes. Millions of people are suffering in the current crisis of capitalism. At a comparable distance into the depression period of the 1930s, Communist organizers were already mobilizing thousands of people in the streets, effectively fighting evictions, and playing a major role in organizing the unorganized. Viewed as its counterpart, the meager accomplishments of the U.S. left in a wide range of struggles are embarrassing. Yet, no one has adequately summarized that experience and drawn the conclusion that what is wrong is the entire set of assumptions about class politics in the United States. Until those conclusions are drawn and the struggle to redirect left politics is begun, the suffering will continue and the spectre of right-wing forces able to manipulate the discontented will loom larger.

Few would deny that we are currently living in a political climate that is defined by a new cold war. Within academic circles, we are beginning to see the right-wing attack on Marxist intellectuals. Moreover, the mass media has now defined anything "terrorist" or "evil" in the world as being "Marxist." And in the academy itself, sociologists are moving away theoretically from Marx, and in an often arrogant fashion are emphasizing the failure of classical Marxism to explain contemporary events (see, for example, Aronowitz 1981). Instead of moving to redefine the theory within the framework of historical materialism with its central focus on relations of production and reliance on the working class as the historical agency for socialist transitions, many of these sociologists have returned to their Weberian classics and no longer even speak of late capitalism, but rather of post-capitalist or post-industrial society.

The recent trends within "Marxist" sociology with its side-tracking of some basic elements of Marxist theory and methodology is bound to have little, if any, strategic influence. Yet, as McNall writes in Chapter 10, the analytical tools of Marxism have much to offer to our understanding not only of past and present conditions but of the mechanisms for large-scale social change. The articles that follow, while each reaching its own particular conclusions about a range of recent work in sociological theory, share a basic point of view—the importance of linking social theory to political strategy. Through these articles we hope to provide an arena for continued debate in areas such as class analysis, social movements, race and ethnicity, and large-scale social transformation. For it is only through continual debate, combined with active involvement in concrete struggles, that the promise of Marxism can be recaptured.

REFERENCES

Aronowitz, Stanley. 1981. *The Crisis of Historical Materialism*. New York: Praeger.

Insurgent Sociologist. 1977. "Editorial" 7, 1 (Winter).

Jessop, Bob. 1982. *The Capitalist State*. New York: New York University Press.

Lembcke, Jerry. 1984. "The Fight Against Shutdowns: Youngstown Steel Mills Closings." *Antipode* (Fall).

Skocpol, Theda. 1980. "Political Response to Capitalist Crisis: Neo-Marxist Theories of the State and the New Deal." *Politics and Society* 10, 2.

Szelenyi, Ivan. 1986. "The Last Frontier of the Marxist Urban Sociologist?"

Contemporary Sociology 15, 5 (September).

Therborn, Goran. 1976. *Science, Class, and Society.* London: New Left Books.

Wallerstein, Immanuel. 1982. "Crisis as Transition." In *Dynamics of Global Crisis,* by Amin, Arrighi, Gunder Frank, and Wallerstein. New York: Monthly Review Press.

1

Crisis and Vitalization: An Interpretive Essay on Marxist Theory

Albert Szymanski

It is the thesis of this paper that the development of Marxist theory from Marx's and Engels' earliest works to today can best be understood as: (1) a series of periods in which the theory's interaction with revolutionary movements has led it to be formulated; and (2) a series of cycles that have reflected an oscillation between orthodox categories and open and eclectic formulations. That is, the long-term development of Marxism can be roughly modeled as a helix, rather than a static system, linear trend, or back-and-forth movement between the same two poles.

The common contemporary characterization of Marxist theory as in crisis must be understood in terms of both of these long-term developmental trends. Neither the worth of Marxist concepts and theories nor the real need for reformulation can be adequately grasped without a proper historical understanding of the theory's origins, relevance, and potential for future change. Above all, the development of Marxist theory must be understood as a product of the mass movements that have been the primary "carriers" of Marxism since the mid-nineteenth century. These mass movements rise and decline in response to the contradictions of capitalist society.

This article originally appeared in *Science & Society* 49, 3 (Fall 1985):315–31, under the title, "Crisis and Vitalization in Marxist Theory," and is reprinted with permission of the publisher.

Therefore, Marxist theory is both energized and deenergized, as well as forced specifically to confront the particular nature of each revolutionary conjuncture. This discipline can be expected to reoccur for as long as mass movements pulsate and respond to the particular contradictions of the societies of which they are a part.

The development of Marxist theory has not occurred in a mechanical fashion according to any inherent logic. Its growth rather has been at root a response to the sentiments and concerns of its adherents. In periods of deeply felt social and political crisis, orthodox revolutionary notions have credence. In periods of stability and prosperity, open eclectic formulations have made more sense. In times when the movements of industrial workers in the West have been on center stage, formulations of mainstream Marxism reflect the problems of such movements. In times when the movements of peasants, or the struggle between states with different social systems have been on center stage, reformulations of Marxism have reflected the particularities of this reality. In short, Marxism is neither a stable dogma nor a manifestation of a long-term linear force. Its development, rather, is at core and in the last instance a manifestation of the historically specific pulse of the societies in which it occurs.

Like any other system of ideas, Marxism has been a product of the social and political currents of its time. And, like other systems, once formulated it can have, and of course has had, great effect on historical development. This paper will first discuss the cyclical oscillations of the center of gravity of Marxist theory, then discuss the secular trends that correspond to the particular problems posed by each period in its development.

THE CYCLICAL ASPECT OF MARXIST THEORETICAL DEVELOPMENT

The development of Marxist theory perhaps can be seen as repeating a basic cycle of four phases: (1) a period of energization or impetus; (2) a period of formation/reassertion of revolutionary and materialist theory; (3) a period of the watering down of revolutionary formulations; and (4) a period of the predominance of explicit "revisionism."

Phase I: This is the time of a rapid growth of revolutionary movements provoked by a crisis in society. Such movements are categorized by a "storm the heavens" mentality, high levels of enthusiasm, idealism, and the belief that qualitative changes can occur through active intervention. Everything is possible. During this phase systematic theory normally is little developed or at least not generally accepted. Moralism and naiveté typically predominate. In this period the energy is generated to create or elaborate a theory of society, crisis, struggle, and transformation that can: (a) explain the causes of peoples' unhappiness, and (b) guide social change. The drive to develop or renovate theory at this stage becomes most pronounced after the first wave of enthusiasm fails to realize the anticipated results, and as a consequence, more materialist explanations are sought.

Phase II: In this period the seminal theoretical works, often written as pamphlets, polemics, or manifestos in Phase I, are developed and elaborated, usually by young activist leaders of the early period, into comprehensive theoretical and empirical works encompassing the earlier experience. This is the time of the highest level of integration of revolutionary theory and practice. The mass movements initiated in the earlier phase still have most of their energy and enthusiasm. But now it has been disciplined by organization and guided by theory. At other times revolutionary theory seems to be hollow and irrelevant to mass movements.

Nevertheless, the fact that theorists now have the time to work out elaborate analyses reflects the fact that the underlying social crisis is easing and the enthusiasm of the masses is slowly (or in some cases because of violent repression, not so slowly) fading. It is during this period that the prevailing discourse is one of class analysis, mode of production, revolution, dictatorship of the proletariat, vanguard party, historical materialism, science, political economy, dialectics, contradictions, discipline—that is, the classical categories of orthodox historical materialism prevail. Such Marxist classics as *Capital* (Marx 1867), *Anti-Dühring* (Engels 1878), *Imperialism* (Lenin 1916), *State and Revolution* (Lenin 1917), *History and Class Consciousness* (Lukacs 1923), *The Prison Notebooks* (Gramsci 1929–1935), *The Accumulation of Capital* (Luxemburg 1913), *The History of the Bolshevik Revolution* (Trotsky 1932), *One Dimensional Man* (Marcuse 1964), *Monopoly Capital* (Baran and Sweezy 1966), *Classes in Contemporary Capitalism* (Poulantzas 1974) were written in such periods. In some cases publication occurs with a considerable delay; for example, Marcuse and Baran and Sweezy's 1960s works had been germinating for 25 years.

Phase III: During this period the disjunction between theory (revolutionary) and practice (reformist) that began to appear toward the end of Phase II becomes dominant. While the intellectuals, theorists, and leaders formed in the revolutionary upheavals of Phase

I continue to produce the newspapers, articles, and so forth that set the intellectual tone of left discourse, the practice of mass movements is now clearly reformist in orientation, reflecting the prevailing noncrisis atmosphere of relative prosperity, peace, and lack of repression.

In this period the verbal discourse is still one of orthodox Marxism, but the substance of that discourse, as reflected in the real meanings of words and theories, undergoes a fundamental transformation in the direction of idealism, eclecticism, voluntarism, subjectivism, democracy, reformism, and evolutionary politics. Emphasis increasingly is on gradualism, openness, downplaying of the role of the working class, culture, individualism, lack of discipline, *even* while orthodox language and mode of argument is still current. For example, idealism would be expressed as "ideas are material force." Quotations from Marx and Lenin are used to show that the level of discipline and unity in a party should be low; that women, ethnic minorities, or the middle class are as central as the working class in the axis of political movement; that class analysis is only part of the truth; that Marx was in favor of freedom of the press, and was above all a good democrat, and so forth.

In this period Marxism loses its edge (reflecting the loss of revolutionary energy and will to storm the heavens) characteristic of the early period. But theorists continue to give lip service to what is becoming a hypocritical and increasingly transparent enterprise. Perhaps the most well-known practitioner of this approach was Karl Kautsky. Perhaps this was also true of most of the mass Communist parties of the advanced capitalist countries and those intellectuals on their periphery in the late 1950s and the 1960s.

Phase IV: The transition from Phase III to Phase IV is the period of true crisis in Marxist theory. On the one hand, it is apparent to large numbers of those who have been schooled in Marxist orthodoxy that their concepts and discourse now have little relevance to contemporary political reality. Historical materialism is rejected. Large numbers of open, nondogmatic, and usually younger intellectuals rediscover a wide range of perspectives that had long ago been dismissed as well as develop new syntheses of other orientations with remnants of Marxist ideas. Democracy, idealism, and individualism are in the air. The crisis in Marxist theory is intensely felt. All is open for reexamination. A creative wind sweeps away all dogma. As the increasingly artificial enterprise of the previous period collapses, the unity of theory and practice is restored, now around an explicitly reformist practice and revisionist theory.

The minority who persists in adhering to orthodox categories in spite of the withering of the mass movements that had once made them vital adopts a siege mentality. The issue of why no revolution and what accounts for the fading of the mass movement becomes central. Various factions and sects blame insufficient revolutionary analysis, leadership, or organization for the failure. Here there is sectarian squabbling rather than fundamental reexamination of categories.

The cost of maintaining a revolutionary materialist analysis is the crystallization of the disjunction between critical theory and practice. The corollary of this disjunction is dogmatism (the assertion of theory in the absence of relevant practice), sectarianism (the incessant squabbling about theory without the discipline of practice and mass movements to resolve issues), and practical irrelevance (as the leadership of mass movements largely passes to those with revisionist theory). Revolutionary materialism, now encased in a hard shell, has rigidified. But irrelevance nevertheless keeps alive the seeds of what once was a vital, creative, and powerful force.

During this period the strength of the success at leading mass movements (a good practical sense for how to advance reforms) is precisely its weakness (the absence of critical understanding and the loss of imagination). Likewise its theoretical weakness is precisely its strength (theory does not get in the way of the practical pursuit of short-term gains). Exactly the contrary is true of the now sectarian revolutionary Marxism. Its weakness (relative lack of integration into popular massive movements) allows it to preserve its strength (critical categories, a long-term vision with few illusions about the nature of capitalism and imperialism) unencumbered by trying to win elections or attempting maximum short-run growth. Likewise, its strength is its weakness. Its long-term and critical vision encased in a dogmatic shell inspires few workers, while sectarian disputes about the causes of the failure of revolution to materialize and of the various Marxist grouplets to grow disillusions even many of the remnants of the hard core.

Edward Bernstein (1899) was the first to formulate the basic principles of the fourth phase within the Marxist tradition. His book could have been written in the late 1920s, in the late 1950s, or in the late 1970s (and in essence was by others). Its arguments make sense both to those leading mass movements and to intellectuals in times of prosperity, peace, and stability. It is equally true, however, that in times of mass revolutionary energy and surges of imagination the book has appeared as a parody, for example, in 1919, 1945, and

1969, since it is now so out of phase with the experience of the mass movements and left intelligentsia. How quickly the wheel turns.

Bernstein (1899) laid out, in language that today sounds fully contemporary, virtually all of the basic ideas that again and again in Phase IV of the cycle of Marxist theory become predominant. Bernstein (1899, p. xxiv) argued that capitalism has become a permanently stable system and that no great future crisis is to be expected. This is a claim that rings true in 1900, 1928, 1960, or 1978, but that is discordant in 1918, 1933, 1945, or 1968 (and which has relatively little resonance with the experience of the less-developed capitalist countries at any point in the twentieth century).

> In all advanced countries we see the privileges of the capitalist bourgeoisie yielding step by step to democratic organizations . . . a social reaction has set in against the exploiting tendencies of capital [Bernstein 1899, p. xxv].

> As soon as a nation has attained a position where the rights of the propertied minority have ceased to be a serious obstacle to social progress, where the negative tasks of political action are less pressing than the positive, then the appeal to a revolution by force becomes a meaningless phrase [Bernstein 1899, p. 218].

While fitting the experience of most workers and intellectuals in Western Europe and the United States immediately prior to World War I, as well as in the latter part of the 1920s, the 1950s, and the 1970s, such claims in the Europe of the 1930s, or in most of the less-developed countries of the world for the last 100 years, have little resonance.

Bernstein was the first to celebrate abstract democracy and freedom in counterdistinction to the orthodox Marxist emphasis on the dictatorship of the proletariat within the Marxist tradition (Bernstein 1899, pp. 143–46). His arguments could equally well have appeared in 1925, the 1950s, or the late 1970s. Bernstein's claims in Germany in the 1933–45 period, or for that matter in almost all of Europe in the late 1930s, as well as in the majority of all capitalist countries today, could only bring sardonic laughter.

Bernstein (1899, pp. 28–40) also made a strong case against the labor theory of value, historical materialism (pp. 6–18), class analysis (pp. 18–28), and the leading role of the working class (pp. 54–73 and esp. p. 221). Indeed virtually all the basic arguments of the reformists and progressives of the 1980s were more or less fully developed in 1899, and are reasserted again in the late 1920s as well as in the 1950s and early 1960s. Just as Bernstein's argument has rung true among open-minded intellectuals in so many earlier periods, it has often been periodically swept aside by revolutionary waves of energy and imagination.

Just as Bernstein's book has been republished to find a new mass audience, and/or been written again by others in the periods in which it is appropriate, so too the basic revolutionary works of Marx and Engels, whether in their original authorship, or as written again by others. Lenin, for example, wrote for a second time the basic position of Marx and Engels on the state in his booklet *State and Revolution* (1917). The basic theses of both were reasserted for the third time in numerous pamphlets published by the various Communist parties in the 1940s. Once again they were written in the late 1960s and early 1970s, for example, Poulantzas (1968)—this last in a version appropriate for contemporary intellectual discourse.

When Bernstein's discourse is current, the discourse of Engels and Lenin, the 1940s Communist parties', or Poulantzas' on the state are dismissed as dogmatism or Stalinism (Jessop 1982); just as in the period immediately following social crisis the discourse of Bernstein and democratic reformism is dismissed as superficial. In some ways the same books are written, confined to the mice, and eventually rediscovered again (and again).

The development of the New Left over the 1960s was a classic illustration of the cyclical process. Largely evolving out of the social democratic tradition (in the United States out of the Socialist party-related League for Industrial Democracy), with little or no influence from the Marxist tradition, the discourse of the mainstream of the student movement changed from that of "democracy" in the first half of the 1960s to that of revolutionary Marxism by the end of that decade (see Students for a Democratic Society's *Port Huron Statement* and *America and the New Era*). While such terms as "imperialism," "capitalism," "revolutions," "working class," were scoffed at in the early 1960s because of their dogmatic, sectarian, and inappropriate air, after 1966 they very rapidly became central. The revolutionary youth movement regenerated a revolutionary language that now seemed quite appropriate. The liberal rhetoric of the early 1960s in fact was now laughed at and discredited by the mainstream of the New Left, just as the use of SDS rhetoric of 1970 came to be by Western intellectuals in the 1980s. Indeed by 1980 things had once again turned full circle from where they were a decade before. Bernstein's ideas now resonate (once again).

THE SECULAR ASPECT OF
MARXIST THEORETICAL DEVELOPMENT

In addition to its cyclical oscillation between orthodoxy and reformism, Marxist theory has developed in response to the particular problems faced by popular movements during each revolutionary upsurge since 1848. Marxist theory can thus be categorized in terms of five (or five and a half) periods, each of which experienced a cycle of the type described above. These periods (roughly) classified by their beginning revolutionary upsurge are 1843-49, 1864-71 (the half period), 1884-1906, 1917-21, 1935-49, and 1967-70. (The timing of these periods is, not surprising, somewhat different in different parts of the world capitalist system, as all movements do not peak precisely at the same time.) The distinctive problems faced by the popular movements that reflect the primary contradictions of each of these conjunctures have left their mark on the development of Marxist theory.

In some ways the cyclical aspect of Marxist theory (or at least the first three phases of the cycle) can be traced in the works of Marx and Engels themselves. Marxism originated in the 1840s in the seminal works of Marx and Engels, works that were mostly tempered in the emerging revolutionary movement in Germany that led up to the revolution of 1848-49. Their involvement in revolutionary activities as youth was the energy behind such earlier works as *The Economic and Philosophical Manuscripts* (Marx 1844), *The German Ideology* (Marx and Engels 1845), *On the Condition of the Working-Class in England* (Engels 1845), and the work that culminated this period, *The Communist Manifesto* (Marx and Engels 1849).

With the crushing of the revolutionary movement in 1849, Marx and Engels went into life-long exile. Marx retreated to the library of the British Museum where he spent the balance of the next 15 years. It was in these years—1850-65—that Marx did the bulk of the research and writing of his magnum opus, the various drafts of the volumes of what eventually began to be published as *Capital* in 1867. The principal impetus for this project was to give a scientific, and hence predictive, basis for the revolutionary working-class movement. Marx was driven to understand what had precipitated the revolutions of 1848 and to predict both the return of revolutionary crises and the potential course of such future revolutions (so that revolutionaries could more effectively act to ensure their success).

In this period of latency of the revolutionary movement, the predominant theoretical ideas soon became those of reformism, for example, the notions of Lassalle became predominant in the German working-class movement, while trade unionism replaced Chartism in the United Kingdom. The post-1849 period was, in fact, a period of peace, prosperity, and gradual formal democratization of society (as exemplified in the expansion of the franchise and the growth of social welfare and popular education). It is then no surprise that reformist rather than revolutionary ideas came to predominate in the reemerging mass movements. Nor is it a surprise that Marx and Engels persisted in their revolutionary materialism in relative isolation.

Over the course of the last half of the 1860s, culminating in the events of 1871 in Paris, there was a revival of working-class radicalism. The First International Working Men's Association within which Marx became active was organized to assist the working-class movement in different countries in 1864. But the violent suppression of the Paris Commune in 1871 and its repressive reverberations around the world cut short this incipient rebirth of the radical working-class movement. After 1871 Marx once again returned to his desk to spend the rest of his life primarily on his theoretical work.

Engels, however, who outlived Marx by 12 years, from the mid-1880s came to play a central role in the emerging mass revolutionary working-class movements. The Second International Working Men's Association was formed in 1889. The German Social Democratic party was legalized in 1890 and adopted a fully Marxist program at its Erfurt Conference in 1891. Marxism soon became the predominant working-class political perspective throughout most of Europe.

This was a period of rapid industrial growth and militant class conflict, as well as the period of the 1905 Revolution (which gave impetus to both Bolshevik formulations in the Russian Empire and to a reassertion of Luxemburg's revolutionary analysis in Germany). This period saw perhaps the most violent class conflict in U.S. history, witnessing many militant and violent strikes, as well as the founding of the Industrial Workers of the World (1905). It also gave birth to the American Socialist party (1901) which grew rapidly in membership until reaching its peak in 1912. In Britain the Labour party became a major party. In Germany the Social Democrats increased their vote until they became the largest party in the Reich. In France this was a time of militant strikes and the rapid growth of the multitendency radical left.

In this period, as in the previous waves of working-class upheavals, the development of Marxist theory occurred *outside* universities. Marxist theory throughout the nineteenth and early twentieth centuries (in fact, for the most part until after World War II) was developed by those organically involved with mass movements (in Gramsci's term, by organic intellectuals). Engels, of course, was at the center of the emerging Marxist movement. Luxemburg was a leader of the German and Polish Social Democrats. Lenin was central in the Bolshevik faction. In terms of milieu, emotional attachments, and monetary support, the leading theorists of this second revolutionary wave were attached to the class movement whose indigenous ideology they expressed.

The handful of academic radicals (mostly progressives and populists) such as Thorstein Veblen, Charles Beard, and Scott Nearing in the United States, and J. A. Hobson in the United Kingdom, suffered persecution for their convictions, especially during the period of reaction during and immediately following World War I, when the movements that they reflected were repressed.

Since the German movement was the most massive, it first became sensitive to the pressures toward reform. Thus, it was in Germany that the first historical "crisis" in Marxist theory developed. Bernstein's *Evolutionary Socialism* appeared in 1899 and revisionism thereafter grew in strength. Although energized by the 1905 events in the East, the revolutionary politics of Luxemburg lost ground as the German reality seemed ever more remote from the violent class conflict perspective she articulated, until in the 1914 vote for war credits for the German war effort only two Social Democratic party (SPD) representatives voted with her faction.

As the massive militant working-class thrust of 1885–1906 subsided in most Western countries, the massive Socialist parties they had created became increasingly reformist. For example, in the United States "Big Bill Haywood," the leader of the activist left of the Socialist party, was expelled in 1912 as part of the drive for respectability.

The first theoretical crisis of Marxism was manifest in polemics between such creative revolutionaries as Luxemburg, the verbally orthodox such as Kautsky, and explicit revisionists such as Bernstein. The whole world was watching. Similar currents were manifest elsewhere. In Russia there was a rift between the revolutionary and rather orthodox Bolsheviks (who, however, put more emphasis on will, discipline, and leadership than was traditional) and the reformist Mensheviks, which culminated in their formal 1912 split. Although, as their name indicates, a majority at the time of their formation in 1903, with the waning of the energizing experience of the 1905 revolution the Bolsheviks soon became a minority as relative prosperity gave credence to the Mensheviks. In the years immediately preceeding World War I the categories of revolutionary Marxism were everywhere ringing more hollow as the Bolsheviks in Russia and Luxemburg in Germany came to fight an increasingly defensive battle. Times, however, were about to change abruptly.

The third wave of massive revolutionary energy occurred in the wake of the crisis provoked by the war among the advanced capitalist countries (1914-18) in general and the aftermath of the Bolshevik Revolution in Russia in particular. The incredible destruction of human life and the extreme strains the war placed on the working class and peasantry throughout Europe resulted in a sudden end to prosperity and democratization, as well as to the optimistic illusions about capitalism. The militant left grew rapidly as disillusionment with the war spread and the economic contradictions of capital once again became manifest.

In face of the growing crisis in Russian society, the imaginative and inflammatory discourse of the Bolseviks now resonated with the sentiments of workers, peasants, and soldiers: Peace, Land, and Bread. All Power to the Soviets. A complete break with the past. The overthrow of the old ruling classes. Socialist Revolution. Such sentiments carried the day. Reformism was swept away by the revolutionary tide. Indeed, the Bolshevik Revolution marked a qualitative transformation of Marxist theory (as well as a reassertion of orthodox categories).

The revolutionary wave provoked by the World War and the Bolshevik Revolution subsided in the 1921-23 period, giving way to another period of peace and prosperity, and as a result the withering of revolutionary enthusiasm. As the Marxist cycle moved into the second phase, reformism seemed to make sense once again. However, the Bolshevik Revolution and the practical problems it faced reverberated among intellectuals around the world. As a result, the period of the mid- to late 1920s was the most creative since the time of Marx.

It was the revolutionary upsurge of 1917-21 that produced the works of Lukacs (especially *History and Class and Consciousness*), Gramsci, the early Karl Korsch, the early writing of the Critical Theory School, as well as the Marx-Freud synthesis of Wilhelm Reich. Lukacs and Gramsci, in fact, were consciously trying to articulate Leninism and the experience of the Bolshevik Revolution in Western Europe—thus the centrality of discipline, the party, revolutionary will, military and ideological hegemony, illegality, the seizure of power and so forth in their writings. It might be said that both were also translating Lenin so that intellectuals could understand him.

As the wave of the revolutionary crisis of 1917-21 finally broke among the intelligentsia in the late 1920s, Marxist theory went through its second historical crisis. Some theorists of the early period came to renounce revolutionary analysis as many now became embittered, while the new Communist movement became increasingly sectarian. Some moved first to experimental, eventually reformist, and finally uncritical perspectives (e.g., the critical theory tradition in Germany). Some went mad (e.g., Wilhelm Reich). Many others accepted the new orthodoxy of the increasingly disciplined Communist parties, suppressing their tendency to innovate in order to be part of the still rather significant mass political movements.

The predominance of reformist ideas in the 1920s and early 1930s gave way in the latter part of the 1930s and especially throughout the 1940s to a renewed wave of revolutionary mass energy. As a result, the popularity and influence of orthodox Marxism once again grew rapidly, both among working-class movements and intellectuals.

The Western country with the strongest Marxist traditions and movement was the first to witness the revitalization of Marxism corresponding to the rebirth of revolutionary mass movements—Germany in 1929-33. It was in this period that most of the best of the early essays of Fromm, Marcuse, Adorno, and Reich were written. It was this period as well which inspired later works such as Neumann's *Behemoth* (1944) and Marcuse's *Reason and Revolution* (1941). In fact, this period was echoed in the works of Marcuse not published until the 1950s and 1960s (as well as in the works of Paul Baran). The economic crisis of the 1930s soon gave birth to popular upsurges throughout the world and thus to a radicalization of the intelligentsia.

In Europe and much of Asia it was the immediate experience of the war against fascism, especially involvement in the resistance and in the ground swell of militance and imagination that immediately followed liberation, that more than anything else inspired a new generation of revolutionary intellectuals. In face of the discrediting of traditional liberal and conservative ideologies by the experience of fascism, many young intellectuals were ready to take Marxism seriously. All for a moment seemed possible. Imagination reigned among intellectuals and activists alike. For the first time Marxism became a major force in universities around the world.

A new generation of critical intellectuals, radicalized by the Great Depression and the following great democratic and socialist upsurge of the latter days of World War II and the immediate postwar period, briefly came to have major significance in U.S. academic life. Indeed this was the first period when there were more than a handful of pretty much isolated and idiosyncratic leftists in U.S. academia. This was the generation, not only of Seymour Martin Lipset, Nathan Glazer, Daniel Bell, et al., who moved toward liberalism in response to the waning of the popular movement and the serious intellectual repression (as well as academic rewards) of the 1950s, but also of C. Wright Mills. Mills who, counter to the intellectual current of his time, *continued* to move left, established for himself a unique position as an idiosyncratic critical intellectual whose works lived on to inspire the early stages of a rebirth of creative radical ideology in the 1960s.

The strong role the Communist parties played in this period as a result of the defeat of Germany by the Soviet Union and the leading role they played in the resistance in most countries (including China and Vietnam) temporarily gave these parties enormous prestige both among working people and intellectuals. This period has left a major theoretical legacy that is vital to this day.

The vitalization of Marxist theory in the wake of the upheavals of depression and war took the form of the assertion of the categories and theories developed within the Communist International over the last part of the 1920s and first half of the 1930s (largely presented in the documents of the Sixth and Seventh International Congresses of that organization held in 1928 and 1935, respectively). The principal concepts, other than the reassertion of the classical orthodox notions of class, class struggle, state, political economy, materialism, and dialectics, included the newer notions of the synthesis of nationalism with Marxism presented forcefully in Dimitrov's writings, and manifest in the practice of the popular fronts and especially in the success of the Communist parties in Yugoslavia, China, and Vietnam. Other major innovative contributions of this period included: (1) The idea of two stages to revolutions, and of four class alliances in achieving the first stage, where capitalism was not yet developed—a strategy that seemed to work well not only in China and Vietnam, but also in the extremely backward rural societies of Eastern Europe (e.g., Romania, Bulgaria, Poland, Hungary). (2) The new theory of imperialism, which became dominant in the Communist movement in 1928 and which argued that imperialism *underdeveloped*, rather than as Marx, Luxemburg, and Lenin had argued industrialized, the less-developed countries, came to flower in diverse manifestations both in Europe and throughout the less-developed countries. For example, one of its most influential descendants, dependency theory, captured the imagination of non-Marxist and Marxist intellectuals alike in

Latin America, Europe, and elsewhere. (3) The idea that centralized planning with heavy emphasis on industry was the most efficient and rapid path to modernization and increased living standards for the less-developed countries, that is, that the Soviet model of socialism showed the way for the poorer backward countries, not only of Central Europe, but also for China, Vietnam, and the rest of the less-developed countries. (4) The theory of popular (protracted guerrilla) war as a principal strategy for working people to seize power. The experience of guerrilla warfare of the anti-fascist resistance in Europe and East Asia, especially in Yugoslavia and Albania, and perhaps above all the experience of the Communist parties in China and Vietnam meant that in many circles protracted guerrilla warfare replaced the classical notions of insurrection and general strikes as the most commonly debated and discussed strategy for seizing power.

In the advanced countries, the idea of protracted war was supplemented by the willingness to carefully use parliamentary forms in the transformation of societies, for example, the idea of people's democracies in Eastern Europe, and the nonbloody (but armed) seizure of power in Czechoslovakia in 1948 after the resignation of the centrist ministers.

This period saw the reopening of the peasant question. While pre-World War II Marxism had a significant anti-peasant component, the events of popular war throughout Europe (especially in the east, e.g., Yugoslavia, Albania, Greece) and above all the revolutionary role of the Vietnamese and Chinese peasantries in East Asia, and the need to construct popular democracies in the new, largely rural, socialist countries, all refocused Marxist attention on the revolutionary potentialities of peasants.

Impetus was also given to the mode of production debate. Whereas other schools of orthodox Marxism generally either considered the whole world to be capitalist (or about to become so) or gave little attention at all to the less-developed countries, the Comintern in the 1920s and 1930s gave central attention to the question of modes of production in the less-developed countries. In fact, it worked out and periodically reworked an elaborate schema of tribal, feudal, semi-feudal, and capitalist formations with much attention given to the articulations among them. Indeed, the theory of two stages and four classes, as well as that of the peoples' democracies were integrally dependent on such analyses of articulated modes of production.

More than in any other period of revitalization of Marxist theory, the intellectual products of this period were, in Gramsci's term, a product of collective intellectuals. While before the war the debates within revolutionary Marxism could be clearly associated with individuals—Luxemburg, Plekanov, Kautsky, Lenin, Trotsky, Bukharin—after that period this is no longer the case. This reflects the fact that the distinctive ideas of this period were organizationally more related to the mass movements than has been the case in any other period *before or since*. It is now generally difficult to identify an individual Marxist as the primary source of a given idea or theory, even when an individual party leader's name (e.g., Stalin, Mao, Tito, Ho Chi Minh) may have appeared as the author of a given polemic, manifesto, or pamphlet.[1] It should be noted that the publicly expressed ideas attributed to such individuals change as a reflection of changing sentiments within parties. This indicates the collective nature of their production.

In fact, in the post-war generation (up to the birth of the New Left in the late 1960s), perhaps the most vital intellectual debates occurred among collective intellectuals and those close to them, as well as in the form of ex-adherents' criticisms of the leading collective intellectuals. This included the Trotskyist tradition, strong in England and in a few other countries, whose polemics with "Stalinism" focused attention on many key issues. The split between the Soviet Union and China after 1958 had a major resonance among European intellectuals such as Althusser, Bettleheim, and Poulantzas. In fact, it was a major inspiration for the opening of many new debates in Marxist theory such as the nature of the Soviet Union (and other socialist societies), revolutionary strategies (the role of the countryside, peasants, etc.), and the transition to socialism (especially inspired by the Cultural Revolution in China). The Cuban Revolution and the unique position it put forth through most of the 1960s (e.g., expressed in the works of Ernesto "Che" Guevara and Regis Debray) and its challenges to both the Soviet and Chinese orthodoxies reverberated throughout the intelligentsia of both the less-developed and the advanced countries. In fact, together with the experience of the Chinese Revolution, it played a major role in the revitalization of revolutionary ideas in the late 1960s in the West as well as in the less-developed countries.

Over the course of the 1950s, revolutionary enthusiasm waned as prosperity, peace, and social stability returned (supplemented in the early 1950s by a significant level of repression, both in the West and the East). As a result creative revolutionary theory and imagination also waned. Consequently a crisis in Marxist theory was precipitated.

The siege mentality of the Soviets and the orthodox parties (produced in fact by a U.S.-organized siege of both) in the post-1947 period facilitated the crystalization of narrowly orthodox Marxism and the temporary stagnation of creative thinking. Dogmatism and sectarianism became the mode of discourse. The decade or two from 1947 must then be contrasted with the innovative (if disciplined and collective) reformulations of orthodox Marxism that had occurred in the previous three decades.

In the 1960s Eurocommunism emerged with its explicit rejection of the discourse of orthodox Marxism and adoption of ideas similar to those of Bernstein and the social democracy of the late 1920s. Meanwhile the discourse of revolutionary Marxism became encapsulated in the smaller Communist parties loyal to a classical version of Soviet Marxism, in some countries such as France and Britain some Trotskyist grouplets, and by the late 1960s—especially in France, Germany, Italy, and the United States—the new Maoist sects.

Once again, the waning of the revolutionary movement resulted in the bifurcation of the mass movement and orthodox theory, with the mainstream of both the working-class movement and the progressive intelligentsia rejecting orthodox Marxism because it now made no sense of their experience. Currents of existentialism, a greatly watered down "critical" theory, the "beatniks," and other romantic and subjectivist ideologies now caught the fancy of the intelligentsia. Everything was up for reexamination. "No one" was a Marxist anymore.

In the U.S. state repression and social pressure manifested in the milieu of intellectuals took its toll. The minority who did not surrender their radicalism in the 1950s were mostly dismissed from their positions or forced out of academia (e.g., Paul Sweezy). Perhaps the only (fairly) orthodox Marxist of note to survive the 1950s in U.S. universities was Paul Baran who, in spite of his harassment and isolation from the faculty and students of Stanford, hung on to both his job and sanity until 1964 when he died at the age of 54.

The non-Marxist radical, C. W. Mills, was able to hold out for only so long against the tide of criticism that was engulfing him. Totally isolated in the academy of the 1950s, his iconoclastic behavior was only partially effective in protecting him from the immense pressure of conservatism. Without colleagues or students, engaging in ever more controversial battles, increasingly out of step with his intellectual milieu, he, not surprisingly, suffered two heart attacks and died prematurely at age 46 in 1962. A stubborn victim of the withering away of the wave of energy and imagination that had propelled him on his persistent and lonely course. An illustration of the immense power of social forces on intellectuals. The exception that proved the rule.

The fifth generation of imagination and revolutionary energy overlapped with the last stages of the degeneration of the previous wave. The locus of revolutionary energy and the Marxist practical and theoretical movement had now moved out of Europe to Asia and Latin America, especially to Cuba, Vietnam, and China. The resonance of the new Third World revolutions was felt most acutely in Europe among the new generation of young intellectuals, rather than among the working class and older intellectuals who had been formed in the late 1930s and 1940s. The Cultural Revolution in China peaked in 1967-68; the Cubans were most militant in 1967-68; Che died fighting in Bolivia in 1967; the Tet offensive occurred in Vietnam in 1968; the mass student upheavals in the United States and France peaked in 1968 and 1969.[2]

Developments in Cuba (1960-68) and China (after 1958 and especially during 1965-70), both of which deviated considerably from the Marxist orthodoxy of the time, played a central role in the development of the distinctive ideas of this period. While Vietnam was widely respected, its theory was that of the Comintern of the 1930s—a fact little appreciated at the time.

The Cuban Revolution of 1959 and its transformation into Marxist socialism in 1961 began a new era in Latin America. The peasant and guerrilla insurgencies were magnified in the growth of intellectual Marxism throughout the continent. The revival of the war of national liberation in Vietnam after 1956 and its intensification over the course of the 1960s (with the ever increasing U.S. attempt to suppress it) captured the imagination of intellectuals worldwide.

Developments in China, namely the Great Leap Forward of 1958-59, and above all the "Great Proletarian Cultural Revolution," had an even greater impact. The Chinese developments, which were led by a new generation of energetic Chinese youth, captured the imaginations of large segments of Western intellectuals who had never been enthusiastic (or who had long since lost their enthusiasm) for Soviet Marxism. Chinese, Cuban, and Vietnamese communism seemed like the *real* things: nonbureaucratic, imaginative, democratic, militant. Third World revolutions had an immense impact on the development of Marxist theory.

In the advanced capitalist countries the burst of Third World revolutionary energy was reflected in the renewed respectability of revolutionary Marxism. "Everyone" (at least among younger intellectuals) was once again a "Marxist." The central debates again occurred in the terms of Marxist discourse. The terms revolution, class, class analysis, imperialism, popular war, contradiction, dialectics once again (rapidly) gained currency, while youth now scoffed at the older liberal ("end of ideology") discourse that had been so fashionable in the 1950s. Democracy, elections, parliament, reform, liberalism, and so forth became terms of derision. The New Left of the advanced capitalist countries was extra-parliamentary and anti-liberal (in imitation of the movements they admired in China, Vietnam, and Cuba).

A new wave of organizations and publications were launched within which the revived left developed its ideas. In the United States virtually every major academic discipline established a radical organization in the 1968–71 period—perhaps the most persistent and influential being the Union of Radical Political Economists. A score of new left journals were established which have continued to publish: for example, *Socialist Revolution* (which appropriately changed its name to *Socialist Review* in the mid-1970s); *The Insurgent Sociologist; Politics and Society; Radical America; Telos* (which in the mid-1970s renounced its Marxist origins); and *Science for the People* being just a few of the better known. It was striking to browse through a good left bookstore's collection of journals in 1983 and see that most of the left periodicals were in volume 14 or 15. The generation of 1968 thus left a continuing intellectual legacy, just as had the early generation of the late 1930s and 1940s, of which the survivors into the 1960s in reasonably healthy form were *Monthly Review* (1949), *The Guardian* (1948), and *Science and Society* (1936).

Like other reassertions of revolutionary Marxism, the wave of the late 1960s too had its innovations. These on the one hand reflected the Third World epicenter of its inspiration, and on the other its largely middle-class basis among European and North American youth. The concept "Third World" (which implied being qualitatively different from both Western capitalism *and* Soviet Marxism) became virtually universal. "Liberation movement," inspired by the National Liberation Movement of Vietnam, came to be applied to virtually every progressive movement—to the "Women's Liberation Movement," the "Gay Liberation Movement," and even the "Sociology Liberation Movement." Anti-authoritarianism and experimentation with all kinds of new life styles took inspiration from young people's perception of the anti-authoritarianism of China and the militant anti-U.S. imperialism of the Latin American and Southeast Asian guerrillas (even though such sexual and life style experimentation was the furthest thing from any of the Third World movements' minds). The facts that "people of color" were in motion in the Third World and the 1960s' Black rebellion in the United States made the issues of race and nation central political and theoretical concepts. During the 1970s, as the energy of the sixties revival faded, new concepts were given impetus, for example, the women's movement.

Once again, as in the immediate post-World War I period, emphasis in the early stages was on will and imagination, in fact the works of Lukacs and Gramsci were rehabilitated and given a significantly more voluntarist—and individualist—reading than before. In the later stages of the revival the emphasis on discipline and party also reappeared— only now Lenin and Mao were being read instead of Lukacs and Gramsci. Critical theory was revived with a heavy emphasis on Freud. Marcuse's work *Eros and Civilization* as well as his *One Dimensional Man* became extremely influential (as did, to a somewhat lesser degree, Reich's work).

On the most sophisticated level the revived revolutionary energy of the 1960s became manifest in the restatement of orthodox Marxism in the works of Louis Althusser (and to a somewhat lesser extent the works of Nicos Poulantzas) in France. Althusser was a militant of the French Communist party throughout the 1960s and early 1970s. His earliest work, which began appearing in 1962, was a critical response to the liberalization of Marxism that had become current among Western intellectuals in the last half of the 1950s; for example, Hegelianism, humanism, historicism, existentialism, eclecticism. He was at first a product of the previous wave, but his popularity and influence snowballed with the growth of the New Left over the course of the 1960s, finally peaking in the early 1970s after the peak of both the Third World revolutions and the popular New Left movements. Thus Althusser became part of the new wave of revolutionary theory.

Althusser, more than any other single individual, manifested the rebirth and creative restatement of traditional Marxist orthodoxy in language that the young intelligentsia could appreciate. He too was able to translate Lenin into language that the intelligentsia could understand. His translation was, of course, different from that of Lukacs—who did an equally revolutionary, but more voluntarist and romantic translation. The work of Lukacs, Gramsci, and the young Korsch could capture the imagination of the young Western European intelligentsia in both the early 1920s and the late 1960s because of its emphasis on "storming the heavens," illegality, revolutionary discipline, and revolutionary will. The work of Althusser, because of its structuralism, however, found a more limited audience. In fact, Althusserianism, even at its early 1970s peak, always had to contend with the strong (and usually stronger) revolutionary Marxist interpretations that stressed will rather than structure, and that much more than Althusser (and Poulantzas) were open to life style experimentation, Third Worldism, guerrilla warfare, cultural experimentation, and individualism, for example, New Left readings of critical theory, Reich, Lukacs, and Gramsci.

Nevertheless, Althusser (and Poulantzas) gave tremendous credibility to the reconceptualized orthodox Marxist discourse of materialism, class analysis, working class, ruling class, ideology, the state, state monopoly capitalism, and so forth. Althusser's framework of "determination in the last instance," ideological state apparatuses, relative autonomy, and so forth gave a very sophisticated depth to the basic orthodox Marxist categories. Once again, the most sophisticated European intellectuals could defend orthodox Marxism with a discourse that could stand up to (if not intimidate) their voluntarist, individualist, and idealist opponents. After 1968, Cuba slowly adopted the Soviet model, while reducing its support of Guevarist adventures in Latin America. The Vietnamese Revolution was victorious in 1975. The Cultural Revolution in China lost steam and was reversed after 1969. Black rebellions ceased in the United States. The student movement died as apathy once again reigned on college campuses. The 1970s in the advanced countries were a period of peace, (relative) prosperity, law and order, and "democratization." In fact, it was one of the least repressive and stable periods in history. On the other hand, it should be noted, repression had never been greater in most of Latin America and Southeast Asia, where the revolutionary movements of the 1960s were crushed under vicious military dictatorships.

With the waning of revolutionary energy, Marxist theory once again entered a period of crisis, as the old questions and answers were no longer felt to be appropriate. Crisis was in the air as everything was once again up for reexamination and debate. New interpretations, at first largely within the discourse of Marxism, but increasingly without, prevailed. Western intellectuals, as they had in the 1950s, again turned away from revolutionary Marxism. As always happens, the content of discourse changed before its terms did. Throughout most of the 1970s virtually everyone still called themselves "Marxist." But the term and its associated discourse lost almost all content. But by the late 1970s in France and soon thereafter in the rest of the West, a wide variety of individualistic, humanistic, empiricist, and reformist ideologies became dominant. Even the theological categories of hermeneutics and semiology became popular.

Althusser and Poulantzas, who for a brief few years were the docents of the intellectual left, soon fell into disrepute as "dogmatists" and even "Stalinists." The fall down exerted tremendous pressure on them to recoup some of their prestige, and being mortals they first responded with essentially reformist reworkings of their earlier insightful orthodoxy. Poulantzas went over to essentially reformist political analysis in his last book (1978), while Althusser became publicly critical of the French Communist party for "Stalinism" and eventually left it. They lost what had made them great. Unable to either keep their bearings in a sea of hostility or reorient themselves in a world in which it was no longer chic to be Marxist, the first went mad, murdering his wife, and the second killed himself.

Their demise as intellectual figures left Parisian high fashion in the hands of explicit non-Marxists such as Lacan and Foucault (who now became the rage). As had happened in the immediate aftermath of the 1968 events, when respect for the French carried Althusser and Poulantzas around the intellectual world, the demise of respectable French orthodox Marxism soon too swept the intellectual world. "No one" was a Marxist anymore.

The terms and concepts central to Phase II of the cycle: class, materialism, economic crisis, imperialism, mode of production, proletarian leadership, ruling class, and class analysis now rung increasingly discordant. Democratization, self-management, parliamentary struggle, culture, multi-determinancy, the leading role of intellectuals and/or women, discourse, semiology, deconstruction now resonated with the times.

While at first this new content was forced into the old Marxist terms, for example, socialist "self-management" or full democracy for all; intellectuals are the "new working class"; women (including professionals) are the "true proletariat"; the class struggle occurs within the state; culture is a material force; to focus on mode of production determinism is economism which neglects the role of the politics; surplus labor is a more rigorous conceptualization of exploitation than surplus value, and so forth. But soon the stretching of the Marxist categories past the breaking point became apparent, and the old terms were increasingly abandoned in favor of new. The discourse of class, material force, party, proletariat, socialist, value and exploitation theory, and so forth is now simply dropped as unnecessary dogmatic baggage (which it clearly *is*). Humanism, empiricism, voluntarism, eclecticism, and idealism were now explicit and proudly displayed.

The discourse of revolutionary Marxism now became crystallized in Trotskyist, Maoist, and pro-Soviet sects, whose leaders, after a moment of leading massive demonstrations around 1968, became increasingly isolated from mass struggles (which now were led by confirmed social democrats). Once again the separation of revolutionary Marxist theory and mass movements in the West became complete.

The attack on those still defending the orthodox Marxist ramparts has often used traditional Marxist epithets, now given a new content. This has proven to be a very effective tactic. While a decade before they would have self-confidently dismissed such criticism as liberalism and immediately gone over to the offensive, they now often cower defensively in the face of attacks on them for economism, Stalinism, dogmatism, vulgar Marxism, reductionism, mechanical Marxism, being undialectical, and even sexism, racism, and elitism. Powerful rhetoric indeed.

CONCLUSION

In summary, the development of Marxism has been marked by both a cyclical movement back and forth between revolutionary orthodoxy and reformism and a secular trend that has moved in jumps followed by plateaus, with each stage corresponding to the particular problems of a powerful revolutionary movement. The major innovations in Marxist theory, it must be noted, have tended to occur during periods of orthodoxy when, together with the reassertion of certain basic concepts such as class, revolution, state, and materialism, a new set of concepts and theories are introduced to deal with the newly emergent problems of historical development and revolutionary practice. Thus, in spite of claims to openness and synthesis with other systems, periods of reformism have, in fact, been the least creative, tending to replicate earlier ideas, for example those of Bernstein (1899), rather more closely than the ideas of new orthodoxy replicate those of Marx or Lenin.

In fact, it is during the periods of orthodox predominance that both imaginative and truly critical theoretical notions prevail. It is, then, that Marxist ideas are most different from (as a result of being more critical of) prevailing ideologies, as well as most likely to entail new imaginative insights. In contrast, during periods of the predominance of reformist (and eclectic) notions and syntheses that openness results in the dulling of Marxism's critical edge (as its notions become more like those of the ideological mainstream) as well as less imaginative and insightful (for the same reason).

These facts are only apparently ironic. Reality is hidden by ideology of both the orthodox and the revisionists; the first claims legitimacy on the basis of its adherence to classical ideas, and the second claims its legitimacy on the basis of being open. But a close examination of the development of Marxist theory reveals a very different reality. This suggests that it is from the needs and experience of revolutionary movements, not the heads of intellectuals, that theoretical advance springs.

The state of Marxist theory, both in universities and mass movements, is fundamentally a product of the condition of social movements and the crises of which they are in turn a product. In periods of crisis, revolutionary sentiments revive and sharp periods of class conflict ensue. The energy and imagination of working people spill over to the intelligentsia. Orthodox, critical, and imaginative Marxism is reborn and approaches hegemony. Marxism regains its edge when it again becomes responsive to revolutionary movements.

It is no accident that many of those in the West who are today adherents of orthodox Marxism have ties to the vital mass movements of the less-developed countries such as Pakistan, Latin America, Southern Africa, the Mideast, or the Philippines.

In the advanced countries, periods of the hegemony of revolutionary Marxism have corresponded to the presence of strong movements that arise in the wake of serious and protracted economic crisis and even more so in the train of war. It can thus be predicted that the current predominance of open and reformist Marxism will be reversed with either protracted economic depression or warfare, either a war against Third World insurgencies such as that in Vietnam, or a less than total atomic war. Class warfare of the old time variety might well be expected to be reborn in the train of the tremendous social dislocation and frustrated expectations that such events would entail. In fact, a rebirth of revolutionary movements in the advanced countries may well generate imaginative innovations in Marxist theory on the order of those that followed in the wake of the Bolshevik Revolution.

NOTES

1. See Szymanski 1979, chap. 10 and 1984, chap. 7 for a thorough treatment of Stalin, the cult of personality, and his role in the Communist movement. This analysis is too complex to repeat here, and the issue is too emotionally charged to summarize briefly.

2. The Portuguese Revolution of 1975 should be considered a belated part of this wave since it was in good part provoked by the revolt against anachronistic Portuguese colonialism in Africa.

REFERENCES

Althusser, Louis. 1970. *For Marx*. New York: Vintage.

Althusser, Louis, and Etienne Balibar. 1970. *Reading Capital*. London: New Left Books.

Anderson, Perry. 1976. *Considerations on Western Marxism*. London: New Left Books.

———. 1980. *Arguments Within English Marxism*. London: New Left Books.

Baran, Paul, and Paul Sweezy. 1966. *Monopoly Capital*. New York: Monthly Review Press.

Bernstein, Eduard. 1961. *Evolutionary Socialism*. New York: Schocken.

Engels, Frederick. 1845. *On the Condition of the Working Class in England*. Moscow: Foreign Languages Publishing House.

———. 1962. *Anti-Dühring*. Moscow: Foreign Languages Publishing House.

Gramsci, Antonio. 1928-35. *The Prison Notebooks*. New York: International Publishers.

Jessop, Bob. 1982. *The Capitalist State*. New York: New York University Press.

Lenin, V. I. 1916. *Imperialism: The Highest Stage of Capitalism*. Moscow: Foreign Languages Publishing House.

———. 1917. *The State and Revolution*. Moscow: Foreign Languages Publishing House.

Lukacs, Georg. 1971. *History and Class Consciousness*. Cambridge, MA: MIT Press.

Luxemburg, Rosa. 1963. *The Accumulation of Capital*. New York: Monthly Review Press.

Marcuse, Herbert. 1955. *Eros and Civilization*. Boston: Beacon.

———. 1960. *Reason and Revolution*. Boston: Beacon.

———. 1964. *One Dimensional Man*. Boston: Beacon.

Marx, Karl. 1867. *Capital*, Vol. 1. Moscow: Foreign Languages Publishing House.

———. 1964. "Economic and Philosophical Manuscripts." In *Karl Marx: Early Writings*, edited by T. Bottomore. New York: McGraw Hill.

Marx, Karl, and Frederick Engels. 1947. *The German Ideology*. New York: International Publishers.

———. 1962. "The Communist Manifesto." In *Selected Works in Two Volumes*. Moscow: Foreign Languages Publishing House.

Newmann, Franz. 1966. *Behemoth*. New York: Harper & Row.

Poulantzas, Nicos. 1973. *Political Power and Social Class*. London: New Left Books.

———. 1974. *Classes in Contemporary Capitalism*. London: New Left Books.

———. 1978. *State, Power and Socialism*. London: New Left Books.

Szymanski, Albert. 1979. *Is the Red Flag Flying: The Political Economy of the Soviet Union Today*. London: Zed Press.

———. 1984. *Human Rights in the USSR*. London: Zed Press.

Trotsky, Leon. 1932. *History of the Russian Revolution*. New York: Simon and Schuster.

2

New Classes and Old Theories: The Impasse of Contemporary Class Analysis

Peter Meiksins

One of the most significant legacies of the rebirth of critical sociology in the 1960s was a renewed interest in "class" as a concept, which had fallen into disrepute in the complacent 1950s. Sociologists of the period reacted to the apparent affluence and stability of their society with an analysis we can now, with hindsight, refer to as "the myth of classlessness." They explicitly denied the validity of the Marxist approach to the interpretation of social structure, especially its insistence on the centrality of exploitation and class conflict to the process of historical development. Instead, they argued, class divisions, ideology, poverty, and other causes of social conflict were diminishing in U.S. society. Far from polarizing, U.S. social structure was becoming increasingly complex and pluralistic as affluence was extended to all segments of society. In this context, questions about the causes and nature of social conflict were perceived as unimportant; attention instead focused on the process of social mobility and on the mechanisms by which Americans had become "convinced" of the fundamental soundness of what had been dubbed "industrial society."

Although there were occasional challenges to this orthodoxy (Mills 1957), the myth of classlessness remained influential well into the 1960s, extending even to the last of the "critical" sociologists still active in the United States (Marcuse 1964). However, as social conflict reappeared and intensified both at home and abroad, this analysis became increasingly difficult to sustain. The result was the rebirth within the emergent New Left of an interest in class analysis.

In part, this represented a return to an older critical sociological orthodoxy. New Left social theorists clearly were attempting to deny the myth of classlessness and to assert the continued value of certain aspects of classical class analyses. Most, for example, insisted on the need to take seriously certain aspects of Marxist theory. While they did not maintain that classical Marxism had all the answers, they looked to it for concepts on the basis of which to build a new, more adequate analysis of contemporary social structure and social conflict.

Nevertheless, it is also true that New Left class analysis represented an attempt to break with this tradition. The common theme uniting most of the major contributors to this new debate on class was a concern to describe and understand *new* patterns of social structure and conflict. In particular, discussion centered around what has been variously called "the new middle class," "the new class," "the new working class," "the service class," and "the professional-managerial class," that is, the large strata of relatively affluent, nonmanual laborers who had become a distinguishing feature of advanced capitalist societies. For the New Left, these groups could not be analyzed adequately within the categories of classical Marxism. The latter might provide concepts with which to begin such an analysis, but the consensus was that critical sociology needed to go beyond the classics to develop an adequate understanding of contemporary social structure. As a result, recent critical studies of class have tended to take the form of an extended debate on how to *modify* classical Marxist concepts so as to make sense of these new phenomena.

In sum, one of the hallmarks of the last 20 years of radical sociology has been the desire to reject the myth of classlessness and to reassert the importance of class to both social analysis and political action. After 20 years of intermittent discussion, however, this new debate on class has begun to lose some of its impetus. No consensus has emerged as to the nature of the new middle class. And a growing number of radical social theorists have despaired of the concept of class altogether, taking refuge either in the new social movements or in the new vogue for studies of discourse and deconstructionism (Wood 1986). It is increasingly clear that the debate on class initiated in the 1960s has now reached an impasse.

This paper will argue that the impasse was inevitable, given the theoretical origins of the entire discussion. It is undeniable that New Left theorists identified the crucial problem for contemporary class analysis—the appearance of the "new middle class." And it is also true that they were sincerely committed to restoring the concept of class to its rightful place in intellectual and political discussion. Ironically, however, New Left theorists rendered themselves incapable of developing an adequate class analysis of contemporary capitalist societies because, in the end, they accepted many of the central points and methodological assumptions of the 1950s' sociology they sought to criticize. Two traditions had a particularly strong effect on contemporary debates. First, the new debate on class has been profoundly affected by the tradition of academic studies of social stratification. While most of the participants in this debate would see Marx, rather than Weber or Parsons, as their intellectual antecedent, it remains true that their theoretical approaches to class often owe more to the latter than to the former. Second, the myth of classlessness, although emphatically denied by most radical sociologists, has proven impossible to escape—as we shall see, many contemporary sociologists, in the very act of rejecting this myth, are able to do so only on its own terms.

NEO-MARXIST CONCEPTIONS OF
THE NEW MIDDLE CLASS

The new middle class quickly emerged as the central preoccupation of New Left theorization on contemporary capitalist social structure. While there was little agreement as to the nature of these strata, there was general consensus that they were new and that they represented a fundamental challenge to classical Marxist theory. Marx, so the argument went, had foreseen an increasingly polarized social structure, with a dwindling group of rapacious capitalists on the one side confronting a growing mass of proletarians on the other. Mainstream social scientists of the 1950s had pointed to the apparent contradiction between this view and the reality of growing numbers of middle-class professionals, managers, and technical employees. New Left theoreticians, while rejecting the myth of classlessness that grew out of this analysis, took seriously its critique of classical Marxism. Capitalist social structure had changed, and a new type of class analysis was needed to make sense of it—otherwise, the academic critique of Marxist social theory would remain unanswered.

A bewildering variety of interpretations emerged out of this desire to respond to the mainstream critique. It would serve no useful purpose once again to review in detail the progress of this debate (cf. Abercrombie and Urry 1983; Carter 1985; Oppenheimer 1985). What needs to be emphasized, however, is that when these interpretations are analyzed closely it is striking how unanimous they were about the fact that the new middle class was fundamentally different from the traditional working class.

Perhaps the first New Left analysis to develop was the theory of the new working class (Mallet 1969; Gorz 1967). Pointing to an upsurge of industrial militancy and ultimately to May 1968 in France (and subsequent events in Italy and elsewhere), this argument attributed to affluent middle-class groups a significance directly opposite to that emphasized by the myth of classlessness. This new working class of technicians and other highly educated groups represented a new revolutionary force, distinct from the traditional working class. For Gorz, Mallet, and others, they were different, but they were a breath of revolutionary fresh air—militant, articulate, independent, and deeply committed to democratic socialist ideas of liberation and self-management.

This interpretation did not last. In the face of political disappointment and a series of highly critical empirical studies (Gallie 1978; Low-Beer 1978; Nichols and Beynon 1977), even its proponents soon changed their tune (Gorz 1976). In the process, the idea long propounded by mainstream social science that the new middle class represented a fundamental political and theoretical *problem* for socialists found its way into the New Left. Theoretical discussion now centered on the question of the precise difference between the new middle and working classes and on describing the manner in which its existence *complicated* patterns of class conflict.

One variant on this theme was articulated in the influential work of Nicos Poulantzas (1975). His view was that a very large, broadly defined "new petite bourgeoisie" had developed within contemporary capitalist societies. Although he recognized that there were significant social differences between the traditional petite bourgeoisie and this new group of mental, unproductive, and supervisory workers, he nevertheless felt that in ideological and political terms the two groups were quite similar—for example, they shared a strong commitment to individualism and a kind of nonsocialist anticapitalism. Within capitalist society, the two petites bourgeoisies constituted a kind of unstable swing group, oscillating politically between the opposing forces of labor and capital. Poulantzas's approach did not prove popular. It was widely criticized, among other things, for reducing the size of the working class to miniscule proportions (Wright 1976, p. 23). However, it was influential in the sense that later contributions to the debate on the new middle class generally accepted his view that they were politically "in the middle."

This was certainly true of the widely accepted view that new middle-class groups were in some sense ambiguous (Wright 1978; Carchedi 1977). Analyses such as these pointed to the complex structural position of the new middle class. Its members shared certain characteristics of the working class, such as selling their labor-power in exchange for a wage. But they also shared certain characteristics with the bourgeoisie: partial control over the means of production, skill, or investment (Wright 1978), or performing the "function of capital" (Carchedi 1975). In political terms, this made them problematic. Carchedi (1975) saw them as more susceptible to capitalist ideology than the working class, but he argued that they could be won over to the working class if political and ideological conditions were right. Wright (1978, p. 108) seemed to agree: "Because contradictory locations have contradictory class interests, they are objectively torn between class forces in the class struggle and can potentially be organized into more than one class capacity. Class struggle itself therefore determines to a large extent the degree to which the complexities of the class struggle are reproduced at the level of class formation."

A second major theoretical tendency, which rejected the notion that new middle-class groups were ambiguous and instead adopted a modified version of Poulantzas's view, also was rooted in the basic assumption that these groups were a new political problem Some New Left analysts defined the new middle class more narrowly than Poulantzas, excluding groups such as clerical workers or low-level technicians on the grounds that they were objectively too similar to the manual working class. However, they did conclude that there was a relatively small group of privileged, highly educated professionals and managers in the middle levels of capitalist society who were distinct from both labor and capital. Lebelling them variously as "the professional-managerial class" (Ehrenreich and Ehrenreich 1978), "the service class" (Abercrombie and Urry 1983), or "the new class" (Gouldner 1979; Stabile 1984), these theorists saw them as a kind of technocratic force within capitalism. That is, their expertise, credentials, and privileges placed them in partial opposition to both the democratic values of the labor movement and the irrationalities of a society controlled by the bourgeoisie. In the final analysis, their interests seemed to incline them toward a society dominated by experts. Like certain neo-conservatives (Bruce-Biggs 1979), then, these radical social analysts saw this group as complicating traditional patterns of class conflict.

NEO-MARXISM AND THE WORKING CLASS

In sum, New Left analysis of the new middle class has generally accepted the proposition (which it shares with mainstream social science) that this group, however defined, is fundamentally different from the working class and, as such, is particularly problematic from the point of view of the socialist movement. We shall discuss the difficulties inherent in this view in a moment. However, before we do, let us consider the related question of New Left analyses of the traditional working class.

While there has been considerable discussion of the New Left's view of the new middle class, less has been said about its approach to the working class. In one sense, this is not surprising since, with the exception of the burgeoning literature on the labor process stimulated by Harry Braverman's *Labor and Monopoly Capital* (1974), there have been very few major theoretical or empirical studies of this group from within the contemporary left. Nevertheless, two distinct views of the working class are implicit in most of the major contributions to the new debate on class.

One view accepts, to a great extent, the central proposition of the myth of classlessness—the idea that the working class has accommodated itself to contemporary capitalism. Such an argument can be seen clearly in discussions of the new working class. In emphasizing the revolutionary potential of new working-class elements, Gorz, Mallet, and others were simultaneously emphasizing the inability (and perhaps unwillingness) of the traditional working class to break out of its capitalist straitjacket. Similarly, the emphasis on the revolutionary character of the Third World that has been the hallmark of the theorists associated with *The Monthly Review* in the United States (Sweezy 1972) also contains an element of despair regarding the proletariat under advanced capitalism. This school of thought tends to play down the possibility of revolutionary working-class movements in advanced capitalist countries—the working class has succumbed to blandishments of an affluent, wasteful consumer society. If a challenge to capitalism is to be mounted, it will have to come from the impoverished workers and peasants of the Third World.

Finally, one can detect a similar view of the working class in the enthusiasm for the early work of Georg Lukacs and for the writings of the Frankfurt school that characterized much of the New Left. For all their emphasis on class consciousness and the revolutionary character of the working class, Lukacs' essays in *History and Class*

Consciousness (1971) remain pessimistic; he is unable to describe the concrete mediations between the reified working class under capitalism and its potential as a revolutionary agent (Meszaros 1972). The pessimism of the Frankfurt school theorists was even more explicit. For example, Marcuse's critique of capitalism (1964) coexisted with his apparent conviction that the working class was just as much a prisoner of one-dimensionality as everyone else. For this group of the New Left, the prospects of a revolutionary working class in advanced capitalist societies were slim indeed; as such, they had either consciously or unconsciously accepted a major component of the myth of classlessless.

Other New Left theorists saw the working class in a rather different light. If one considers the various analyses of the new middle class outlined above, it is clear that all of them implicitly or explicitly regard the working class as politically unambiguous and unproblematic. The argument that the new middle class *is* politically problematic relies on precisely this assumption. To provide just one example, how could Wright argue that the ambiguity of new middle-class groups rested on their differences from the working class (i.e., on the characteristics they shared with the bourgeoisie or petite bourgeoisie) unless he were implying that the absence of these differences would make them unambiguous? For these theorists, it was given that the traditional working class was at least potentially militant, revolutionary, socialist, and so forth. They thus rejected the portion of the myth of classlessness that emphasized the accommodation of the working class to contemporary capitalism. However, this remained an article of faith, an assertion. Little or no attempt was made to ground it in a theoretical analysis or to explore, either empirically or theoretically, the conditions for militancy in the contemporary working class. Even the major exception to this statement, Braverman's *Labor and Monopoly Capital* (1974), has been severely criticized for its neglect of working-class consciousness and resistance (Friedman 1977; Edwards 1979). Consequently, New Left social theory has not really developed a systematic response to mainstream sociology's critique of the classical Marxist analysis of the working class in contemporary capitalist society.

CRITIQUE

What this brief summary of the last 20 years of radical class analysis suggests is that the refutation of the myth of classlessness has been incomplete. Virtually all New Left theorists accept the proposition that the new middle class does require us to reject the classical Marx-ist two-class model of capitalist social structure. And mainstream sociology's critique of the Marxist analysis of the *working class* re-mains unanswered—segments of the New Left accepted this critique as valid, while others have simply asserted, without actually demon-strating, that it was wrong. The various theories discussed above have been criticized in detail elsewhere (Meiksins 1986a; Carter 1985; Oppenheimer 1985; Abercrombie and Urry 1983); no attempt will be made to repeat these criticisms here. Instead, let us focus on the fundamental question: Has this incomplete refutation of the myth of classlessness led to a useful radical analysis of contemporary class structure?

The ultimate test of New Left class analysis, given its emphasis on the distinctiveness of the new middle class, must be its ability to *define* and *describe* this distinctiveness. Yet, nowhere in the debate on contemporary class structure do we find a theoretically consistent basis for distinguishing between working-class and new middle-class employees. Indeed, at times we encounter a type of class analysis that is reminiscent of the mainstream sociology it is supposed to re-fute. This is particularly true of those analyses that try to distinguish between the middle class and the working class by focusing on vari-ables such as income, skill, and other measures of privilege. In es-sence, such analyses argue that middle-class employees differ from the working class because they possess larger amounts of skill, or that they are in a superior material situation. This is why, for example, many recent neo-Marxists have sought to exclude *deskilled* non-manual laborers from the middle class. Probably the most theoretical-ly sophisticated variant of this type of argument is Erik Olin Wright's (1978) work on "contradictory class locations," in which degrees of control over the labor process, investment, or the means of produc-tion are used to measure the boundaries among classes and contradic-tory locations.

There can be no doubt that autonomy, income, skill, and other similar factors are important influences on people's self-conception and their sense of their place in the social structure. However, this does not entitle us to say that they define class. Radical sociologists have generally been critical of their mainsteam counterparts for "re-ducing" class to such factors on the grounds that they confuse in-equality with class. Reliance on variables such as income or skill makes decisions about where to draw the line between classes arbi-trary, since they are not characterized by sharp breaks. The same criticism may be levelled at radical sociologists who employ analogous arguments. We are entitled to ask, for example, just how deskilled does one have to be to be considered part of the working class?

The second important approach to class analysis within the New Left employs a curious kind of functionalist argument. This represents a sharper break with conventional sociological analyses of class; but the resulting "class map" is not adequately justified theoretically. Guglielmo Carchedi (1977), who is probably the leading proponent of this kind of analysis, derives his functionalist argument from several passages in Marx's *Capital* (1967) where a distinction is made between the labor of supervision and the labor of coordination within a collective labor process. The labor of coordination is necessary labor that would have to be performed in any collective labor process, while the labor of supervision is made necessary solely by the exploitative character of the capitalist mode of production. Within contemporary capitalist organizations, according to Carchedi, some employees are engaged exclusively in direct production or the labor of coordination, others perform only the labor of supervision, and a third group performs a mixture of these two functions. This last group is Carchedi's new middle class.

Carchedi's approach has influenced a number of more recent contributions to debates on the new middle class (Carter 1985; Abercrombie and Urry 1983). However, it is not at all clear that his fundamental assumptions can be sustained. Thus, the key to his distinction between working class and middle class is his functional analysis: to be working class, one cannot perform the labor of supervision. But it is difficult, if not impossible, to apply this kind of distinction to the stratification of actual workplaces. Many conventional working-class jobs clearly involve an element of what Carchedi would call supervision. For example, as Michael Burawoy (1979) has argued, even forms of worker resistance can include a disguised element of self-supervision that allows the production of surplus-value to take place. Nor is it clear that there is a class difference between an engineer who is designing a new product (presumably necessary labor under any mode of production) and one who is designing a new system of organization for the production process involved in making that product (which might involve at least an element of supervision). In short, Carchedi's implication that the functionally mixed positions will be located in the middle does not correspond to the reality of workplaces. As a result, it does not give us a theoretically consistent criterion that could be used to distinguish between new middle-class and working-class employees.

Thus, none of the major theoretical tendencies within the New Left debate on class provides a consistent, workable criterion for distinguishing between the classes they claim to have identified within capitalist social structure. Nor have they been able to demonstrate empirically the existence of radically new patterns of class conflict within contemporary capitalist societies or of qualitatively different attitudes among the new middle class. A brief consideration of two issues should suffice to indicate the weakness of their approach.

First, as we saw earlier, many New Left discussions of the new middle class assert that such elements have a natural predisposition toward various kinds of technocratic ideologies. Yet, there have been very few attempts, and even fewer successful ones, to show that this is the case in reality. One of the few New Left studies of new middle-class ideology is Donald Stabile's (1984) recent work, which focuses largely on engineers. He attempts to demonstrate that early 20th century U.S. engineers were attracted to the kind of technocratic ideas attributed to them by Veblen (1919). Yet, his account is singularly unpersuasive. It is equally possible to regard the ideas he describes, such as scientific management, as the response of a vestigial petit bourgeois group within the engineering profession to their loss of independence within corporate bureaucracies (Meiksins 1984). Moreover, since the early 20th century, most U.S. engineering ideologies have taken the form of either an explicit defense of capitalism (often rejecting technocratic ideas outright) or a fairly conventional preoccupation with improving the material position of the engineer (Meiksins 1986b). All in all, there is little evidence that engineers, a classic new middle-class group, have shown any special interest in technocratic ideologies.

When it comes to working-class ideologies, as we have already seen, New Left theorists tend to assume a lack of ambiguity. While most are aware that the average blue-collar worker is not a militant socialist, there does seem to be a fairly widespread assumption that the barriers to the development of such a consciousness within the traditional working class are *qualitatively* less important than they are among the new middle class. Yet, without intending to minimize the ideological complexity of the latter, one must ask whether this assumption does justice to the reality of traditional working-class attitudes. For example, there is considerable evidence that blue-collar workers are internally divided as a group and are not, on the face of it, radically more solidary across workplace or occupational lines than middle-class workers (Nichols and Armstrong 1976). Similarly, Duncan Gallie's (1978, 1983) work on national differences in perceptions of class has demonstrated that one cannot assume that there is anything simple about the development of class consciousness among traditional manual laborers. Again, this is not to suggest that the attitudes of new middle-class employees are either simple or unambiguous; but it does indicate that they do not have a monopoly on either complexity or ambiguity.

No one would argue that there are no differences at all between various kinds of employees, especially between those who are privileged and those who are not. But New Left social theorists have been too careless in assessing the *nature* of those differences. Certainly one can show that the new middle class is more likely to vote for conservative or middle-of-the-road parties, or that they are less liberal on certain political issues (Wright 1985). But does this make them a distinct class? To begin with, we have yet to see a satisfactory demonstration that voting patterns or answers to survey questions are useful measures of class. And even if we had such a proof, it would have to be noted that there are plenty of conservatives within the traditional working class. How are we to understand *their* class position?

It should be added that there are also important *similarities* between the attitudes of the working and new middle classes. For example, both groups show a persistent interest in improving the terms and conditions of labor. In his analysis of class and class conflict, Marx emphasized such similarities among various kinds of wage-laborers, arguing that they were linked to the fundamental conflict of interest between the employer and the employees he or she exploits. It may be that this is less important to class analysis than the attitudinal differences emphasized by the New Left. But this cannot be assumed; *it must be shown theoretically*. New Left class theorists have not succeeded in doing so.

All in all, very little in the way of empirical studies of ideology and class conflict has emerged from the New Left; and what little there is has not been particularly persuasive. This remarkable hiatus deserves explanation. To an extent, it is the result of the New Left's partial acceptance of mainstream sociology's analysis of contemporary class structure. Thus, since they accept at face value the notion that the new middle class is different, the real task is not to describe its ideology. This has been accomplished from their point of view. Rather, the task is to explain theoretically *why* it adopts different attitudes, hence the preoccupation with discovering criteria by which one could distinguish between the new middle and working classes.

However, this still leaves us with the question of why the New Left accepted so uncritically the received wisdom that the new middle class was different. The answer lies in the fundamental weakness of the entire New Left approach to class analysis. As I have argued elsewhere (Meiksins 1986a), the greatest failure of New Left approaches to class is that they fail to identify fundamental conflicts of interest among the various classes they describe. This is in sharp contrast to Marx's approach, which identifies the conflict of interest inherent in the exploitative character of capitalist relations of production as the cause of class in capitalist society. For Marx, there was a clear and ineradicable conflict of interest between exploiter and exploited which constantly tended to erupt into various forms of class struggle. It followed from this that social analysis had to begin with this fundamental conflict and trace the process by which it shaped actual historical conflicts and patterns of ideological development. The great advantage of this approach is that it focused theoretical attention on class as a process of conflict, not as a system of classification. It emphasized the *link* between the fundamental social relations of capitalism and the diverse patterns of conflict found in capitalist societies. Marx's analyses of social conflicts (e.g., Marx 1964) did not arbitrarily assert that certain ideological configurations were classes; rather, they carefully described the connections between conflicting relations of production and existing patterns of class conflict.

In contrast, and despite the occasional pronouncement on the need to analyze the process of class *formation* (Przeworski 1977) and the almost ritual reference to E. P. Thompson's notion of class as "a process," New Left theoreticians have shared with their mainstream counterparts an exceedingly static conception of class. They remain taxonomies (and not especially neat taxonomies at that) that establish neither why patterns of conflict among *groups* of people should develop within capitalist society nor why existing conflicts or ideological configurations are classes. Instead, New Left analyses tend to start with the assumption that the new middle class is ideologically different and then argue back to observed sociological differences among them and other social groups. But they do not establish that there is a fundamental conflict of interest between these groups (Meiksins 1986a). For example, what is the conflict of interest between those who have partial control of the labor process and those who do not (leaving aside the question of how to *distinguish* between them)? Does one exploit the other? [See the discussion of Erik Olin Wright's recent (1985) work below.] Similarly, can one identify clear conflicts of interest between supervisors and those they supervise? At first the answer appears to be yes, but what of those who supervise and are themselves supervised? Bureaucratic organizations involve many layers of supervisory authority. Does each represent a separate class? If not, why do we regard relations of super- and subordination as constituting class in one case but not in others? Once again, the precise nature of the conflict of interests involved remains unclear.

The New Left's failure to focus squarely on fundamental conflicts of interest as the basis for class places them in a Weberian theoretical framework. Their class analyses are really taxonomies: They classify individuals into classes that are ill-defined groups with similar attributes rather than groups that arise on the basis of fundamental conflicts of interest. Since classes are not the product of fundamental conflicts of interest, it follows that conflict among classes is not necessary (as it was not for Weber). Instead, it arises only sometimes, for essentially contingent reasons.

The problems with this approach are fairly obvious. First, we must ask what makes these groups classes. There are innumerable kinds of social differentiation. Why are certain ones—skill, income, or whatever—singled out and called class? Perhaps more importantly, it presents class conflict as something less than a fundamental reality in capitalist societies. This may allow New Left theorists to draw intricate class maps. But, unlike Marx's analysis of exploitation, it does little to respond to mainstream sociology's view that contemporary capitalist societies are characterized by *inequality*, not class conflict.

THE DENOUEMENT

Thus, what began as an attempt to refute the myth of classlessness ended by reproducing many of the limitations and weaknesses of its adversary. While New Left theorists have insisted on the importance of class analysis to an understanding of contemporary society, the actual result of their labor has not been fundamentally different or markedly superior to mainstream sociological analyses of inequality. Most importantly, they have not been able to undermine the central arguments of their adversaries: They have replicated their static analyses of class structure, and they have accepted, without adequate theoretical or empirical justification, several significant points in their critique of classical Marxist class analysis.

In the past few years a sense that radical class analysis has reached an impasse has begun to develop. A number of radical social theorists have become disillusioned with the theoretical constructs of the New Left's approach to class and have sought to formulate new approaches to the interpretation of contemporary social structure and politics.

While some of these appear to be virtually complete rejections of New Left orthodoxy, the break is more apparent than real. As we shall see, these "new" directions in radical social theory are natural outgrowths of the theories they criticize. As a result, they incorporate many of the same weaknesses we have been discussing.

Three emergent themes in contemporary approaches to social class are of particular significance. First, there is a view, which has gained wide acceptance in many parts of the left, that emphasizes the growing polarization of advanced capitalist societies. This approach can be traced back to Braverman's (1974) seminal work, but it has become considerably more explicit in the 1980s. In essence, the argument is that the harsh economic climate of the 1980s has eroded the position of much of the new middle class. Employees who have traditionally enjoyed a comfortable, privileged existence (including home ownership, high salaries, good career prospects, and work conditions) now find it increasingly difficult just to maintain their position. The result is the gradual disappearance of the middle class. A small portion of it (the so-called "yuppies") has been spectacularly successful, but most of the middle class is slipping slowly toward the working class (Blumberg 1980; Johnson 1982; Oppenheimer 1985). For some of the adherents of this point of view, at least, the prospects for socialism have been enhanced by these developments.

This is not the place to enter into an extended critique of the polarization thesis. Suffice it to say that there is some debate as to whether the polarization is as marked or as permanent as some analysts have argued. For example, Mike Davis (1986) argues that the U.S. middle class may use its political power to maintain its position at the expense of those below them. Moreover, as Davis' argument implies, the political optimism concealed in analyses of the declining middle class may be seriously misguided. It does not necessarily follow that a loss of privilege will lead to a middle class willingness to join hands with the labor or socialist movements. On the contrary, there are many historical examples of privileged workers blaming their difficulties on the less privileged rather than on their employers. Consider how craft workers or professionals have traditionally responded to a decline relative to less skilled workers in their real wages.

Most importantly, this analysis perpetuates a number of the old theories of both the Old and New Left. It obviously resurrects the notion that capitalist society is going to polarize in a simple and clear-cut way an argument that has proven extremely easy to defeat in the past. Given that the empirical evidence in favor of the polarization thesis is open to interpretation, and given that it deals with a relatively short period of time, one must be concerned that it, too, will be impaled on the obvious complexity of capitalist social structure.

Also implicit in this argument is a rather familiar understanding of the effects of economic privilege. Proponents of the polarization thesis are reluctant to see privileged employees as part of the working class. Thus, it is only when they begin to *lose* their privileges that they become a potentially progressive political force. There is a strong family resemblance between this argument and "Third World-ist" or Marcusian pessimism about the politics of an affluent working class. The only difference is that more recent analysts hope that this numbing affluence cannot be maintained indefinitely.

A second, extremely important current in recent critical analysis has been a virtual rejection of the concept of class altogether. Many social critics, some of whom (e.g., Jones 1983; Gorz 1980) were once important contributors to the New Left literature on class, have concluded that existing class analyses are no longer useful for understanding contemporary social structure or for informing political movements. In arguing thus, many of the elements of the myth of classlessness are resurrected and "turned on their head." Some (Gorz 1980; Kitching 1983) echo earlier conservative notions about the spread of affluence to large segments of the population, adding only that this will create a new revolutionary class not mired in the "realm of necessity." Others (Laclau and Mouffe 1985; Mouffe 1983) suggest, in an argument strangely reminiscent of 1950s-style pluralism, that class is no longer the primary division in contemporary society. Instead, capitalist societies are divided by race, gender, and a variety of other cleavages; the political conclusion is that the new social movements are a better hope for radical social transformation than traditional class politics. The problems with such analyses are many; as has been pointed out elsewhere (cf. Wood 1986; Meiksins and Wood 1985), they attempt to ground radical politics in a complete rejection of the Marxist conception of history while at the same time failing to provide a workable alternative. What needs to be emphasized here is the continued reproduction within radical social theory of significant elements of mainstream sociological analysis.

Finally, there is the recent work of Erik Olin Wright (1985). Unlike the previous two tendencies, Wright's work is important not because it has gained political adherents, but because it is the first New Left approach to class that attempts to make use of the concept of exploitation. As a result, it appears to overcome many of the characteristic limitations of the last 20 years of radical class analysis. In reality, however, it too fails to go beyond the type of class analysis the New Left set out to criticize. It will not be possible here to provide a complete critique of Wright's complex book. Instead, let us concentrate on three central parts of his argument: the definition of exploitation, the argument that there are several types of exploitation, and Wright's approach to class consciousness and ideology.

Wright's definition of exploitation, which forms the core of his approach to class analysis, departs radically from Marx's. Following John Roemer, he constructs a theory of exploitation within a game theory paradigm; individuals or groups are said to be exploited if they would be "better off" under different circumstances and if some other group that benefits from the status quo compels them to remain within the confines of the existing "game" (Wright 1985, pp. 63-9). Modifying Roemer somewhat, Wright (1985, p. 83) identifies four types of exploitation: 1) feudal exploitation, in which labor-power is unequally distributed; 2) capitalist exploitation, in which means of production are unequally distributed; 3) statist exploitation, in which "organization assets," that is, control over the manner in which the production process is organized, are unequally distributed; and 4) skill exploitation, in which skills and credentials are unequally distributed. Within contemporary capitalist societies, Wright finds as many as 12 classes, which are defined by their status as exploiter or exploited along the last three dimensions outlined above.

Although Roemer's definition of exploitation is cast in terms of property relations, it tends to boil down to a matter of distribution (Carchedi 1986). Thus, propertyless wage-laborers under capitalism, who are obliged to sell their labor-power in exchange for a wage, are exploited because they would be better off under a system where they received "their per capita share of society's assets" (Wright 1985, p. 69). There are a number of obvious problems with this definition of exploitation. First, despite Roemer's (and Wright's) insistence that the exploiter must compel the exploited to remain within the game, there is some doubt as to whether exploitation constitutes a social relationship from their point of view. Thus, actual exploiters need have no actual contact, either direct or indirect, with the people they are said to exploit. They need only benefit economically from the system to be called exploiters. The fundamental insight of Marxist social theory—that capitalist exploitation occurs through the mechanism of a social relationship, an "exchange" between wage-laborer and capitalist—is obscured by this approach (Wood 1987). Wright attempts to get around this difficulty by insisting that one must add to Roemer's definition of exploitation the proviso that "the welfare of the exploiting class *depends upon the work* of the exploited class" (p. 75). But even this qualification leaves open the possibility that exploitation could be defined simply in terms of the distribution of rewards. One can see this most plainly in his discussion of "skill exploitation." Despite his awareness that no social relationship may exist between skilled and unskilled (p. 185), despite his suspicion that this may not correspond to a class distinction (p. 85), and despite his willingness to consider the possibility that skill distinctions may simply be a form of differentiation *within* the working class (p. 95), Wright insists on retaining this as a type of exploitation within his theoretical framework because of the inequality of rewards received by these two categories of employee.

The distributional focus of Wright's approach to class is also apparent in his attempt to develop an empirical test of the validity of Roemer's theory (chapter 5). Despite his awareness of the dangers of equating income inequality with class, Wright is prepared to use it as a kind of indicator: "Since the concept of class used throughout this analysis is rooted in the concept of exploitation, there should be a direct relationship between our matrix of class locations and income" (p. 193). He never makes clear why this should be the case; nevertheless, he goes on to argue that the theoretical class categories he develops on the basis of Roemer's analysis more accurately predict the distribution of income in Sweden and the United States than do other theories. But what does this prove? Wright is unwilling to equate income and class, although the logic of his argument does seem to imply this. As a result, his demonstration demonstrates very little. It is as if he had said: 1) here are some class categories generated by theory A; 2) since this classification is consistent with data that have no clear connection to theory A, theory A is demonstrated. It is unlikely that Wright would endorse an argument of this type; one can only conclude that he is in fact trapped by a distributional definition of class.

In addition, the Wright/Roemer analysis of exploitation fails to do justice to the character of the labor process under capitalism. As Marx pointed out, capitalism tends to create collective labor processes within which *groups* of workers, not individuals, are engaged in the production of value and surplus-value (Marx 1967). Different individuals within the labor process may be more or less highly rewarded, but it is the group, not the individual, that is exploited. From Wright's point of view, it is quite conceivable that the more highly paid portions of the collective laborer would be exploiters of those with whom they "cooperate" in producing surplus-value for capital.

Finally, as Carchedi (1986) has pointed out, the Wright/Roemer definition of exploitation is fundamentally unhistorical. It tends to blur together historically distinct forms of exploitation because of its focus on questions of distribution rather than production relations. Moreover, the test of exploitation they propose—"would the individual be better off under other circumstances?"—is also unhistorical. For example, we are asked to compare the situation of individuals under capitalism to a hypothetical situation where each receives a per-capita share. Yet, this hypothetical situation is hopelessly abstract. As Marx (1968) noted, the historical transition from capitalism to socialism would not and could not be marked by such absolute equality because the legacy of capitalism (inequalities of ability, skill, etc.) made this impossible. And when the transitional phase was completed, reward would be based on *need*, not per-capita share. Given this, it is conceivable that even highly privileged workers under capitalism would be better off under socialism, especially if we allow that the productive forces could be developed sufficiently to allow for high levels of affluence for the majority of the population. Roemer and Wright thus drastically oversimplify the process of historical change; in the process, they import into their analysis the kind of abstraction characteristic of marginal utility economics and lose the historical specificity of Marxist social theory. They also echo the familiar theme, first developed by mainstream sociology, that a degree of privilege is enough to place one outside the working class.

It should already be evident that Wright's new approach, like those of most other New Left theorists, takes us away from the issue of class interests and relations of conflict and toward the question of inequality that has been the staple of mainstream sociology. Given the way he defines class, we are forced, once again, to ask where we should draw the line. How much income does one have to have, or how much better off does one have to be under the current game, to be considered an exploiter? The answer to this question is inevitably arbitrary unless one can demonstrate, as Wright's approach does not, that there is a divisive relationship of conflict beneath the distribution of rewards. Carchedi (1986) is thus correct when he suggests that Wright's matrix is more a matrix of *occupational groups* than of classes.

Wright's discussion of "organization assets" echoes the familiar technocratic theme that has been a mainstay of New Left commentary on the new middle class. When he posits a form of exploitation root-ed in control over the organization of the production process, he seems to be looking for a kind of technocratic group within capital-ism that might emerge, after the abolition of capitalism, as a new exploiting class. (He points to the experience of Soviet-type societies in this connection.) He suggests that managers in capitalist societies have interests that are different from those of the capitalist class and that they constitute a possible threat to capitalist domination (p. 89).

Yet, there is little evidence that managers are distinct from capital-ists in this sense. Carchedi (1986) is correct when he notes that it is hard to imagine what meaning "organization assets" could have under capitalism, apart from the theoretically distinct (for Wright) question of effective control over the means of production. In other words, if someone controls the means of production, they *automatic-ally* control organization assets. Moreover, innumerable studies have shown that there is little difference sociologically between managers and owners (viz. Nichols 1969); if anything, the evidence suggests that the distinction between ownership and management has been blurred, resulting in their fusion into a "global capitalist," to use Carchedi's (1977) phrase.

Finally, let us consider Wright's approach to class consciousness and ideology. In his empirical test of his theoretical framework, Wright uses a number of "attitudes" as indicators of class conscious-ness. As with income, he is aware of the dangers inherent in this, but he argues that the degree of bias introduced by using survey ques-tions is not that great (p. 143). But this really begs the question. The main problem with using attitudes to measure class consciousness is that they are static (Carchedi 1986). That is, such measures do not allow us to grasp the developmental potential contained within a particular attitude or opinion. From this point of view, the "undevel-oped" forms of class consciousness, such as Luddism or individual sabotage that Marx and Engels described in *The Communist Manifesto* (1964), or that Gramsci (1971) referred to as "common sense," might be interpreted as evidence of an *absence* of working-class consciousness and, thus, of the nonworking-class character of their adherents. In contrast, Marx and Engels or Gramsci might see these as the beginnings of class consciousness, containing the germ of something more. Wright's approach to consciousness and ideology thus reproduces the characteristic lack of attention to process and development that we have seen in other New Left class analyses.

This approach to class consciousness leads him into a rather tortured argument in support of the characteristic New Left assertion that the new middle class is different, even when his evidence suggests that it is not. Although he found in his empirical study of Sweden and the United States (chapter 7) that there was a general tendency for pro-working-class sentiment to be strongest in the most unambiguously proletarian positions, he notes that this association was much stronger for the United States. In Sweden, pro-working-class sentiment had a broader base, extending into segments of the workforce with significant skills and/or organization assets. Indeed, he presents evidence that many Swedish new middle-class elements identify with the working class more than do U.S. proletarians. However, Wright does not see this as evidence of greater working-class unity in Sweden:

> Above all, perhaps, the effectiveness of the Swedish labour movement in massively unionizing white collar employees and even substantial segments of managerial employees, has heightened the degree of perceived community of interests among wage earners in different class positions. This does not imply that the objective basis of conflicts of interests among wage earners in different classes has disappeared, but simply that their common interests as capitalistically exploited wage-earners have assumed greater weight relative to their differential interests with respect to organizational and credential exploitation" [p. 279].

Yet, this is not a convincing interpretation of these results. It does not make much sense to argue, as Wright appears to do, that very similar attitudes are the consequence of working-class status in one case (U.S. proletarians) and not in another (Swedish new middle-class groups). Moreover, Wright also finds that the degree of working-class sentiment among *proletarians* is stronger in Sweden than in the United States. This suggests that the appearance of such attitudes is problematic even for unambiguously proletarian groups.

All in all, it is difficult to interpret these results within Wright's framework for class analysis. In contrast, a more developmental approach to class consciousness can make more sense of them. Following Marx and Gramsci, we could argue that class consciousness starts in a relatively undeveloped form (individualistic forms of opposition, occupational consciousness) that may develop into something broader. The fact that a type of employee does not identify with the broader working-class movement, thus, does not mean that these workers are structurally different. As a result, we can explain the greater working-class orientation of the Swedish new middle class as evidence of their having *developed* the germ of class consciousness inherent in occupational consciousness into a larger sense of class. Similarly, the lower level of working-class identification among U.S. proletarians is the result of the different history of class conflict in the United States. In sum, such an approach allows us to understand the ambiguous attitudes of all kinds of employees without ignoring the element of working-class consciousness inherent in them.

This brief critique of Wright's book has omitted many important issues that warrant further discussion. The point that needs to be emphasized, however, is that his new approach is not as new as it appears. Many of the familiar themes of New Left class analysis are central to his argument: a tendency to conflate class and inequality; a lack of attention to class conflict with a corresponding tendency to arbitrarily draw class maps; a tendency to assume that a degree of material privilege is inconsistent with working-class status; and a tendency to assume, despite the lack of concrete evidence, that the new middle class is qualitatively different from the traditional working class.

CONCLUSION

In sum, radical class analysis continues to be a prisoner of the sociology it ostensibly criticizes. It continues to propose a static model of class structure (despite a renewed interest in exploitation). And it continues to echo conventional notions about the nature of social structure—increasing affluence, plural social cleavages, the decline of class, or radical politics requires an immiserated working class. Except for their *assertion* of the importance of class, it is hard to see how we have advanced very far beyond conventional sociological theory with these analyses.

The obvious question that needs to be asked is why radical class analysis has emasculated itself. Why has it taken on so much of its opponents' views, especially when, as we have seen, these borrowings involve severe theoretical and empirical problems? The easy answer involves pointing to the context in which this theorizing takes place. Some would argue that these theories are the work of academics working in universities, cut off from the political movements they describe. Inevitably, their theories take on an academic character as debates with more conservative colleagues, the need to get tenure, the desire to get funding, and other pressures affect them. It is indeed tempting to accept this argument, particularly when one notes how frequently Marxist academics are praised for being Weberians in disguise (e.g., Mann 1986). However, this conclusion does an injustice to many of the theorists we are discussing who remain deeply committed to and involved in political activities of various kinds. In looking for an explanation of this type of theorizing, one needs instead to look precisely at the *political* agenda that lies beneath it. Two important political assumptions are central to New Left theorizing about class. They are not always present together, but one or the other (or on occasion both) is crucial to the development of all of the theories we have been discussing.

First, implicit in many of the theories we have considered is a deep-seated pessimism about the prospects for a viable socialist movement in advanced capitalist countries. This is rooted in the assumption that affluence is inimical to socialist politics—an assumption that Marx might have found rather odd, given his expectation that socialism would develop first in the most advanced capitalist countries. New Left theorists tend to see themselves as writing in a political vacuum, as describing a reality that is not promising soil for the development of socialism. Occasionally they allow themselves to hope for a fissuring of this affluent society (as in the polarization thesis described earlier) that would place socialism on the agenda once again. Or they speculate about the possibility of building a socialist movement, not around the working class, but around a loose coalition of classes and strata with fundamentally different interests (Meiksins 1986a). But in general, their theories are tinged with pessimism about the political prospects for the West. As such, Perry Anderson's (1976) analysis of Western Marxism in general is particularly applicable to them.

The second political theme running through New Left analyses of class, sometimes coexisting with the first, sometimes replacing it, is a fundamental *ambivalence* about what a socialist revolution led by the working class would be like. An important element of certain New Left class analyses is the argument that the traditional working class is not a *desirable* agent for socialist politics. This is clearly evident in the work of the new working class theorists, with their emphasis on the superiority of new working-class elements over the stodgy, traditional proletariat. It is also present in those theories that were inspired by discussions of reification and one-dimensionality—what kind of socialism could emerge from *this* soil? Most recently, of course, this view has found its most explicit expression in the proponents of the new social movements. (The link between the two periods has been personified by the career of André Gorz.) Such theories openly reject the traditional working class as the agent of social change on the grounds that it is too "materialistic" or too "limited," and look instead to other social forces to lead the socialist movement.

What unites these two apparently opposing political philosophies is a redefinition of socialism as a *moral* project, not a historically rooted possibility. Whether it is because they have concluded that a socialist agency no longer exists, or because they disapprove of the agency that does exist, New Left theorists have moved away from the fundamental Marxist insight that socialism is the self-liberation of an actually existing working class. For Marx, socialism was not a utopia with no connection to existing reality, a mere glimmer in the social critic's eye. It was a materially given possibility, placed on the historical agenda by the creation of a class whose liberation from exploitation *required* the abolition of exploitation itself. The New Left has accepted, either consciously or unconsciously, many of the arguments that mainstream social science has mounted in opposition to this view. For them, the working class cannot be the agency of socialist revolution, either because it is not large enough, or because it is too prosperous to want liberation, or because it is too materialistic. New socialist constituencies must therefore be found, either to be added to the traditional working class or actually to replace it. But these new constituencies are in a different relationship to socialism than was Marx's proletariat. Either, like the new social movements, their "interest" in socialism is vague and unspecified (Wood 1986), or, like the new middle class, they are said to have *no*, or at best a partial, material interest in socialism (Wright 1985). Consequently, socialism is redefined, not as the self-liberation from material exploitation of the working class, but as a moral project involving vaguely defined forms of "democracy" or "self-determination" to be effected by amorphous coalitions of widely differing social groups. As has been pointed out elsewhere (Meiksins and Wood 1985; Wood 1986), this redefinition of the socialist project has extremely grave political consequences.

It follows naturally from this political pessimism that the New Left would develop the kind of class analysis that it has. They have accepted the proposition that the working class is no longer an adequate revolutionary force and much of the rest of the myth of classlessness. Where they *differ* from mainstream sociology is in politics—they disagree about the desirability of the status quo and hold out the hope of some kind of socialism. In their hands, class analysis is not ultimately a means of undermining the myth of classlessness.

It is rather a way of *redefining* the conclusions of that myth to make it consistent with a revised socialist politics. It should not surprise us, then, that New Left social theory mirrors so much of mainstream sociology: It is attempting to use the same analysis to argue for different political conclusions.

Yet, as we have seen, it is not at all clear that this analysis is correct. Many questions about the nature of contemporary social structure remain unanswered (and unanswerable) within this theoretical approach. The real question radical class analysis ought to be asking is how can we defeat the myth of classlessness. It will not be possible here to develop a full answer to this question. Let us simply outline some of the key questions on which an effective radical class analysis must focus.

First, as Erik Olin Wright has correctly concluded, attention must be refocused on the nature of capitalist exploitation. The myth of classlessness proposes a view of society as essentially harmonious; the existence of exploitation denies this view because it creates a structural conflict of interest that cannot be abolished within the limits of capitalism. However, simply asserting that exploitation exists is not enough; nor, as we have seen, does Wright's and Roemers's elaborate redefinition get us very far. Instead, we need to confront several important issues that may require us to amplify, but not to reject, the basic Marxist analysis of exploitation. For example, consideration must be given to the nature of exploitation within a collective labor process. If the production of commodities and services involves heterogeneous groups of workers, often arranged into hierarchies, how does this affect exploitation? Is it possible that even those with significant managerial and supervisory responsibilities within these hierarchies are exploited? Further, attention must be given to the relationship between privilege and exploitation. The New Left, as we have seen, has rather uncritically accepted the view that material privilege is incompatible with exploitation. Yet, Marx long ago argued that, within limits, wages and working conditions could improve while at the same time the production of surplus-value continues. This is clearly the implication of Marx's (1967) discussion of skilled labor. This issue must be reconsidered in the light of the proliferation of a variety of privileged nonmanual laborers in contemporary capitalist societies. It may be that they, too, are exploited in Marx's sense (i.e., they perform surplus-labor), even if they are not oppressed in the traditional sense of the word.

In addition, attention must be refocused on the sociology of class conflict. The New Left has done little to explore the links between the basic exploitative mechanism of capitalism and the development of class conflict. Instead, it has often accepted prevailing myths about the consciousness of the contemporary workforce and the proposition that the absence of working-class militancy signifies a fundamental change in social structure. As we have seen, this begs all of the important questions. How does the experience of exploitation, which is necessarily experienced on an individual basis, lead to the development of group action and attitudes? What is the link between undeveloped forms of class consciousness and the organization of a militant, unified working class? Are there any objective barriers (hierarchy, the heterogeneity of the working class, etc.) that impede this process? How do capitalist institutions (the state, the educational system, etc.) intervene in and impede this process? Finally, given the heterogeneity of the working class (differences of income, skill, gender, race, authority, etc.), how do different types of workers react to the experience of exploitation and how can this heterogeneity be overcome?

These questions cannot be answered, or even asked, within the type of class analysis developed by the New Left. Instead, all of these questions require that we restore Marxist class analysis to its place at the center of radical social theory. This remains a capitalist society, and Marxism remains the only theoretically coherent account of class and class conflict under capitalism. A century of historical development may have brought about changes in capitalism that require further analysis. But we will not be able to make sense of them if, like the New Left, we shift discussion onto the terrain of the opponents of class analysis.

REFERENCES

Abercrombie, Nicholas, and John Urry. 1983. *Capital, Labour and the Middle Classes.* London: Allen and Unwin.

Anderson, Perry. 1976. *Considerations on Western Marxism.* London: New Left Books.

Blumberg, Paul. 1980. *Inequality in an Age of Decline.* New York: Oxford University Press.

Braverman, Harry. 1974. *Labor and Monopoly Capital.* New York: Monthly Review Press.

Bruce-Biggs, B. 1979. *The New Class?* New Brunswick, NJ: Rutgers University Press.

Burawoy, Michael. 1979. *Manufacturing Consent.* Chicago: University of Chicago Press.

Carchedi, Guglielmo. 1977. *On the Economic Identification of Social Classes.* London: Routledge and Kegan Paul.

————. 1986. "Review Article: Two Models of Class Analysis." *Capital and Class* 29:195-215.

Carter, Bob. 1985. *Capitalism, Class Conflict and the New Middle Classes.* London: Routledge and Kegan Paul.

Davis, Mike. 1986. *Prisoners of the American Dream.* London: Verso Books.

Edwards, Richard. 1979. *Contested Terrain.* New York: Basic Books.

Ehrenreich, John, and Barbara Ehrenreich. 1978. "The Professional-Managerial Class." In *Between Labour and Capital,* edited by Pat Walker, pp. 5-45. Montreal: Black Rose Books.

Friedman, Andrew. 1978. *Industry and Labour.* London: MacMillan.

Gallie, Duncan. 1978. *In Search of the New Working Class.* London: Cambridge University Press.

————. 1983. *Social Inequality and Class Radicalism in France and Britain.* London: Cambridge University Press.

Gorz, André. 1967. *Strategy for Labor.* Boston: Beacon Press.

————. 1976. "Technology, Technicians and Class Struggle." In *The Division of Labour,* edited by André Gorz, pp. 159-89. Hassocks, Sussex: The Harvester Press.

————. 1980. *Farewell to the Working Class.* Boston: South End Press.

Gouldner, Alvin, 1979. *The Future of the Intellectuals and the Rise of the New Class.* New York: The Seabury Press.

Gramsci, Antonio. 1971. *Selections from the Prison Notebooks.* New York: International Publishers.

Johnson, Dale. 1982. *Class and Social Development.* Beverly Hills: Sage.

Jones, Gareth Stedman. 1985. *Languages of Class.* London: Cambridge University Press.

Kitching, Gavin. 1983. *Rethinking Socialism.* London: Methuen.

Laclau, Ernesto, and Chantal Mouffe. 1985. *Hegemony and Socialist Strategy.* London: Verso Books.

Low-Beer, John. 1978. *Protest and Participation.* New York: Cambridge University Press.

Lukacs, Georg. 1971. *History and Class Consciousness.* London: Merlin Press.

Mallet, Serge. 1969. *La Nouvelle Classe Ouvrière.* Paris: Editions du Seuil.

Mann, Michael. 1986. "Classes, Swedes and Yanks." *Contemporary Sociology* 15:837-9.

Marcuse, Herbert. 1964. *One-Dimensional Man.* Boston: Beacon Press.

Marx, Karl. 1964. *Class Struggles in France 1848-1850.* New York: International Publishers.

————. 1967. *Capital.* New York: International Publishers.

————. 1968. "Critique of the Gotha Programme." In *Selected Works,* by Karl Marx and Friedrich Engels, pp. 311-31. Moscow: Progress Publishers.

Marx, Karl, and Friedrich Engels. 1964. *The Communist Manifesto.* New York: Monthly Review Press.

Meiksins, Peter. 1984. "Scientific Management and Class Relations: A Dissenting View." *Theory and Society* 13:177-209.

————. 1986a. "Beyond the Boundary Question." *New Left Review.* 157: 101-20.

————. 1986b. "The Myth of Technocracy: The Social Philosophy of American Engineers in the 1930's." Paper presented to SHOT Conference, Pittsburgh.

Meiksins, Peter, and Ellen Meiksins Wood. 1985. "Beyond Class? A Reply to

Chantal Mouffe." *Studies in Political Economy* 17:141–65.

Meszaros, Istvan. 1972. *Lukacs' Concept of Dialectic.* London: Merlin Press.

Mills, C. Wright. 1957. *The Power Elite.* New York: Oxford University Press.

Mouffe, Chantal. 1983. "Working Class Hegemony and the Struggle for Socialism." *Studies in Political Economy* 12:7–26.

Nichols, Theo. 1969. *Ownership, Control and Ideology.* London: Allen and Unwin.

Nichols, Theo, and Peter Armstrong. 1976. *Workers Divided.* London: Fontana.

Nichols, Theo, and Huw Beynon. 1977. *Living With Capitalism.* London: Routledge and Kegan Paul.

Oppenheimer, Martin. 1985. *White Collar Proletariat.* New York: Monthly Review Press.

Poulantzas, Nicos, 1975. *Classes in Contemporary Capitalism.* London: New Left Books.

Przeworski, Adam. 1977. "From Proletariat into Class: The Process of Class Formation from Karl Kautsky's *The Struggle* to Recent Debates." *Politics and Society* 7:343–401.

Stabile, Donald. 1984. *Prophets of Order.* Boston: South End Press.

Sweezy, Paul. 1972. "Marx and the Proletariat." In *Modern Capitalism and Other Essays,* by Paul Sweezy, pp. 147–65. New York: Monthly Review Press.

Veblen, Thorstein. 1919. *The Engineers and the Price System.* New York: Mac-Millan.

Wood, Ellen Meiksins. 1986. *The Retreat from Class.* London: Verso Books.

———. 1987. "Rational-choice Marxism: Is the Game Worth the Candle?" *New Left Review* (forthcoming).

Wright, Erik Olin. 1978. *Class, Crisis and the State.* London: New Left Books.

———. 1985. *Classes.* London: Verso Books.

3

Class and Class Capacities: A Problem of Organizational Efficacy

Jerry Lembcke

INTRODUCTION

As the crisis of U.S. capitalism deepens during the closing decades of the twentieth century, the need for the U.S. socialist movement to formulate strategy and tactics that will lead to a transformation of the national political economy becomes more pressing. Central to the discussion of an agenda for change has to be the role of the U.S. working class in a socialist transformation. This paper begins with the recognition that the most influential organizations within the U.S. left have relegated the working class to an increasingly marginalized role. The paper reexamines the theoretical work on which the socialist movement is premising its strategical choices and attempts to reformulate the most important propositions.

There are two theoretical problems central to the question of the working class as the historical agent of socialism. One involves the relationship between capitalist development and class capacities. Two lines of argument on this question can be found within recent studies of the U.S. working class. The dominant position, taken by those associated with the New Left traditions of the 1960s and 1970s (Aronowitz 1970, 1983; Braverman 1973; Ehrenreich and Ehrenreich 1976) and supported by work done on the European working class (Amanzade 1984; Gorz 1982), has contended that as capitalism developed, the economic, cultural, and political capacities of the working class to struggle for socialism were diminished. The alternative

64

position, consistent with classical Marxist theory, argues that advancing proletarianization is a factor that enhances class capacities. The Marxist position has received some support from Gedicks' (1976) study of radicalism in the Finnish-American community, urban political economic studies (Tabb and Sawyers 1983), and from studies of working-class voting behavior done by Hamilton (1972) and Szymanski (1978). The Marxist position has remained vastly underdeveloped, however. With a few exceptions (e.g., Beneson 1985), there have been few attempts to critique the New Left position from a Marxist perspective.

The second theoretical problem concerns the conceptualization of class capacities. Offe and Wiesenthal (1980) made clear the distinction between capitalist class sources of power (accumulated capital) and working-class sources of power (the unity or "association" of workers). But Offe and Wiesenthal did not elaborate the specifics of associational or working-class organizational logic, with the result that non-Marxist formulations of class capacities have continued to dominate the literature. Essentially these formulations have been drawn from pluralist traditions. Within that tradition power is equated with individual sovereignty based upon the control of production. As a notion of *class* capacity, it is appropriate to the petty bourgeoisie under capitalism (i.e., petty bourgeois class capacity *is* derived from control of the production process) but it is inappropriate as a conceptualization of working-class capacities. It is nevertheless the case that petty bourgeois conceptualizations of class capacities (e.g., Stone 1975) have continued to dominate the radical literature on working-class capacities. Because the voluminous "work process" literature is framed in ways tangential to the organizational needs of the working class, New Left-vintage theory in this area has been largely ignored, leaving practical organizational developments to be influenced by bourgeois theory; for example, unions, thinking they can fight capital with capital, pursue bigger treasuries, purchase professional expertise, and seek high-tech solutions for their problems.

This paper is a contribution to the development of a Marxist theory of working-class capacity. It proceeds by reviewing the historical and political context out of which New Left-era scholarship arose. It is then argued that in key respects, the work of radicals failed to break with the political and theoretical problematic established by pluralist social theorists. Specifically, the relationship between class and organizational behavior formulated by Lipset, Trow, and Coleman (1956), and the subsequent framing of the organizational question as one of democracy rather than class capacities, has never been rejected.

Finally, the paper moves to a reformulation of the union organizational question. It is argued that the organizational question can be more productively posed as a problem of class capacity than as one of union democracy. Three bodies of literature are synthesized in this effort: the work in logics of collective action (e.g., Offe and Wiesenthal 1980; Lembcke and Howe 1984); studies of class formation (Gordon, Edwards, and Reich 1982) and class capacities (e.g., Therborn 1983); and organizational studies done within the "strategical choices" framework (e.g., Child 1972 and Cornfield 1986). Following Therborn's (1983, p. 38) suggestion, this paper replaces the conventional concern with static class properties and formal organizational structure with questions about the "capacities of a given class to act in relation to others and the form of organization and practice thereby developed." The paper adopts Therborn's (1983, p. 41) position that "The fundamental power resource available to the working class, therefore, is its *collectivity:* especially its capacity for unity through interlocking, mutually supportive and concerted practices" (emphasis in original).

This paper takes the discussion beyond the current level by attempting to give greater specificity to the notion of class capacities. In this paper I argue that *working class* capacity is an *organizational* variable—that is, the essential "resource" mobilized in pursuit of working-class objectives is neither pecuniary, as it is for the capital-

Figure 3.1.   Conceptual Dichotomies of Class and Class Capacities

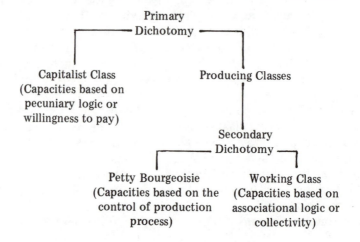

ist class, nor control of production, as it is for the petty bourgeoisie, but rather organizational structure. Therborn's notion of collectivity materializes, in other words, through organizational forms.

Moreover, some organizational forms maximize working-class collectivity while others frustrate or block it. The working class must not only consciously pursue an organizational form that advances collectivity but it must also oppose attempts by the capitalist class to impose organizational forms that atomize the working class. The struggle over organizational forms thus becomes an important dimension of the class struggle, and the study of class capacities becomes, in key respects, a study of organizational forms.

CAPITALIST DEVELOPMENT AND CLASS CAPACITIES

During the twentieth century the U.S. working class has been shaped by three trends. In the workplace, the displacement of craft and skilled labor by mass production techniques has allowed the employment of large numbers of unskilled workers; culturally, the integration of diverse ethnic strains produced by the centralization of production facilities and the constant infusion of petty bourgeois ideology has precluded the development of a clear-cut working-class consciousness; politically, the increasing intervention of the state in the regulation and management of the economy has added to the complexity of class relations and complicated the formulation of working-class strategy and tactics.

The first of these trends, the deskilling or degradation of labor, has been the focus of most studies of the U.S. working class done during the past 15 years. The dominant thesis has been that as monopoly capitalist forms of work, community, and political organization encroached upon earlier organizational forms, the capacity of U.S. workers to struggle in their own interest was undermined. In a seminal piece, Katherine Stone (1975) argued that the source of power for steel workers in the late 1800s was their monopoly of skill and knowledge of the production process. The institution of mass production techniques and the separation of the knowledge of how steel was made from the workers themselves was the key to breaking worker control of the industry. Addressing the relationship between culture and class formation, Stanley Aronowitz argued in *False Promises* (1973) that a nascent labor radicalism based on the homogeneity of the native-born craft workers was blunted by the arrival in the United States of the polyglot, unskilled workforce demanded by monopoly capitalism. More recently (1983), he has portrayed the "technical intelligentsia" as the modern day equivalent of the nine-teenth century craft workers in terms of its ability to play a leading role in social change. The increasing role of the state in the manage-ment and regulation of the private economy has been emphasized by Piven and Cloward (1982), among others, as a key to understanding the failure of U.S. workers to achieve socialist reforms in times of crisis.

There is no doubt that the rich historical detail provided by these studies has improved our understanding of an important dynamic of monopoly capitalism. But the theoretical implication of these studies is that the cutting edge of history lies at the interface between monopoly and competitive (or even precapitalist) forms of organiza-tion. As such, they lead to agendas for further research that elevate the central importance of the labor aristocracy and the petty bour-geoisie in the class struggle and to strategical thinking that is reactive and protectionist. The failure to identify the dialectical properties of the capitalist development process has produced a kind of static and unimaginative quality in the U.S. socialist movement that will at best be able to frustrate monopoly capitalism without being able to advance socialism. In short, the contemporary scholarship upon which many currents of the U.S. left base their actions has failed to identify the ways in which the capitalist development process pro-duces the conditions for socialism and, by failing to do so, has failed to move the historical agenda to the stage of monopoly capitalism versus socialism.

The theoretical implication of these studies can be appreciated best against the backdrop of Marx's and Engels' attempt to describe the capitalist development process as a dialectical process and there-fore as a historical force the long-term effect of which was to em-power the working class. The Marxist assertion that capitalism would produce its own grave diggers is not supported by either the logic of the work process analysts or by their empirical work. The practical consequence of these studies is that the casting of the working class in a central role for contemporary socialist strategies would be mistaken precisely because the degradation of work under capitalism has rendered the working class decreasingly capable of independent action. Consistent with these conclusions, many socialist organiza-tions have targeted middle-class and new working-class segments of the population for their organizing activities.

While it is true that Marx and Engels did not provide the concen-tration of detail on the work process that has emerged in the last decade, it is nevertheless true that the corpus of their work contains a clear effort to identify the contradictory relationship between the development of class relations under capitalism and the development of working-class capacities.

The notion of proletarianization is based on the Marxist understanding of exploitation. Marx argued that the source of all profit lies in human labor and that if the capitalist is to earn a profit it must come from the unequal distribution of returns on production. Because the capitalist controls the means of production and hence the sale and distribution of products, the capitalist returns less to the workers than what the worker actually produces. This is called exploitation, and the rate at which capitalists extract surplus from the labor of their workers is called the rate of exploitation, which Marx expressed as

$$\frac{\text{surplus}}{\text{variable capital}}$$

The capitalist is also in competition with other capitalists, both nationally and internationally. There is a constant pressure to produce for a lower selling price. This means getting more out of the productive process for the same or lower costs. It means workers will have to produce more without receiving a commensurate increase in wages, which means an increase in the rate of exploitation. The first way to do this is to increase the ratio of constant capital (machinery and raw materials) to variable capital (wages)—what Marx called the organic composition of capital. The second is to increase the scale of production—what Marx called the centralization of capital.

Proletarianization captures the human and social effects of capitalists' efforts to maintain an acceptable rate of exploitation. Increasing the organic composition of capital most directly affects workers by displacing their jobs through mechanization and automation; the quality of the remaining jobs is also diminished. Accident rates in manufacturing, for example, have increased as production processes have become more capital intensive.

While Marx and Engels were by no means oblivious to or unconcerned about the dehumanizing effects of the proletarianization process, they also saw it as a contradictory process that would ultimately strengthen the working class. "All political economists of any standing," wrote Marx in *Capital* (1967, p. 447), "admit that the introduction of new machinery has a baneful effect on the workmen in the old handicrafts and manufactures." Early worker struggles were fueled by resistance to the brutal imposition of machine technology and their desire to return to previous forms of production.

In *The Communist Manifesto*, Marx noted that workers "direct their attacks not against the bourgeois conditions of production, but against the instruments of production themselves; they destroy imported wares that compete with their labour, they smash to pieces machinery, they set factories ablaze, they seek to restore by force the vanished status of the workman of the Middle Ages" (Marx and Engels 1972, p. 42). But in Marx's view the past could not be restored and he characterized continuing efforts to do so as "utopian." Many of Marx's writings during the period of the First International were criticisms directed at followers of Michael Bakunin and Ferdinand Lassalle whose efforts to form associations of individual producers (cooperatives) as a hedge against capitalism he saw as an extension of the utopian tendency.

Marx and Engels saw in the emergence of capitalist production something far more profound than the radicalization of workers. Capitalism, "with all the miseries it imposes upon [workers] . . . simultaneously engenders the material conditions and the social forms necessary for an economic reconstruction of society" (Marx and Engels 1972, p. 186). With the loss of individual control over production and the workplace, social individualism was broken down and the groundwork was laid for the collective struggle of workers for the social ownership and control of capital.

Marx and Engels did not write in any detail about the specifics of union organizational forms. It is clear from their general theory, however, that they viewed proletarianization as a favorable development for working-class capacities. Marx wrote,

> The real fruit of [workers'] battle lies, not in the immediate result, but in the ever expanding union of the workers. This union is helped on by the improved means of communication that are created by modern industry, and that places the workers of different localities in contact with one another. It was just this contact that was needed to centralize the numerous local struggles, all of the same character, into one national struggle between classes. . . . This organization of the proletarians into a class, and consequently into a political party, is continually being upset again by the competition between the workers themselves. But it ever rises up again, stronger, firmer, mightier [Marx 1972, p. 43].

Engels (1975, p. 418) emphasized the contradictory effects of the centralization of capital and labor in industrial cities:

> If the centralization of population stimulates and develops the property-holding class, it forces the development of workers yet

more rapidly. The workers begin to feel as a class, as a whole; they begin to perceive that, though feeble as individuals, they form a power united. . . . The great cities have transformed the disease of the social body, which appears in *chronic* form in the country, into an *acute* one, and so made manifest its real nature and the means of curing it [emphasis added].

The processes of capitalist development proceeded unevenly, however, and that unevenness was reflected in the uneven development of the working class. "The more the factory system has taken possession of a branch of industry," noted Engels (1975, p. 529), "the more the working-men employed in it participate in the labour movement; the sharper the opposition between working-men and capitalists, the clearer the proletarian consciousness in the working-men." In locales and regions where technology lagged behind and the centralization of workers did not occur, the individualized precapitalist artisanal forms of production persisted. The "small masters" occupy a middle ground between "proletarian Chartism and shopkeepers' Radicalism," according to Engels.

Several points applicable to the general thesis of this paper can be derived from the Marxist position as outlined here. First, it is absolutely clear that for Marx and Engels, the proletarianization of labor attendant upon the development of capitalism entailed the simultaneous development of working-class capacities to transform the class relations of capitalism. Second, it is evident that for them, the representation of individual economic and political rights under capitalism was not the principal objective of working-class organization. Rather, the objective was the empowerment of the working-class struggle. Finally, there emerges from the outline a working-class strategical agenda of unifying the broadest possible elements of the working class, including the unemployed and the marginally employed. This is the key point because in the context of current struggles it becomes the criterion by which we can specify the most efficacious form of union organization.

In the United States the culmination of capitalist development in the unionization and political mobilization of millions of industrial workers during the 1930s lent credibility to the Marxist thesis that the industrial proletariat would be a leading socialist force (Gordon, Edwards, Reich 1982). During the 1930s working-class movements like the Congress of Industrial Organizations (CIO) became rallying points for not only workers but many middle-class activists. As a consequence, the notion of proletarian democracy was more than an academic issue at the outset of the Cold War—it was a material force to be reckoned with. The political context in which the post-war union democracy studies were done, in other words, demanded that the credibility of the basic Marxist theory of capitalist development and class formation be challenged.

POST-WAR LABOR STUDIES

Prior to the late 1940s, union organizational studies were the purview of labor historians, many of whom worked within a framework established by institutional economics. Most of these studies focused on the unions affiliated with the CIO and emphasized the factional struggles between communists and noncommunists within the unions. A major theme of these studies was that the Communist party influence destroyed democracy in unions. In 1938, for example, Benjamin Stolberg wrote that the rank and file in the CIO was rebelling against the party's "complete disregard of all union democracy" (Stolberg p. 155). Writing about the International Woodworkers of America in 1945, Vernon Jensen likewise counterposed communist presence in the union to rank-and-file democracy.

Although the notion of union democracy employed by the labor historians was very vague and undertheorized, it was framed in a way that had specific political implications. The assumption of the studies was that unions represented the material interests of their members against the interests of capital and that, generally speaking, unions that were controlled by their members were democratic; unions that were controlled by "outside" forces were considered undemocratic. In their accounts of the CIO, historians conventionally treated communist unionists as agents of foreign interests or "outsiders," and it was on this basis that they were considered to be an undemocratic influence.

Implicit in this approach to the question of democracy within unions was the understanding that the relationships between union and nonunion groups (including employers) and various factions within unions involved an element of power that was exercised in pursuit of group interests. Moreover, the careful documentation of the socioeconomic bases of the factions provided by these studies made it possible to account for organizational differences in class or class-fractional terms.

Framed in this way, union organizational studies were sure to remain politicized because it would always be possible to challenge on empirical grounds someone else's conclusions about what (or who) was or was not democratic. They were, in other words, asking promising questions, and although their own ideological biases prevented them from acknowledging the conclusions that their data pointed to, it was only a matter of time before someone else would. Moreover, the empirical evidence usually did not support the Cold War contentions that the communist movement was alien and anti-thetical to "democracy": communists were indeed indigenous to the factories and communities they organized, and in case after case it was the constitutional rights of communist unionists that had been violated by their opponents; the key actors in the purges of the late 1940s were often trade union professionals, leaders of liberal movements outside the unions, state agencies, and employers, not the rank and file (Levenstein 1981; Lembcke 1984; Keeran 1980). In short, the logic behind the purges of the Cold War period was anything but democratic, and the energy that propelled them appeared to emanate from everywhere but the industrial working class. This framework left open the possibility that not only were industrial workers capable of democracy but that nonworking-class elements were quite capable of undemocratic behavior—possibilities that made the relationship between class and democracy a fit subject for study. In the context of the Cold War this framework was clearly too dangerous; a new framework that would depoliticize the questions of union democracy was needed. Liberal sociologists accommodated this agenda.

Sociology and Union Democracy

The most important of the union democracy studies was that done of the International Typographical Union (ITU) published as *Union Democracy* in 1956 by S. M. Lipset, M. A. Trow, and J. S. Coleman. Lipset et al. viewed their study of the ITU as important for what could be learned that would be applicable to political processes in the larger society. They used the ITU case as an exception to prove Michels' (1962) "iron law of oligarchy": in the absence of counter-vailing forces, individuals will seek to maximize their power and influence in organizations. They defined democracy as the "possibility that an official can be defeated for reelection" (Lipset, Trow, Coleman, p. 453) and concluded that the ITU was democratic by this criteria. It had been able to maintain its high level of democracy, moreover, because three conditions checked the natural human and organizational propensities toward oligarchy: the ITU was small, its members (printers) were relatively high status workers, and its governance system (the two-party structure) was pluralistic (pp. 452–

3). Stated in theoretical terms, Lipset et al. found union democracy to be positively associated with political pluralism and the status of members, and negatively associated with size.

Radical Critiques of Union Democracy Studies

On its own terms, those of political pluralism, *Union Democracy* had a number of problems. In the first place, Lipset et al. conceptualized their dependent variable (union democracy) in a way that isolated it from social relations external to the union. By their definition a union could be democratic even if its leadership positions were filled by a succession of persons having no connection with or interest in the union's members; and a union could be considered democratic even if its leadership positions were filled by a succession of persons having no connection with or interest in the union's members; and a union could be considered democratic without reference being made to the adequacy of its performance in representing worker interests. In short, neither the relationship of the leaders to the members nor the relationship of the union to the larger society were germane to the notion of union democracy as it was conceptualized in this study.

Lipset et al. assumed away the criticism of their narrow conceptualization by saying that a union that did not represent its members would not be able to hold the allegiance of its members and would therefore cease to exist. Thus, a union that was democratic by their criteria was assumed to also be representative of worker interests in other social, economic, and political arenas. More recent research done by Valentine (1978), however, found little association between the level of union democracy (as defined by the pluralists) and the efficacy of unions as representatives of worker interests.

With the notion of democracy conceived as narrowly as it was, it was easy to demonstrate quantitative relationships between it and similarly narrow independent variables like size; but even a slightly broadened notion of democracy such as that employed by Faunce (1967) dissolved the certainty of the relationship. The narrowness of the conceptualization was typical of post-war "abstracted empiricism" that reduced its subject to psychological explanations and failed to relate sectors of society to one another. As a consequence, the ITU study led to conclusions that may or may not have been "true" but that had little "genuine relevance" and that functioned in a way that "eliminate[d] the great social problems and human issues of our time from inquiry" (Mills 1959, pp. 62, 73).

Fewer studies could have had less "genuine relevance" than did *Union Democracy.* Indeed, what is most remarkable about the ITU study is the absence of its authors' attention to the ideological issues and political factionalism that was tearing the North American union movement apart while they were doing their work. With whole internationals being expelled from the CIO, with the Canadian border being sealed to left-wing unionists, and with hundreds of union activists facing prosecution under various pieces of Cold War legislation, the question of governance structures *internal* to unions was hardly *the* issue. What *Union Democracy* did provide was a deflection of attention away from the real issues.

The main contribution of subsequent liberal and radical critiques of the ITU study was to move the questioning away from purely formalistic notions of union democracy into a framework that recognized the conflicting interests of union members and employers. Despite some attempts to reconceptualize the organizational problem in terms of social relations (e.g., "logics of collective action"), however, the term "union democracy" has generally been retained to refer to both formal organizational structure and representational efficacy. Moreover, the failure to question more fundamentally the pluralist assumptions of the union democracy studies has resulted in many of those assumptions being carried over into contemporary radical and neo-Marxist studies.

For activists, the confusion has meant that organizational theory has been essentially irrelevant. In the absence of any theory to guide practice, reform efforts have been sporadic and ad hoc; demands have been inconsistent from one reform effort to another and sometimes contradictory in light of the overall objectives of the union. It is safe to say that while nearly everyone, incumbents and insurgents alike, lays claim to the plank of union democracy, it has become a purely normative expression with increasingly vague meaning.

TOWARD A MARXIST THEORY OF
CLASS AND ORGANIZATION

Because radical sociologists never really focused their critique in a theoretical way, neither they nor the reform movements they have influenced have broken with the fundamental premises of pluralism. Specifically, (a) the relationship between class and organizational forms found in *Union Democracy* has never been criticized; (b) the assumptions made by the pluralists about the relationship between organizational size and democracy has not been reexamined; and (c) the ideological bias of Lipset et al. has not been subjected to an empirical critique.

Class and Democracy

Having no empirical base on which to stand, Lipset et al. dismissed the notion of proletarian democracy on philosophical grounds.

> Aristotle . . . suggested that democracy can exist only in a society which is predominantly middle class . . . that only in a wealthy society with a roughly equal distribution of income could one get a situation in which the mass of the population would intelligently participate in politics and develop the self-restraint necessary to avoid succumbing to the appeals of irresponsible demagogues. . . . Applying this proposition to trade-union government, we would expect to find democracy in organizations whose members have a relatively high income and more than average security [p. 14].

In other words, Lipset et al. theorized the relationship between class and organizational forms just the opposite from Marxist theory: The conditions for union democracy are most favorable in industries and occupations where working conditions most closely approximate those of middle-class occupations; those industries and occupations that are most working class, on the other hand, are least likely to produce democratic unionism.

Lipset et al. bolstered their argument by adopting a philosophical notion of democracy consistent with Cartesian methodology and Rousseauan social philosophy. "In the Cartesian world . . . phenomena are the consequences of the coming together of individual atomistic bits, each with its own intrinsic properties, determining the behavior of the system as a whole. Lines of causality run from part to whole, from atom to molecule, from molecule to organism, from organism to collectivity" (Levins and Lewontin 1985, pp. 1-2). Applied to human society, the Cartesian view held that the individual was ontologically prior to the whole, and that methodologically one can understand society only by reducing it to the characteristics of its parts—individuals. Individualism, as a social philosophy, met the needs of an emergent capitalism and thus came to be the ruling ideology of the new ruling class.

Lipset et al. premised their analysis of organizational behavior on this Cartesian model. A democratic organization was thus one in which individual sovereignty was maximized. The authors never examined the historical correspondence between capitalism and Cartesian reductionism; nor did they acknowledge that organizational models based on individual sovereignty have an ideological bias that reflects a specific bourgeois class interest. Finally, there was no recognition in *Union Democracy* that a different organizational logic might be spawned by the interests and historical experience of the working class.

Post-war radical theory accepted this pluralist formulation. In *New Men of Power* (1948), C. Wright Mills described U.S. workers as "underdogs [who] lack the hardy self-confidence and capacity for indignation common to middle-class people" (p. 267). Through Mills' influence on the New Left, the same class bias was carried into later studies. Throughout the 1960s and 1970s the dominant theme of working-class studies (e.g., Braverman 1974; Ehrenreich and Ehrenreich 1976; Marglin 1974; Aronowitz 1973; Piven and Cloward 1982) was that monopoly capitalism undermined the capacity of the U.S. working class. Writing specifically about union organizational forms, Sam Friedman (1982, p. 254) noted about Teamsters Local 208 that the local was exceptionally democratic and militant because of the high level of communication among truck drivers, their high levels of skill and craft identity, and their high pay—all of which were high-status characteristics Lipset et al. said made printers more inclined toward democracy.

There are at least three important problems with this formulation. First, while there is undoubtedly the available empirical evidence to sustain a variety of positions on this question, the record is not nearly as clear-cut as the liberal and radical traditions have presented it. The argument will be made at greater length below that the CIO unions representing the more proletarianized workers were in fact the most democratic even by pluralist standards. Second, the theory implies that capitalism deskills workers, and deskilled workers are less democratic. While the statement is in itself an indictment of capitalism that compels an understanding of how to transform the system, it also implies a logic of causation that is unidirectional and social relationships that are static. As such it does not contain within it a theory of how change in the actual structure of capitalism might occur. It leads to strategies and tactics that are reactive and defensive rather than transformative. Friedman, for example, notes (p. 262) that "capitalism produces strong tendencies toward both union bureaucracy and work degradation" but concludes that "these tendencies need not be absolutely determinant. Workers can resist, and they can win major victories." While this formulation is an advance over that of pluralists who saw bureaucratization as inevitable, its weakness is its failure to identify the contradictory properties of the class struggle that can be built upon for the enhancement of working-class offensive capacities.

Finally, given the long-term trend for capitalism to *eliminate* the kind of job conditions characteristic of printers and truckers (i.e., highly skilled with a high level of control over the work process and high status in the society at large), the prospects for union democracy were dismal. Logically, this theory leads to the conclusion that capitalism itself erodes the conditions favorable to democracy, but liberals and radicals both have evaded the implications of this conclusion. Alternatively, the relationship between worker status and union democracy could be the reverse of the way the authors hypothesized it (i.e., that the greater the proletarianization, the greater the chances for organizational democracy). If, in addition, the dependent variable is conceptualized as an aspect of class capacity rather than formal organizational democracy, the theoretical problem is opened to a vastly broader and more political set of considerations.

These possibilities ran counter to a fundamental class bias in both pluralist and radical scholarship, however, and as a result the propositions were never seriously explored. The emphasis of New Left historiography and the "work process" studies of the radical economists, moreover, laid the groundwork for the assertion of very conservative themes in writing of labor history. If it was craft and skilled workers who were on the cutting edge of history at the turn of the century, and if technical workers are there today, is it not then possible to interpret the CIO period in a way that places American Federation of Labor (AFL) unions and craft/skilled workers at center stage? While most accounts of the period have always emphasized the role of the unskilled workers, left-wing leaders, and community forms of organization, there has been a recent spate of books and articles that portend a rewriting of the period. David Brody (1975), for example, has downplayed the importance of working-class collective action to the period and Robert Zieger (1983) has produced an unblushingly sympathetic account of AFL business unionism. Their work is wholly consistent with New Left premises and the work of Cold War sociology.

In his critique of Braverman, Szymanski (1978, p. 50) argued that the popularity of the work process studies "among professionals and intellectuals at the current time can probably also be explained by the fact that [Braverman] is speaking to our fears, needs and experiences, as well as those of skilled craftsmen. Our jobs are under considerable pressure to break up our traditional privileges and skills and relinquish control to managers, administrators and capitalists. . . . We very much fear losing our relative privileges and being proletarianized." The preoccupation of radical scholars during the 1970s with questions of *control* was a matter of self-interest consistent with their petty bourgeois position. With the demise of radical social movements, the deepening malaise of the labor movement, and intensifying academic repression of the 1970s, the class base for theoretical work and the class composition of theoreticians was increasingly "bourgeoisified." The result has been a rightward drift toward neo-Weberian and neo-classical theory (Wright 1985; Elster 1985; Roemer 1982).

Size as an Organizational Determinant

The inverse relationship between size and organizational democracy has remained one of the most commonly accepted tenets of organizational sociology. Even for Offe and Wiesenthal (1980, p. 81), who in other respects move organizational theory into promising new areas, size transcends the logic of class as an organizational determinant.

The theory that large size begets organizational oligarchy poses two problems for a Marxist analysis. First, it is based on an assumption derived from neo-classical economics (and, in turn, from the same philosophical premises discussed above) that if the cost to an individual for his or her voluntary association with the organization exceeds the benefits of association then that person's association can only be maintained by organizational mechanisms that compel the association. The larger the organization, argues Mancur Olson (1980, p. 33), the higher the cost-benefit ratio for the individual:

> [in] small groups each of the members, or at least one of them, will find that his personal gain from having the collective good exceeds the total cost of providing some amount of that collective. . . . In such situations there is a presumption that the collective good will be provided. Such a situation will exist only when the benefit to the group from having the collective good exceeds the total cost by more than it exceeds the gain to one or more individuals in the group. Thus, in a very small group, where each member gets a substantial proportion of the total gain simply because there are few others in the group, a collective good can often be provided by the voluntary, self-interested action of the members of the group. . . . Even in the smallest groups, however, the collective good will not

ordinarily be provided on an optimal scale. . . . This tendency toward suboptimality is due to the fact that a collective good is, by definition, such that other individuals in the group cannot be kept from consuming it once any individual in the group has provided it for himself. Since an individual member thus gets only part of the benefit of any expenditure he makes to obtain more of the collective good, he will discontinue his purchase of the collective good before the optimal amount for the group as a whole has been obtained. In addition, the amounts of the collective good that a member of the group receives free from other members will further reduce his incentive to provide more of that good at his own expense. Accordingly, the larger the group, the farther it will fall short of providing an optimal amount of a collective good.

Thus, contends Olson (p. 86), the reluctance of union members to support their unions is "rational" and the explanation for conservative business union leadership lies in "the need for coercion implicit in attempts to provide collective goods to large groups" (p. 71).

The neo-classical argument holds up, however, only if two things are true. (1) It is true if the cost-benefit analysis of participation is calculated in narrowly economic terms, that is, the cost in terms of dues-dollars, income lost due to strikes, and so forth exceeds the income gained through improved wages and fringe benefits. If, however, participation in union affairs is viewed as a form of self-determination in one's work life, it ceases to be a "cost" at all. Likewise, if the notion of "benefits" is understood more broadly than immediate economic gain (e.g., the economic security that comes with having close friends to fall back on in old age as opposed to having to count on individual retirement savings), solidarity with fellow workers gained through union work has to be taken into account. This challenge to neo-classical reasoning is precisely what underlies the current questioning of the "prudent man" formula by which union pension funds have traditionally been invested in the private sector for maximum short-term profit rather than, for example, in low-income housing for union members or publicly owned enterprises that would ensure long-term social security and community stability (Rifkin and Barber 1978). Marxist theory (Lozovsky 1935) has always recognized that the representation of worker interests within the parameters of capitalism is only part of unions' raison d'être; their interests are also the foundation upon which an edifice of revolutionary political and cultural institutions arises. Viewed in this broadest possible way, the satisfaction of worker needs under capitalism becomes secondary to the logic of strategical efficacy in the struggle for the transformation to socialism.

(2) The inverse relationship between organizational size and democracy holds only if workers' behavior conforms to neo-classical notions of rationality, that is, their primary motive is to maximize economic gain and minimize economic costs. If the neo-classical theory is correct, union members' enthusiasm for their unions should be greatest when economic returns are the most certain. But in fact during economic expansion of the post–World War II period, U.S. workers benefitted enormously economically while union membership and participation declined. It can be shown through detailed case studies (Lembcke and Tattam, 1984) that the decline in union participation had virtually nothing to do with size and everything to do with class conflict. It was not the failure to negotiate lucrative contracts that discouraged workers in the post-war years but rather the narrowing of union concerns to wages, hours, and working conditions at the expense of the broader social issues like civil rights and imperialism.

The argument that workers conform to neo-classical rationality could be more a projection of a class-specific bourgeois ethic onto the working class than anything else. If the Marxist assumption that social conditions give rise to social consciousness is true, however, it is logical that the conditions of working-class existence would engender a different consciousness and that one dimension of working-class formation is the displacement of individual consciousness by class consciousness. In the following section it will be argued that in the United States this process has proceeded very unevenly with the result that one finds a range of consciousness among workers and that the internal power struggles in unions can be interpreted as struggles between class fractions rooted in very different material conditions. Specifically it can be shown that those fractions that advocated an economistic agenda resembling neo-classical rationality were precisely the least proletarianized craft and skilled workers.

The second major problem with using size as an independent variable for organizational explanations is that in the context of the post–World War II trends—the increasing concentration and centralization of capital, the centralization of economic planning, and the internationalization of production—it offered no insights into the problem of increasing working-class capacities through union reforms. Firm sizes were increasing, bargaining units were getting larger and more geographically dispersed, and the workforce more heterogeneous. Clearly, in order for unions to effectively represent worker interests, unions had to get larger but, as Lipset et al. posed the problem, the working class had to choose between organizational democracy and organizational efficacy.

There was the same ahistorical and static quality to the pluralists' proposition on size and organization as there was to their formulation of class and organization; for the most part radical and neo-Marxist theory has made no attempt to retheorize the relationship. There has been no attempt, for example, to show that size becomes a determinant of organizational behavior only if allowed to do so. That is, how size is mediated by organizational forms such as representation structures, delegate selection rules, roll call vote processes in conventions, and so forth will determine if and how size effects matters such as leadership selection and rank-and-file enthusiasm for the union, and most important, the union's capacity as an agent of social change.

It will be argued in the next section that the relationship of size to other organizational features cannot be separated from the relationship of class: For the capitalist class, size is positively related to class power but for the working class the relationship is more complex. How union size gets mediated is determined by the balance of political power within the organization (power derived, that is, from sources other than size) and is not in itself a determining feature of organizational behavior. As Child (1972) argued with respect to corporate organizations, the choice of organizational form is an "essentially political process, whereby power-holders within organizations decide upon courses of strategic action. This 'strategic choice' typically includes not only the establishment of structural forms but also the manipulation of the environmental features and the choice of relevant performance standards" (p. 2). In the study of labor unions the relationship between power holders, or leaders, and members of the organization, or rank and file, is especially critical. The historical data (Lembcke and Howe 1986) concur with Child (1972) and Chandler (1962) that strategical choices of organization leaders is a major source of organizational variation.

The Ideological Legacy of Pluralist and Radical Studies

In addition to the class bias in the conclusions of Lipset et al., there was a political bias associated with it. On the matter of political pluralism within unions, the authors argued (pp. 456–7) that a more pluralistic "pattern might have developed in a more clear-cut fashion than it has if a part of the left wing of the labor movement had not been captured by a totalitarian political movement, the Communist Party." They contended that "The Communists, by refusing to play the democratic game, help to break or prevent the institutionalization of internal democratic procedures." Stated as a theoretical proposition one would expect to find the least amount of internal democracy in those unions where communists had the most power.

In fact, neither the pluralist sociologists nor the Cold War historians made any attempt to empirically verify their claims about communist totalitarianism in unions. Lipset tried in a very curious way to base his claim on a single quote from Harry Bridges, president of the International Longshoremen and Warehousemen's Union (ILWU) who was close to the Communist party. According to Lipset (1952, p. 60), Bridges used the following words to defend the Soviet Union at the 1947 ILWU convention: "What is totalitarianism? A country that has a totalitarian government operates like our union operates. There are no political parties. People are elected to govern the country based upon their records. . . . That is totalitarianism . . . if we started to divide up and run a Republican set of officers, a Democratic set, a Communist set and something else we would have one hell of a time." What Bridges meant was that a country where the working class was the ruling class would be denigrated as "totalitarian" by its detractors. But in the context of the Cold War, the word "totalitarian" was already too loaded with negative connotation and Lipset was able to use the quote to denigrate not only communism but working-class organizational autonomy as well. He said, "Bridges believes that there is no class base for opposing political groups within the 'one-class' trade union." For Lipset, Bridges' words confirmed that "one-class" unions were a condition for totalitarianism and since a union is by definition a one-class organization, all unions tended toward oligarchy. Moreover, the Communist party's line on union organization during the 1930s emphasized the autonomy of industrial workers from multiclass organizational forms such as company unions (Keeran 1980). The strategy of industrial worker independence, which had proven enormously successful in the organizing drives that produced the CIO, was dismissed as totalitarian in Lipset's model. In keeping with his philosophical stand that only the middle class was capable of democracy, in other words, Lipset found that unions controlled solely by their own members were undemocratic. There was no empirical basis for such a conclusion, but in the McCarthyist climate of the 1950s it was sufficient for his purposes to be able to associate communists in U.S. unions with Soviet "totalitarianism" and let Cold War imaginations do the rest.

Unfortunately, New Left sociology never redressed the ideological assumptions of Lipset et al. If anything, Mills added fuel to the fire. Of communists in unions, he wrote, "Communist rule within unions

Table 3.1. Direct Rank-and-File Control of Leadership

	Referendum Election of Officers			Provisions for Direct Recall Referendum			Power of Officers to Appoint Other Officers and Staff		
	Yes	Qualified	No	Yes	Qualified	No	None	Limited	Extensive
Communist-led Unions									
UE			x		x		x		
ILWU	x			x				x	
IWA	x			x			x		
Mine-Mill	x			x				x^a	
NMU	x					x	x		
Noncommunist Unions									
UAW		x				x		x^b	
Steel		x^a				x			x^d
UMWA		x^e				x			x
IUE		x^f			x^g		x		
ACWU		x^h				x			x^i

Notes:

a. President's powers of appointment are limited to organizers but the elected executive board members from each district are also staff organizers.

b. The international president "shall fill by appointment all vacancies occurring in the International office except as otherwise provided for in this constitution . . . may appoint a member whose duties shall be to collect and compile statistics . . . may appoint such organizers, field and office workers as may be necessary . . . shall appoint subject to the approval of the International Executive Board one or more competent traveling auditors who shall examine the accounts of all subordinate bodies at least once a year. All appointments or suspensions from office done by the President shall be subject to the approval of the International Executive Board.

c. " . . . no person shall be notified or be a candidate who has not been nominated by 15 or more local unions. . . . The International tellers shall decide the legality of the votes of any local union . . . and all contests growing out of the report shall be filed with the International Executive Board which body shall have the power to decide the contest" (p. 27). The complexity of the United Steelworkers' election procedure is indicated by the length of its constitutional specifications, 12 pages. By comparison, the ILWU specifications of officer elections are one page long.

d. "The International President shall have the authority to appoint, direct, suspend, or remove, such organizers, representatives, agents and employees as he may deem necessary." There is no mention of any need for executive board approval for these presidential actions.

e. The UMWA provisions for elections, recalls, and powers of appointments are almost exactly the same as those for the United Steelworkers.

Table 3.1 continued

f. "A candidate shall be eligible for election only if he has been nominated in Convention by a delegate from each of 10 or more local unions from 3 or more districts, the combined per capita representations of which locals at the convention is no less than fifteen per cent (15%) of the total per capita representation." Only the president and secretary-treasurer are elected in this manner. Other officers, such as trustees, are elected in convention (p. 43). The IUE election procedure is encumbered with legal technicalities to a degree comparable to those of the United Steelworkers and United Mine Workers.

g. To initiate a recall a local "must first receive official endorsements from not less than ten (10) other locals from at least three different districts, comprising twenty-five (25%) percent of the total membership of the Union, as determined by the paid per capita on the average of the three previous months, before submitting the petition to the International trustees" (p. 15).

h. "No person shall be eligible for nomination of election . . . unless, for not less than five years immediately preceeding the date of the convention which nominates him he has been a member of the Amalgamated . . . employed by it, or in a trade or industry within its jurisdiction."

i. The Amalgamated president can appoint representatives, organizers, administrative, technical, and other employees without executive board approval.

Source: Union constitutions.

they control is dictatorial: although they talk the language of democracy, they do not believe or practice democratic principles" (1948, pp. 199–200). In *False Promises,* a book that influenced New Left-generation union activists more than any other, Stanley Aronowitz concluded that unions organized by the communists were conservative and "instruments for the disciplining and control of workers" (1973, pp. 13–14).

In the revival of labor history during the 1970s, virtually no attempt was made to see if the equation of communists and organizational authoritarianism held up empirically. In fact, it probably does not. A review of labor history and union constitutions reveals that in the unions such as the Mine, Mill, and Smelter Workers and the International Woodworkers of America, which were headed by communist leadership, one finds the highest level of rank-and-file participation in leadership selection (see Table 3.1). Moreover, the social base of these left-wing factions was most often the most proletarianized sectors of U.S. industries—a fact that does not square with pluralist and New Left assumptions about democracy and the working class. Their implicit association of the communist movement with a working-class social base was correct, but rather than empirically testing the association between that connection and union democracy, they simply repeated the accepted Cold War assumptions about communist "totalitarianism" and used the equation in a way that supported their thesis that the working class was not a historical agent likely to advance social democracy.

RETHEORIZING THE
UNION ORGANIZATION PROBLEM

An attempt to build a Marxist theory of union organization must go beyond a critique of pluralist limitations and reestablish the centrality of class as an explanatory variable. Such an attempt must be able to demonstrate that the long-term trend of capitalism to proletarianize larger numbers of workers is a condition that is more favorable to the establishment of a unionism that represents the objective interests of the working class. It must be able to show empirically that control by the *more* proletarian factions are positively associated with this more efficacious form of organization. But a theory that only demonstrates an instrumental relationship between the class/class fraction social basis of an organization and its organizational form would also be inadequate. What is needed is a theory that relates the internal logic of organizational forms to the social forces external to the organization. We need a structural understanding that is able to show how class, understood in a relational and dialectical sense, is played out through the struggle over organizational forms. In other words, Marxist theory must go beyond establishing an association between class and formal forms of organization and show the nature of that form of organization is—that is, objectively, working class.

The remainder of this paper is devoted to a preliminary attempt to formulate a theory of union organization that advances beyond the pluralist theory critiqued above, and that is consistent with Marxist theoretical principles. In general, it is argued that tension between capitalist attempts to fragment workers and workers' attempts to unify through unions provides the central logic that shapes union organizational forms. In skeletal form, the theory that emerges is as follows: (a) the dependent variable, "union democracy," is reconceptualized as the level of working-class organizational capacity operationalized as forms of organizational logic that range from working class (i.e., the association of human resources) to capitalist-like (i.e., the merging of financial resources); (b) the main independent variable is the class character of the organization. This variable ranges along a continuum from unions with very proletarianized memberships and high levels of rank-and-file control to unions whose members are skilled craftspersons and whose leaders and staffs are less proletarian and have high levels of autonomy from the rank and file.

Reconceptualizing the Dependent Variable:
From Organizational Democracy to Organizational Capacity

A reconceptualization of union democracy must begin by breaking the subject out of the confining organizational constraints given it by pluralists and neo-Marxists. A union can be neither democratic nor undemocratic on its own terms; the notion of a democratic organization has meaning only in the structural context in which it is set. Its definition implies an understanding of the social relations that bring the organization into being historically and the function of the organization in the chemistry of social forces acting to reproduce or dissolve the social structure.

The relationship between unions and other institutional forms and their general function within the class structure can be understood within a theoretical framework established by Offe and Wiesenthal (1980, p. 76). They argue that "the positions of a group in the class structure . . . not only lead to differences in power that the organizations can acquire, but also lead to differences in the associational practices, or logics of collective action, by which organizations of capital and labor try to improve their respective position vis-à-vis each other." They contend further (p. 80) that the difference between capitalist and working-class forms of organization "lies in the fact that [the former] depends upon its ability to generate the members 'willingness to pay' whereas the [latter] depends, in addition, on its ability to generate its members' 'willingness to act.' " Extended to an analysis of union organizations specifically, the Offe and Wiesenthal theory suggests that unions could be placed on a continuum ranging from those with more capitalist-like organizational practices (i.e., those that rely on the mobilization of financial resources to achieve their objectives) to those with more working-class–like associational practices (i.e., those that rely on mobilizing human resources).

Although Offe and Wiesenthal are not writing specifically about unions, the meaning for a definition of "union efficacy" would seem to be clear: a union functions in an efficacious fashion if it is effective in advancing working-class interests against those of the capitalist class. Moreover, "interests" is understood in an explicitly relational and class specific way: the objective of union activity is the enhancement of working-class capacities to transform the social relations of production under capitalism. While capitalists' organizational power lies in the merging of their capital or money resources, the real source of working-class power lies in the collective power of union members, which cannot be merged but only associated. Thus, it is only through the "collective deliberation" of members of the organization that the collective interest—to maximize associational power—can be optimized. In this model, then, the dependent variable is understood to be a dimension of class capacity that manifests itself through organizational forms.

In Lembcke and Howe (1986) we were able to operationalize "associational practices" as forms of representation within unions that were based on unit rule and "fiscal" or pecuniary practices as representation proportional to per-capita financial contribution. We found the latter form to be characteristic of conservative, AFL craft unions, and the former to be typical of radical, CIO industrial unions.

The Independent Variable—Class

For the most part contemporary radical theorists have concluded that capitalist development has worked to the detriment of the working class. Marxists, moreover (e.g., Szymanski 1978), have generally restricted themselves to analyses of class and political (i.e., electoral) behavior or to the problems of specifying class boundaries (e.g., Wright 1979). By reformulating the relationship between class and organizational capacities and broadening the scope of class analysis, we arrive at a strategical agenda that is very different from that currently followed by the mainstream of the U.S. left.

This method operationalizes class as the level of proletarianization. Both objective and subjective indicators of proletarianization are used. First, in terms of industrial development, traditional indicators of objective proletarianization are levels of capital-to-labor ratios, horsepower-to-labor ratios, and measures of productivity such as the ratio of value-added to wages (Gordon, Edwards, Reich 1982). A survey of major industries indicates that the unions organized according to associational logic are located in industries with the highest level of industrial development and, therefore, the most proletarianized workforces (see Table 3.2). The International Union of Mine, Mill, and Smelter Workers Union, for example, had an organizational structure that was very associational (and very democratic by pluralist standards) and it was in an industry that had a horsepower-to-worker ratio of 23.5, which is two times greater than the coal mining industry (9.83) which gave rise to one of the

Table 3.2. Frequency Distribution and Gamma on Proletarianization and Logic of Collective Action for CIO Unions

Logic of Collective Action	Highly Proletarianized	Moderately Highly Proletarianized	Indeterminant Class Identity	Moderately Lowly Proletarianized	Lowly Proletarianized	Total
Associational Logic	2	2	3	2	1	10
Mixed Logic	1	1	1	3	1	7
Pecuniary Logic	0	0	0	2	2	4
Total	3	3	4	7	4	21

Gamma = .56 (significant at the .01 level).
Source: Compiled from union constitutions.

most pecuniary-oriented (and least democratic by pluralist standards) unions, the United Mine Workers of America (UMWA).

While it is possible to demonstrate the correspondence between the level of proletarianization and organizational logic at the global level of whole industries, it is very seldom the case that disagreements over organizational form are expressed at that level. Thus, it is not possible to identify the concrete logic of those struggles without examining the factional struggles over organizational questions that were waged within particular unions. It can be shown that within the UMWA, for example, the level of proletarianization was greatest in Illinois coal fields from which the left-wing opposition to John L. Lewis' autocracy perennially came (Dubofsky and Van Tine 1977, p. 157; U.S. Department of Commerce 1940, pp. 242, 260). Likewise it was from the *least* proletarianized regions of Connecticut that the opposition to Mine-Mill's democratic left-wing administration came during the 1940s. By carefully examining the record (e.g., convention transcripts) of those fights, the logic behind the positions taken becomes apparent. At the factional level of analysis, moreover, it is possible to associate the positions taken by factions with their respective levels of proletarianization.

Conducting the analysis at the factional level also allows the relationship between organizational logic and the objective indicators of proletarianization outlined above to be validated through an examination of more subjective indicators. In a previous case study (Lembcke 1984), for example, it was found that the change from an associational logic of organizational form to a pecuniary logic in the International Woodworkers of America (IWA) followed a power struggle within the union. Moreover, what appeared to be personal and ideological differences between union leaders and factions in the fight were in reality struggles between fractions of the working class whose historical roots were deeply embedded in the uneven development of the lumber and wood products industry.

The historical and social characteristics of the class fractions that vied for power within the IWA have been presented in detail elsewhere (Lembcke 1984). The "conservative" fraction was based in a region that had received Oregon Trail pioneers in the mid-1800s who had brought with them aspirations to be independent farmers. These farmer-workers were most often German, and they had seldom had previous industrial experience. The mills they worked in were small and located in rural areas. The first form of unionism these workers knew was the craft form, represented by the American Federation of Labor (AFL) which established a foothold in the Portland, Oregon area during the 1880s.

The other faction was based in the northern Washington and British Columbia region which had not been opened for wood products production until the last decades of the century. In that region Scandinavian workers, many of whom were immigrants who brought with them previous trade union experience, entered mills that represented a monopoly form of industry (e.g., Weyerhauser). These workers, whose conditions offered little hope of social mobility, were exposed to an industrial form of unionism [represented by the Industrial Workers of the World (IWW)].

By examining union convention proceedings, it is possible to associate positions taken on organizational questions, and the distribution of votes by individuals and local organizations, with their respective social bases as described above. Based upon case studies like these, it is possible to associate the most proletarianized fractions of the working class with forms of collective action most consistent with the associational logic described above; it is also possible to associate the least proletarianized fractions with forms of collective action most consistent with pecuniary or capitalist logic described above. It is also through this method that we can see the strategical significance of organizational choices (Child 1972) and appreciate the enduring consequences (Cornfield 1986) of those choices.

SUMMARY AND CONCLUSIONS

In the presence of widespread activist interest in the questions about working-class organizational efficacy, the attempts by Marxist theorists to contribute to the discussions have been minimal. In the wake of Braverman's 1974 work, Marxists and other radical scholars wrote prolifically on problems related to the organization and control of work processes. These studies have enormously enhanced our understanding of the class struggle at the point of production. But because the objective of these studies has been to gain a better comprehension of the logic of management's control of the workplace, their meaning and utility for informing the practice of activists working for organizational reform of unions themselves has remained derivative and limited.

For the most part, theorizing about problems of strategy and tactics for union reform movements have remained locked within a problematic established by pluralist social theorists. This paper has attempted to understand the failure of radical and neo-Marxist theoretical work to inform the practice of labor union activists as a failure to break with the assumptions and conclusions of pluralism.

It has been argued that a break with the pluralist tradition must be made in two very specific ways. First, it is necessary to reconsider the conventional assumptions about the direction in which capitalist development influences working-class capacity. No matter if union democracy is conceptualized in the abstract pluralist sense, or in a relational sense as it is here, it can be shown that the more proletarianized fractions of the working class produce the most democratic and efficacious forms of organization. Second, as this paper has attempted to argue, the conceptualization of class capacities as a matter of *control* of production needs to be reconsidered. That conceptualization, being consistent with the realities of petty bourgeois and professional work life, leads to strategies and tactics useful to that class but irrelevant to the working class. Theoretical work treating working-class capacities as a matter of control, for the most part, has not been translated into meaningful practice, and where it has, it tends to be reactive and protectionist rather than transformative.

This paper has argued that working-class capacities are largely an organizational question—the manner in which the members of the class are associated for class struggle. Forms of organization that minimize the competition between class members and maximize unity are considered to be capacity-enhancing or efficacious forms, while those that invite competition or attempt to substitute sources of power that are naturally more advantageous to the capitalist class (capital) or the petty bourgeoisie (control of production) are considered to erode capacity.

While a retheorizing of union organizations must have as its first objective the establishment of definitions and relationships that correspond logically and empirically to the world they purport to describe, it must be done in the recognition that the relationship between class and organizational form is not one of simple, unidirectional determinism. Union organizational form at any moment represents a balance of class struggle; class is, in other words, a determinant in a structural rather than an instrumental sense. The ability of capital to influence union leadership and organizational forms through economic, ideological, and legal means is an integral factor in the overall logic that shapes union organizations. Ultimately, the test of the theory has to be whether or not those who act on it in practice are able to produce the desired results of representing the interests of union members within the parameters of capitalism as well as increasing the capacities of the working class to transform the class relations that define the capitalist order.

REFERENCES

Allen, V. L. 1954. *Power in Trade Unions*. New York: Longmans, Green.

Aminzade, Ronald. 1984. "Capitalist Industrialization and Patterns of Industrial Protest." *American Sociological Review* 49, 4 (August).

Aronowitz, Stanley. 1973. *False Promises*. New York: McGraw Hill.

————. 1983. *Working Class Hero*. New York: Pilgrim.

Beneson, Harold. 1985. "The Community and Family Bases of U.S. Working Class Protest, 1880-1920: A Critique of the 'Skill Degradation' and 'Ecological' Perspectives." In *Research in Social Movement, Conflicts and Change*, edited by Louis Kriesberg. Greenwich, CT: JAI.

Braverman, Harry. 1974. *Labor and Monopoly Capital*. New York: Monthly Review Press.

Brody, David. 1975. "Radical Labor History and Rank-and-File Militancy." *Labor History* (Winter).

Child, John. 1972. "Organizational Structure, Environment and Performance: The Role of Strategic Choice." *Sociology* 6:2-22.

Cornfield, Daniel B. 1986. "Declining Union Membership in the Post-World War II Era: The United Furniture Workers of America, 1939-82." *American Journal of Sociology* 91, 5:1112-53.

Dubofsky, Melvyn. 1976. "The Origins of Working Class Radicalism, 1890-1905." *Labor History* (Spring).

Dubofsky, Melvyn, and Warren Van Tine. 1977. *John L. Lewis*. New York: Quadrangle.

Ehrenreich, John, and B. Ehrenreich. 1976. "Work and Consciousness." *Monthly Review* 28, 3 (Summer):10-18.

Elster, Jon. 1985. *Making Sense of Marx*. Cambridge: Cambridge University Press.

Engels, Frederick. 1975. *The Condition of the Working Class in England: Collected Works of Marx and Engels* Vol. IV. New York: International Publishers.

Faunce, William. 1967. "Size of Locals and Union Democracy." In *Readings in Industrial Sociology*, edited by William Faunce. New York: Appleton-Century-Crofts.

Friedman, Samuel. 1982. *Teamster Rank and File: Power, Bureaucracy, and Rebellion at Work and in a Union*. New York: Columbia University Press.

Gedicks, Al. 1976. "The Social Origins of Radicalism Among Finnish Immigrants in Midwest Mining Communities." *Review of Radical Political Economics* 8, 3 (Fall).

Gordon, David, R. Edwards, and M. Reich. 1982. *Segmented Work, Divided Workers*. Cambridge: Cambridge University Press.

Gorz, André. 1982. *Farewell to the Working Class*. Boston: South End Press.

Griffin, Larry, M. Wallace, and B. Rubin. 1986. "Capitalist Resistance to the Organization of Labor Before the New Deal: Why? How? Success?" *American Sociological Review* 51, 2 (April):147-67.

Hamilton, Richard F. 1972. *Class and Politics in The United States*. New York: John Wiley.

Jensen, Vernon. 1945. *Lumber and Labor*. New York: Farrar & Rinehart.

Keeran, Roger. 1980. *The Communist Party and the Auto Workers Unions*. Bloomington: Indiana University Press.

Lembcke, Jerry. 1984. "Uneven Development, Class Formation, and Industrial

Unionism in the Wood Products Industry." In *Political Power and Social Theory*, Vol. 4, edited by M. Zeitlin. Greenwich, CT: JAI.

Lembcke, Jerry, and William Tattam. 1984. *One Union in Wood*. New York: International Publishers.

Lembcke, Jerry, and Carolyn Howe. 1986. "Organizational Structure and the Logic of Collective Action in Unions." In *Current Perspectives in Social Theory*, Vol. 7, edited by Scott McNall. Greenwich, CT: JAI.

Levins, Richard, and R. Lewontin. 1985. *The Dialectical Biologist*. Cambridge: Harvard University Press.

Lipset, S. M. 1952. "Democracy in Private Government." *The British Journal of Sociology* 3:47-63.

Lipset, S. M., M. A. Trow, and J. S. Coleman. 1956. *Union Democracy*. New York: Anchor.

Lozovsky, A. 1935. *Marx and the Trade Unions*. New York: International Publishers.

Marglin, Stephen. 1974. "What Do Bosses Do? The Origins and Functions of Hierarchy in Capitalist Production." *Review of Radical Political Economy* 6, 2:60-112.

Marx, Karl. 1867. *Capital*. New York: International Publishers.

Marx, Karl, and F. Engels. 1972. *Selected Works in One Volume*. New York: International Publishers.

Michels, Robert. 1962. *Political Parties*. New York: Dover.

Mills, C. Wright. 1948. *The New Men of Power*. New York: Harcourt, Brace.

———. 1959. *The Sociological Imagination*. New York: Oxford University Press.

Offe, Claus, and Helmut Wiesenthal. 1980. "Two Logics of Collective Action: Theoretical Notes on Social Class and Organizational Form." In *Political Power and Social Theory*, Vol. 1, edited by M. Zeitlin, pp. 67-115. Greenwich, CT: JAI.

Olson, Mancur. 1980. *The Logic of Collective Action* Cambridge: Harvard University Press.

Piven, Frances Fox, and Richard A. Cloward. 1982. *The New Class War*. New York: Pantheon.

Roemer, John. 1982. *A General Theory of Exploitation and Class*. Cambridge: Harvard University Press.

Rifkin, Jeremy, and R. Barber. 1978. *The North Will Rise Again*. Boston: Beacon.

Stolberg, Benjamin. 1938. *The Story of the CIO*. New York: Viking Press.

Stone, Katherine. 1975. "The Origins of Job Structures in the Steel Industry." In *Labor Market Segmentation*, edited by Richard Edwards, M. Reich, and D. Gordon. Lexington, MA: Lexington Books.

Szymanski, Al. 1978. *The Capitalist State and the Politics of Class*. Cambridge: Winthrop.

———. 1978. "Braverman as a Neo-Luddite." *The Insurgent Sociologist* (Winter):45-50.

Tabb, William, and Larry Sawers. 1978. *Marxism and the Metropolis*. New York: Oxford University Press.

Therborn, Goran. 1983. "Why Some Classes Are More Successful Than Others." *New Left Review*, no. 138 (March-April):37-55.

United States Department of Commerce. 1940. *Sixteenth Census of the United*

States. Mineral Industries 1939 Vol. 1. Washington, DC: Government Printing Office.

Valentine, Cynthia E. 1978. "Internal Union Democracy—Does It Help or Hinder the Movement for Industrial Democracy?" *The Insurgent Sociologist* (Fall).

Wright, Eric O. 1979. *Class Structure and Income Determination.* London: New Left Books.

————. 1985. *Classes.* London: Verso/New Left Books.

Zieger, Robert. 1983. *Rebuilding the Pulp and Paper Workers' Union 1933-41.* Madison, WI: University of Wisconsin Press.

4

Bringing Classes Back In: State Theory and Theories of the State

Rhonda F. Levine

The publication of Ralph Miliband's *The State in Capitalist Society* and the ensuing Poulantzas-Miliband debate marked the beginning of a renewed theoretical interest in the capitalist state (Miliband 1970, 1973a, 1973b; Poulantzas 1969, 1976). While Poulantzas and Miliband circumscribed their controversy within a selected range of topics, the debate itself inspired a multitude of separate lines of inquiry that extended well beyond the original confines and in fact opened new terrain to both theoretical and historical investigation. Whereas previously scholars tended to treat the state as either a mere superstructural phenomenon or ignored the subject entirely, today the subject of the state has become a topic of lively debate.

The state debate in Europe, coupled with domestic industrial economic decline, has encouraged some scholars to evaluate various conceptualizations of the state in terms of their relevance for explaining the historical development of the United States. This effort has raised a new set of questions that have shifted the state debate beyond the generalized framework of Marxism and has attempted to advance an alternative formulation of the state that purports to be more historically relevant. This "state-centered" theory has gained

An earlier version of this paper appeared as "Marxism, Sociology, and Neo-Marxist Theories of the State," in *Current Perspectives in Social Theory* 6 (1985). The argument and analysis presented here is elaborated in Rhonda F. Levine, *Class Struggle and the Capitalist State: Industrial Labor, Industrial Capital and the New Deal.* Greenwich, CT: JAI, 1987.

popularity in U.S. sociology, supporting the Weberian notion of the state as an independent organization of political power with a life and structure of its own.

The purpose of this paper is to present a critique of state-centered theory and to propose an alternative "class-centered" approach to the study of the state. The New Deal industrial recovery program serves as the empirical case from which to evaluate these two competing explanations of the state in contemporary capitalism.

STATE-CENTERED THEORY

No one would deny the fact that the role of the state in the post-World War II era has expanded its domain. The complexity of class relations in late capitalism is compounded by the ever-widening role of the state in social and economic matters. For proponents of state-centered theory, the increased role of the state in economic management, in particular, has made plain that analyses of the state and state activity cannot be understood simply in terms of forces that guide "civil society." State-centered theory is distinguished from society-centered theories by locating the state as an autonomous structure with its own logic, separate from social and economic forces.

State-centered theory is best stated and exemplified in the recent work of Skocpol (1985). Borrowing the concepts of "state-centered" and "society-centered" from Nordlinger (1981), Skocpol calls for a break with society-centered theories of the state, arguing that such conceptualizations do not adequately account for the primacy of the state in understanding societal dynamics. Although Skocpol places such strange bedfellows as pluralists, structural-functionalists, and Marxists in the society-centered camp, it is with her critique of Marxist analyses that we are concerned here. Leaving aside the fact that Skocpol's distinction between society- and state-centered approaches ignores the variety and differences within the so-called society-centered camp, state-centered theory purports to present a challenge specifically to Marxist state theory.

For state-centered theory, the state's relationship to the economy and polity is an empirical question. The problem with Marxist analysis of the state, according to Skocpol, is that it assumes without question that "states are inherently shaped by classes or class struggle and function to preserve and expand modes of production," thereby failing to examine empirically the question of state autonomy (1985, p. 4). For Skocpol, state-centered theory allows one to examine the

autonomy of the state and state activity in such a manner as to realize that under certain historical circumstances it is the state that has
the capacity to reshape relationships between groups and classes
within civil society. Marxists, according to Skocpol, ignore that important social change is a consequence of autonomous state activity
and cannot be reduced to class forces.

For Skocpol, society-centered theorists assume that political
struggles and structures can be reduced to socioeconomic conflict
and forces. Marxists, in particular, argue that the state functions to
preserve class domination, ignoring, therefore, that the state has a
logic and interest of its own separate and distinct from class society.
State-centered theory, on the other hand, has two complementary
strategies for studying the state that do not reduce the state to a
mere reflection of societal forces. According to state-centered theory, "states may be viewed as organizations through which official
collectivities may pursue distinctive goals, realizing them more or less
effectively given the available state resources in relation to social
settings. On the other hand, states may be viewed more macroscop-
ically as configurations of organization and action that influence the
meanings and methods of politics for all groups and classes in society" (Skocpol 1985, p. 28). State-centered theory seeks to be a new
"theoretical understanding of states in relation to social structures,"
one which is not likely to resemble Marxist theories. Whereas Marxist
theories are more interested in developing grand theories, Skocpol
writes that state-centered theory provides "solidly grounded and
analytically sharp understandings of the causal regularities that
underlie the histories of states, social structures, and transnational
relations in the modern world" (Skocpol 1985, p. 28).

No doubt, Skocpol's insistence in taking state structures and
state institutions seriously is a well-taken corrective to some simplistic Marxist notions that the state is merely a reflection of the economic base. But Skocpol ignores the variety of Marxist perspectives
on the state (cf. Jessop 1982, pp. 9–20). Even those perspectives that
argue for the relative autonomy of the state, according to Skocpol,
maintain society-centered assumptions by arguing that the state, in
the final instance, is to "preserve or expand modes of production"
(Skocpol 1985, p. 5). What Skocpol seems to misunderstand and mis-
represent here is what most Marxists mean by the concept "mode of
production." As Brill (unpublished) writes,

> A mode of production is not a social or an economic concept but
> political-economic articulation of relations and forces of production.

The state, in this sense, does not function to preserve a mode of production but is rather a more concrete manifestation of a component of the relations of production. The concept of a mode of production attempts to express particular abstract patterns by which social tasks and social products are distributed and integrated. It is a tool for organizing our investigations of concrete social formations, it is not a thing which has a concrete relation to states.

Whereas Skocpol chastises Marxists for not questioning the assumption that classes and class struggle shape the state and state activity, Skocpol herself assumes the independence and autonomy of the state from larger social factors. Accepting the Weberian view of the distinction between society, economy, and the state, Skocpol does not grasp the significance of Marxist analysis that develops concepts that seek to explain what appears to be the separation between the economic, political, and social spheres. In many ways, Skocpol is guilty of what she has accused Marxists of doing: assuming that the state has certain qualities that are, by definition, true. In other words, whereas Marxists assume that the state is part of an overall mode of production and state activity is therefore understood in such a context, Skocpol assumes the separation of the state from social and economic forces, analyzes the state in its own right, and then claims that the state influences and directs change in both the economic and social spheres. Skocpol claims that empirical evidence supports her state-centered approach. Yet, her analysis is carried out within this narrow, one-sided view of the state as an independent organization with its own logic and history. There is little doubt that she will invariably prove what she has already assumed.

By reducing the state to a set of organizations, Skocpol's state-centered theory is limited in the scope of its analysis of large-scale historical change. State-centered theory, like much of mainstream political science, takes the "state" at face value, ignoring deeper levels of analysis that might indeed shed light on the complex relation between the state and larger social and economic forces. For Skocpol, one of the strengths of state-centered theory is that it seeks to develop "middle-range generalizations about the role of states in revolutions and reforms, about the social and economic policies pursued by states, and about the effects of states on political conflicts and agendas" (Skocpol 1985, p. 28). But how, exactly, is state-centered theory useful in actually explaining large-scale social change? Is it really a "new" theoretical approach? Or is it merely the old standard social science critique of Marxism with new words that appear to escape the old language of pluralist analysis? It is to these issues that we now turn.

NEW DEAL AS TESTING GROUND

In a series of articles, Skocpol and associates draw on state-centered theory to demonstrate the significance of state structures in explaining New Deal policies (Skocpol 1980; Finegold and Skocpol 1984; Skocpol and Finegold 1982; Weir and Skocpol 1985; Skocpol and Amenta 1985). Whereas Marxists focus on state structures as embedded in class contradictions, Skocpol centers her analysis on the administrative and bureaucratic capacities of the organization of the state. For Skocpol it is not class conflict or struggles that condition state activity, but rather the structure and activities of the state that profoundly condition the ability of classes to achieve certain levels of struggle, organization, and representation (Skocpol 1985, p. 5). By arguing that all existing conceptualizations of the state fail to consider the specificity of party and state structures, Skocpol conceptualizes the state as independent from the social relations of capitalism and proceeds to analyze the specificity of the structure of the state.

Claiming that her state-centered approach best explains the formulation and implementation of various New Deal policies, Skocpol focuses on the fragmentary character of the U.S. state, the weak national administrative structure, and the nonprogrammatic structure of political parties as the root cause of the limits to New Deal policies (Weir and Skocpol 1985, pp. 132–7). While there is no denying these aspects of the state in the United States, there is little explanation of the forces that initially shaped the structures. By arguing that the determinants of state response to the economic crisis of the 1930s is traceable to the U.S. national administrative arrangements, government institutions, and political parties, Skocpol and her associates obscure the impact of inter- and intraclass conflict on the very structure of these arrangements.

By arguing that state policies are primarily shaped by the development of state structures and party organization, "organizations that have their own historical trajectories and cannot be taken for granted or reduced to manifestations of the current array of social forces," Skocpol and Finegold proceed to analyze the fate of the National Industrial Recovery Act in terms of the administrative weaknesses of the agency designed to implement the act (Finegold and Skocpol 1984, p. 161). While correctly pointing out these administrative weaknesses, Skocpol and Finegold, in their haste to dismiss competing explanations, ignore the importance of the underlying economic processes that shaped the structures of the state in the first place.

In order to unpack Skocpol's (and associates') argument, it is necessary to evaluate how she defines the terrain of analysis and how she understands existing frames of reference. For Skocpol, the Great Depression of the 1930s signalled an economic crisis in the United States. The two striking indices of this economic crisis, for Skocpol, were high and persistent levels of unemployment and stalled business activity, measured by underutilized productive capacity. To be sure, Skocpol's crisis was a capitalist crisis in that it entailed reduced profits, laid off workers, and declining demand. The solution to the economic crisis was centered in expanded demand for war materials that occurred in the late 1930s.

Skocpol's argument conforms more or less to the standard historiographical interpretations. The problem, however, is not so much what she says but what is omitted. The economic crisis of the 1930s was a world depression. It signified an "organic crisis" in that it entailed structural contradictions in the overall mode of capital accumulation and it required a restructuring of the mainstays of the entire productive-reproductive edifice.

The *differentia specifica* that distinguishes this economic crisis was the specific relationship between three overlapping structural barriers to expanded accumulation: (1) an exceedingly high rate of labor exploitation manifested in low levels of consumption on the part of the working class, resulting in problems of profit realization; (2) unregulated competition, leading to problems of investment; and (3) an antiquated matrix of state apparatuses that did not reflect the changing balance of class forces. In short, the dominance of large-scale corporate capital on the economic terrain was not matched by the political practices of a centralized dominant apparatus of the state.

Skocpol does not acknowledge that the organic crisis of the 1930s and its resolution was a crisis of accumulation that both destroyed capital (by eliminating high-cost and extraneous producers) and restored capital on a new footing (by rewarding low-cost producers and accelerating the growth of large-scale corporate capital). This process of structural selectivity occurred "behind the backs" of the social actors enmeshed in the immediate reality of day-to-day politics. Skocpol's narrow and incomplete conceptualization of the economic crisis permits her and her associates to pose the problem of New Deal recovery measures in terms of conscious intervention and the administrative means by which to carry them out. In general, Skocpol argues that various New Deal policies, such as the National Industrial Recovery Act, "failed" to bring about the intended economic recovery because of the administrative weaknesses or lack of state capacity to bring it about. This success/failure dichotomy merely assumes what must be proven. Capital accumulation is a contradictory process. Capitalist growth and recovery certainly meant enormous profits for some. Yet, it also entailed financial ruin for others. No single New Deal policy could have satisfied all capitalist interests.

In their state-centered approach explaining New Deal policies, Skocpol and associates ignore the process of capital accumulation and the internal barriers and contradictions that it engenders. Consequently, the structural limits to state policies are also glossed over. In her haste to prove that the state has an organizational capacity and bureaucratic autonomy of its own, Skocpol operates under a set of undeclared and unsubstantiated assumptions. Consequently, she is able to "prove" what has already been assumed: (1) the state has a true essence, an undifferentiated homogeneity; (2) the state enjoys the capacity to act; and (3) state managers are vehicles for state policy formation and the personification of the state's capacities and powers.

Skocpol's task is made easier because she conflates two levels of analysis that should be kept distinct and concepts that actually have different social meanings. Specifically, Skocpol collapses the analysis of the institutional ensemble comprising the capitalist state with the evaluation of the historically specific political regime under Roosevent. Equally important, she treats the Roosevelt administration, the state, and government more or less undistinguishably. Consequently, she oscillates between levels of analysis, analyzing deep structures with their own biographical origins within the internal frame of reference. The result is a confusing set of critical commentaries that seem merely to skim the surface layers.

These methodological and analytical weaknesses of Skocpol's are made even more pronounced if one seriously looks at the manner in which she dismisses existing frames of reference (cf. Skocpol 1980; Finegold and Skocpol 1984). By lumping together all Marxist and neo-Marxist theories of the state, Skocpol overlooks the fact that these various arguments, under the rubric of "instrumentalism" and "structuralism," employ very different languages, structures of presentation and exposition, and distinctive objects that place them on very separate terrains. In addition, Skocpol and associates at times selectively and even unfairly "reconstruct" their arguments. Perhaps the most glaring illustration of this reconstruction is the unexplained omission of Poulantzas' later works from Skocpol's treatment of what she labels "political functionalism." A composite picture of Poulantzas' work certainly does not lend itself to the specific characterization as the type of "born-again" Parsonian structural-functionalism in Marxist garb as Skocpol would lead one to believe (cf. Jessop 1985). In particular, Skocpol fails to appreciate Poulantzas' distinction between general characteristics of the capitalist state and the specific characteristics of political regimes such as that of Roosevelt. This distinction enables one to argue that the structural relationship between the capitalist state and the process of capital accumulation is carried forward, distorted, and blocked by the actual relations of class forces. The relations of class forces, in turn, is reflected in political parties, state administrations, and state structures. In fact, Poulantzas specifically argues that the state is not a functional monolithic integrated whole, but rather is constituted by class contradictions.

AN OUTLINE FOR A CLASS-CENTERED APPROACH TO THE STUDY OF THE NEW DEAL

In state-centered theory, bureaucratic and administrative arrangements have been excised of any class content or class controversies or conflicts. Bureaucratic structures appear as *sui generis* sets of rules and procedures governing decision making and the policy implementation process. "One cannot take the state as an unproblematic given or reduce it to one of its multiple determinations," Jessop (1982) warns. Skocpol and associates have ignored this admonition. Consequently their analysis of the New Deal has been largely confined to a narrow scope of political decision making.

The work of Poulantzas serves as a starting point for a comprehensive Marxist-inspired theory of the capitalist state. By theorizing general characteristics of the capitalist state as Poulantzas does at the outset (similar to Marx's analysis of capital accumulation found in *Capital*), the particular aspects of the state in historically specific conjunctures can indeed be analyzed. Although all states share certain common characteristics, each state and political regime needs to be examined on its own terms, given the concrete reality of the historical conjuncture. This means much more than merely examining administrative and bureaucratic arrangements. Operating within a Poulantzian frame of reference, Jessop (1982) suggests that an adequate analysis of state activity (1) be founded on the specific qualities of the capitalist mode of production, (2) attribute a central role to the limits imposed by the accumulation process on class forces,

(3) establish the relationship between the political and economic without reducing one to the other or treating them as autonomous from one another, and (4) allow for historical differences in forms of representation, intervention, and internal structures. Because state response to economic crisis is based on the political repercussions of the crisis, it follows that an analysis of the specificity of New Deal policies must take into account the balance of class forces and the dynamic of the class struggle.

Accepting the Marxist premise that capitalism is a contradictory system and that the primary social classes of labor and capital are in antagonistic relationship to one another, the class-centered approach proposed here takes as its starting point a set of propositions: (1) the capitalist state is internally divided by its location within the social relations of production. Since the state is located within the contradictions of capitalism, the state itself is wrought with contradictions and the very contradictions that arise within the state are a product of the basic contradictions of class society; (2) as a consequence of the forces that continuously separate capital into distinctive competitive and antagonistic units, the capitalist state is the political terrain for adjudication of fractions of capital. By being relatively autonomous from various class fractions, state policy serves to mediate between units of capital by attempting to politically unify an otherwise disorganized capitalist class. Moreover, as a consequence of the antagonistic relationship between labor and capital, the capitalist state becomes the arena for assuring a consensus for capitalist rule. State policy simultaneously attempts to unify an otherwise disorganized capitalist class and channel working-class struggles within parameters compatible with capitalist social relations of production, thereby short-circuiting independent working-class political organization; (3) state policies always reflect, in Poulantzas' words, "strategic compromises" (1975, p. 144). Although state policies attempt to maintain class rule by providing the conditions for profitable accumulation, state policies are not formulated nor implemented according to a preestablished functional harmony, but in and through the struggle of antagonistic classes. The particular formulation and implementation of a specific policy are shaped by the dynamic and nature of the class struggle in the particular historical time and setting. Categories like monopoly capital and nonmonopoly capital, fractions of capital, and relative autonomy form the conceptual apparatus through which an analysis of specific historical conjunctures is initiated. By "bringing classes back in," the class-centered approach sidesteps one-sided analyses that reduce a complex process of variable determinations into a unilinear explanation for policy formation and implementation.

A reassessment of the New Deal industrial recovery program from a class-centered approach sheds light on not only the manner in which new Deal policies were formulated and implemented, but also, and perhaps more importantly, on the extent to which New Deal policies provided conditions for a new phase of capital accumulation.[1] The origins and implementation of New Deal policies under the Roosevelt administration represented a bold program of national economic recovery during a period of significant economic collapse, political turmoil, and ideological dissension. Seen retrospectively, New Deal policies appear to exhibit a certain coherent logic. Yet, from the perspective of those policy makers who designed and implemented them, the various policies and programs appeared as a series of ad hoc, almost desperate measures designed to temporarily defend against further economic decline and political rebelliousness (cf. Levine 1987).

Put broadly, various New Deal policies designed to restructure the political and economic order existed in abstraction. Yet the practical possibilities of implementing a particular policy are limited not only by the specific balance of class forces but also by a more complex set of circumstances inherited from the past. The Roosevelt administration inherited a complex set of circumstances that circumscribed its historical possibilities. In particular, the world depression that had ravaged business operations for over three years prior to the Roosevelt administration's political regime had exposed deep structural contradictions in the accumulation process.

When the Roosevelt administration took office, the industrial working class was becoming increasingly restive. Unemployed workers engaged in street demonstrations and marches to demand federal relief and some form of unemployment insurance, while employed workers resisted wage decreases and increases in the number of hours of work for the same pay. Industrial capitalists themselves were hopelessly divided over what caused the Great Depression and what possible routes would overcome its devastating effects. Gerard Swope, president of the General Electric Company, proposed the self-regulation of industry through price-fixing and profit control, some minimal increase in compensation for workers in an attempt to prevent labor discontent, and an easing of the antitrust laws as one route toward economic stabilization. The plan called for greater cooperation between trade associations and the state machinery and dismissal of the fears of monopoly and competition in order that greater stabilization be achieved in the depressed atmosphere of the time (Sobel 1972, pp. 89–90). The Chamber of Commerce, while not agreeing entirely with Swope's plan, supported some sort of business planning and cooperation and, along with the National Association of Manufacturers, supported a revision of the antitrust laws. Smaller-scale industrial capitalists and those not active in the trade associations, however, feared that such plans would only further monopoly growth, a factor they perceived as dominant in explaining the crisis to begin with (Rosen 1977, p. 64; Lund 1933).

While it is true that many industrial capitalists united for a relaxation of the antitrust laws, the political unity of the industrial capitalist class was anything but secure. Even Berle, one of Roosevelt's advisors, recognized that the growth of large-scale corporate capital caused a political differentiation within the capitalist class. Berle wrote to Roosevelt in 1932 noting that the administration would have to initiate an industrial policy that could aid in "regulating and unifying" the capitalist class (Berle 1932). Berle further argued,

> Were the few thousand men running things a coordinated group, you would at least have a government of sorts. Actually, they are in the state of the political feudal barons in France before a centralized French government unified them. . . . Either the handful of people who run the economic system now will get together making an economic government which far outweighs in importance the federal government; or in their struggles they will tear the system to pieces. Neither alternative is sound national policy.

The shift in the balance of class forces engendered a chaotic situation where capitalists—themselves increasingly fragmented both economically and politically—were losing the iron grip that they enjoyed during the 1920s boom period over the working class in general and the increasingly restive working class in particular. Left-wing political groups gained a wider presence among workers at the point of production, and strike activity and work stoppages became the response to wage cuts and work speed-ups (Milton 1982, pp. 25–9; Cochran 1977, pp. 43–81). The various mechanisms through which capitalists had subjected labor to its discipline during the previous decade became unravelled as the depression wore on. The resulting class tensions threatened to add even further to the economic chaos during Roosevelt's first term in office. By the middle of the 1930s, the growing round of strikes was the most visible sign that the industrial working class had actively intervened to determine the future course of industrial production. Work stoppages increased from 637 involving

183,000 workers in 1930 to 2,014 stoppages involving 1,120,000 workers in 1935 (U.S. Census 1975, p. 179). This intervention of the working class meant that whatever policy was pursued for economic recovery was hindered not only by the structural reality of the accumulation process but by the activities of the industrial working class that interrupted the capital accumulation process.

Rather than representing a coherent blueprint that by conscious design established an overall plan for economic recovery, the Roosevelt administration muddled along, tinkering with various programs relating to banking, agriculture, and relief—making every effort to force compromises between antagonistic interests wherever possible and simply imposing a solution when adjudication seemed impossible. The National Industrial Recovery Act (NIRA), with its codes of fair competition setting production and price guidelines for the various branches of industry, was formulated not only to overcome obstacles to accumulation but to politically organize a fractionated industrial capitalist class. The inclusion of section 7a that presumably gave industrial workers the right to organize and join unions of their own choosing was only included as an effort simultaneously to sidetrack the Black Thirty-Hour Bill and to make concessions to industrial labor.

In November 1932, the American Federation of Labor (AFL) convention called for a five-day work week and a six-hour day in an effort to increase employment and purchasing power (Radosh 1967 *ad passim;* Bernstein 1972, pp. 481–3). In December 1932, Senator Hugo Black introduced a bill to Congress that incorporated the demands of the AFL. The Black-Thirty-Hour Bill called for the prohibition of interstate shipments of goods produced by labor working more than six hours a day and five days a week (Leuchtenburg 1963, p. 56). According to Hawley (1966, p. 22), the Black Thirty-Hour Bill "reflected the popular notion that available work should be shared; it enjoyed the support of organized labor; and in an atmosphere of the time, it seemed likely to win the approval of the House as well as the Senate." However, Roosevelt was opposed to the bill, believing that it would lead to an actual decline in purchasing power because of the lack of minimum wage provisions (Himmelberg 1976, p. 196; Hawley 1966, p. 22; Schlesinger 1959, p. 95; Leuchtenburg 1963, p. 56). Roosevelt thought that the best strategy to oppose the Black Thirty-Hour Bill was to present a better proposal for stimulating both industrial recovery and industrial employment. Clearly, the proposed measure would have to include some concessions to organized labor. Not only did the Black Bill incorporate the demands of organized labor, but William Green, president of the AFL, stated that the Black Bill "struck at the roots of the problem—technological unemployment" and went on to intimate that he would call a general strike in support of the 30-hour work week (U.S. Congress 1933, pp. 1–23).

After the Black Bill passed the Senate, Roosevelt instructed Secretary of Labor Frances Perkins to propose a number of amendments to the House Labor Committee, including the establishment of minimum wage levels. Industrial capitalists and organized labor opposed the Perkins' amendments, especially the minimum wage provisions. Harriman of the Chamber of Commerce argued that constructive wage-and-hour legislation should be based on the principles of "industrial self-government" that had been recommended by such organizations as the Chamber of Commerce and the National Association of Manufacturers. These businessmen argued that antitrust laws should be revised so as to allow employers to enter into voluntary trade association agreements covering such things as hours, wages, and unfair competition. Organized labor, through its spokesperson William Green, opposed the Perkins amendments arguing that the bill, if amended, would vest in industrial boards the power to stipulate minimum wages that would eventually become the maximum wage (Hawley 1966, pp. 22–3; Himmelbert 1976, pp. 203–4).

While the Perkins' amendments were being heatedly debated in the hearings before the House Labor Committee, Roosevelt requested that Raymond Moley, a member of his brains trust, review recovery proposals of the Chamber of Commerce, National Association of Manufacturers, and the brains trust. Roosevelt directed Moley to develop a program for industrial stabilization that would be agreeable to both industrial capitalists and organized labor. As the Black Bill was sidetracked in the House and soon became buried in the fervor of New Deal legislative proposals, three separate groups worked on separate drafts of a recovery bill. Out of the confusing and complex drafting process a single recovery measure emerged (see Galambos 1966, pp. 130–6; Roos 1937, pp. 3–40; Leuchtenberg 1963, pp. 56–8; Himmelberg 1976, p. 206). Although the precise manner in which the final draft evolved is somewhat unclear, it is fairly clear why the measure included provisions for a temporary relaxation of the antitrust laws and government support for trade associations along with provisions granting industrial labor the right to organize and bargain collectively. Industrial and trade association leaders and representatives of organized labor were all successful in representing their particular interests to various members of the different groups working on drafting the recovery measure.

The recovery measure, soon to be known as the National Industrial Recovery Act, received the endorsement of both capitalists and organized labor before the final draft went before Congress. Hillman, representing organized labor in the garment industry, and Lewis, representing organized labor in the coal industry, supported business proposals for the suspension of the antitrust laws and argued that industrial codes also protected labor in that they offered "high-wage businessmen badly needed protection from operators who connived to undersell them by exploiting their workers" (cited in Leuchtenberg 1963, p. 57). The AFL viewed the NIRA as a big step forward in industrial economic planning, rationalization, and stabilization. The position of the capitalist class on the NIRA was made equally clear. Hugh Johnson, soon to be head of the National Recovery Administration, spoke with leading industrial capitalists who had come to Washington during the weeks of the final drafting of the NIRA and discussed all phases of the recovery measure, including section 7a, which presumably allowed industrial labor to organize. In general, industrial capitalists, especially those associated with the National Association of Manufacturers, were suspicious of section 7a. However, the wording of the stipulation of union recognition was left rather ambiguous, and capitalists were assured by Johnson that section 7a would not threaten the continuation of the open shop. On the whole, industrial capitalists were willing to accept section 7a in exchange for the passage of the entire bill—especially those aspects that imposed price controls (Kolko 1976, p. 126).

When the final draft of the NIRA was presented to Congress on May 17, the proposal appeared to offer a little to both industrial capitalists and organized labor. Large-scale capitalists received government authorization to draft code agreements exempt from antitrust laws, and small-scale capitalists received government licensing of business practices. Organized labor received section 7a, which presumably guaranteed the right to organize and bargain collectively and stipulated that the industrial codes of fair competition should set minimum wages and maximum hours. Roosevelt recommended immediate action on the proposed recovery legislation and said that the Congress should provide the necessary machinery for "a great cooperative movement throughout all industry in order to obtain wide reemployment, to shorten the working week, to pay decent wages for the shorter week and to prevent unfair competition and disastrous overproduction" (cited in Hawley 1966, p. 26).

Contrary to its design, the implementation of the National Industrial Recovery Act only stimulated disunity among industrial capitalists and militancy on the part of industrial labor. Initially all capitalists expressed the desire to suspend the antitrust laws and to institute codes of fair competition that would provide production and price controls. The regulation of prices and production was thought to be a safeguard for small- and medium-scale capitalists against increased industrial concentration and to provide protection for their individual competitiveness in the market. Hence, these capitalists looked to the state administration for temporary protection against being driven out of the market and forcibly being "bought out" by the larger monopoly firms. However, the actual code drafting process did not coincide with the desires of smaller capitalists. The codes were supposed to include price and production controls which would enable small- and medium-scale capitalists to remain competitive in the market, but the actual codes for numerous branches of industry entailed price and production quotas that were "unprofitable" for small-scale capital. Moreover, the high price controls in some codes reflected the price consumers paid and not the cost of production. Hence, higher prices for commodities were rationalized as a method of maintaining the higher cost of production for small businessmen (Hawley 1966, pp. 58-9).

Labor representation among the code authorities was minimal and wage and hour provisions were plagued with loopholes and exceptions. The mandatory labor provisions provided by section 7a of the NIRA were rarely included in the code provisions and many codes were a result of debate between capitalists and state officials with no labor representation. The interpretation of section 7a was debated throughout the code-making process and, indeed, throughout the life of the NIRA itself. National Recovery Administration (NRA) administrators saw their job to be the "impartial enforcement" of section 7a. Hence, the NRA maintained that it was not within its purpose to organize either labor or management and, while it recognized the right of labor to bargain collectively, it would not "deprive" them of the "right" to bargain individually. Thus, while it would not oppose company unionism, the NRA itself did not provide the machinery to implement section 7a. The NRA developed a National Labor Board (NLB) in response to the wave of strikes in late 1933 which was supposed to enforce section 7a and to settle labor disputes. However, the exact nature of the authority of the NLB over labor disputes was never made explicit, thus, leaving it ineffectual in either aiding labor through the implementation of section 7a, or in settling labor disputes (Rubinow n.d., pp. 67-78). The position of the NRA was ambiguous at best with respect to union organization. Hugh Johnson, administrator of the NRA, argued that "I do not believe that there is any constitutional guarantee of freedom to exploit labor anymore than there is a constitutional guarantee to run a newspaper in a fire trap" (Johnson 1933). Nevertheless, there was little evidence of a marked support of labor, in particular organized industrial labor, in the administration and implementation of the codes of fair competition.

The implementation of the NIRA and NRA policy directives had consequences that were not anticipated by either the capitalist class or organized labor leaders. Ironically, contrary to its design, the NIRA's and NRA's implementation of the act actually worked to disorganize the capitalist class and organize the working class. The issue of monopoly growth and national planning served to intensify the conflicts within the capitalist class, and the debate over the interpretation of section 7a tended to heighten the class struggle between wage-labor and capital.

Rising labor militancy produced a significant realignment of the Democratic party and the implementation of state policies that made crucial concessions to industrial labor such as the National Industrial Relations Act. The class recomposition of the Democratic party and labor legislation favorable to segments of the industrial working class served to diffuse labor militancy by the end of the 1930s, directing the leaders of the newly emergent industrial union movement to accept by the end of the decade a general consensus in support of the existing political and economic order (cf., Milton 1982).

The disunity among industrial capitalists persisted throughout the 1930s with many industrial capitalists criticizing a variety of New Deal programs. Yet, the Roosevelt administration—because it represented the balance of class forces—attempted to put into motion plans for economic recovery that reflected compromises not only between labor and capital, but also within capital itself. Following criticisms by nonmonopoly capital of the implementation of the National Industrial Recovery Act, the Temporary National Economic Committee was established to investigate the growth of monopoly and its repercussions in the industrial economy. Although the Temporary National Economic Committee documented the prevalence of monopoly growth, nonmonopoly capital was unable to alter the process of concentration and centralization of capital. However, conflicts within the industrial capitalist class over the best strategy for economic recovery did unveil to the Roosevelt administration that the bureaucratic structures inherited from previous administrations were inadequate to accomplish the tasks necessary to implement New Deal policies. These organizational forms constituted a structural impediment hindering the nature and type of recovery strategy that was historically possible. As a consequence, the Roosevelt administration was compelled to adjust, improvise, and tinker with the existing framework while at the same time attempting to create new structures. This process was not formalized until administrative reorganization proposals of 1938–39.

Whereas nonmonopoly capital was unable to stimulate changes in the accumulation process, the industrial workers' movement was able to do so. The trajectory of capitalist development changed as a result of the upsurge in workers' militant activities during the 1930s. Labor militancy, by demanding and using collective bargaining through the establishment of unions associated with the Congress of Industrial Workers, made it possible to overcome the resistance of large-scale capital to a fundamental reorganization of wages and consumption. Nevertheless, it was monopoly capital that was able to adjust to these working-class gains. Monopoly capital not only passed on wage gains and benefits acquired by workers to consumers (both nationally and internationally) but also used collective bargaining as a way to ensure labor peace. In the process, monopoly capital was able to dominate crucial state agencies. Increased state economic intervention not only aided in the regulation of competition, but also in providing further investment outlets. The obstacle to capital accumulation of too high a rate of exploitation was temporarily resolved through the institutionalization of collective bargaining and the incorporation of significant industrial unions into the national political bargaining process. Problems of unregulated competition were temporarily resolved through state policies. The political structure was altered to correspond more closely to the imperatives of the accumulation process: monopoly capital came to dominate key agencies, and the industrial union movement was incorporated into a clearly subordinate position on the political terrain vis-à-vis monopoly capital. The incorporation of the industrial union movement into the national political bargaining process and into a more cooperative relationship with monopoly capital via collective bargaining, the resulting ideological consensus for capitalist rule, and the unchallenged political hegemony of monopoly capital all combined to produce the conditions for a new phase of capitalist development. By attempting to resolve class conflicts and antagonisms, the New Deal industrial policies simultaneously created new structural conditions that regulated the objective conditions for capital accumulation and the conditions under which future struggles would be waged.

The class-centered approach proposed here is premised upon the recognition of the multi-layered determinants of New Deal policies. At the specific historical conjuncture (1933-39), the combination of uninterrupted capital accumulation on a world scale symbolized by the Great Depression, the growing rift between capital and labor on the shopfloor, and conflicts within the industrial capitalist class limited the political options available and circumscribed the choice of recovery policies and their implementation. Seen in this light, the state-centered argument of Skocpol and associates offers a one-sided approach to the investigation of the New Deal. The implementation of New Deal programs was certainly impeded by the existing bureaucratic and administrative arrangements, but these arrangements themselves need to be understood in terms of their underlying class content.

CONCLUSION

Over the past 15 years the debates over Marxist conceptualizations of the state and state activity and the evaluation of various theoretical positions vis-à-vis concrete historical developments promised to develop the much awaited analysis of politics and the state in the United States. The peculiarity of intellectual development in the United States had prevented the blossoming of a serious Marxist intellectual tradition. Yet the radical critique of mainstream sociological categories and concepts that shook the profession in the late 1960s and early 1970s had possibilities of breaking down the previous barriers to a serious interest in Marxist analysis. However, once this radical critique came to resemble explicitly Marxist modes of analysis, the anti-Marxist onslaught was once again upon us. Whereas it was commonplace in the previous decade to critique mainstream sociological concepts and categories, in the 1980s it has become rather fashionable to critique Marxist approaches within sociological analysis. This attempt to discredit and dismiss Marxist analysis of sociological phenomena is probably no clearer than that which is embodied within state-centered theory.

State-centered theory purports to be a new theoretical approach to the study of social change, a "paradigmatic reorientation" for the study of social phenomena. It claims to offer a better assessment of empirical reality than existing theoretical approaches, in particular, Marxist approaches. If state-centered theory is seen as a corrective to abstract theorization in the absence of empirical studies, then much is to be gained from such an approach. But the truth of the matter is that state-centered theory *does not* provide the theoretical space requisite to understanding the complex relationships in late capitalism. By beginning an analysis with individual or organization motivations is to deny the more abstract notions of social relationships that constrain individuals and organizations. In her study of the Social Security Act of 1935, Quadagno (1984) has stressed that the historical investigation of New Deal policies—and by implication of state decision making in general—must operate simultaneously on a number of levels of abstraction in order to appreciate the complexity of the translation of political power into economic power. In her words, "political structures cannot be analyzed as autonomous entities but must be considered in terms of their underlying economic dimensions" (Quadagno 1984, p. 645). Quadagno's study of the Social Security Act and my own work on the National Industrial Recovery Act (cf. Levine 1987) are evidence of the fact that indeed one can embark on empirical research and still maintain an understanding of the broader political-economic-social context in which all activity takes place.

If indeed state-centered theory does not offer anything particularly insightful about social phenomena given its narrow, in some respects subjectivist, view, then why has it gained such popularity within U.S. sociology? By arguing that the state—organizations and activity—be placed at the center of the analysis, Skocpol and other proponents of state-centered theory are forced to analyze historical events from the standpoint of individuals within state institutions and state organizations. Such a theoretical position is not incompatible with pluralism and in many ways resembles pluralist analysis. The difference is that state-centered theory has borrowed from Marxism concepts like class conflict and uneven capitalist development, and has cleansed them of their Marxist content, thus making them acceptable to the mainstream of the profession. As Brill (unpublished) writes, "by rigidly maintaining the . . . distinction between society, polity, and economy while emphasizing state institutions Skocpol has preserved basic assumptions and academic boundaries." The reliance on organizational analysis to explain large-scale social change certainly does not bring us any closer to understanding the complexities of modern society. By retreating into traditional academic notions of objects of analysis, state-centered theory adds little to our knowledge of social change. State-centered theory merely represents one more attempt to mystify the backruptcy of mainstream social science discourse. It is time to bring the concept of classes back into its proper place in analysis, as a central analytical tool for understanding social change. For it is only through our understanding of the past through the prism of a class-centered approach that we can begin to understand the present and develop strategies for the future—a future free of exploitation and oppression.

NOTE

1. For a critique of the state-centered approach using New Deal agricultural policies as the empirical case, see Jess Gilbert and Carolyn Howe, "State-Centered vs. Class Struggle Theories of the State: The Case of New Deal Agricultural Policy," unpublished, available in mimeograph.

REFERENCES

Berle, A. A. 1932. Memorandum to Governor Franklin D. Roosevelt, August 15. Berle Papers, Box 15. FDR Library, Hyde Park, NY.

Bernstein, Irving. 1972. *The Lean Years.* Boston: Houghton Mifflin.

Brill, Howard. Unpublished (available in mimeograph). "State Bureaucrats and Capitalists: Theda Skocpol's Conception of State and Society."

Cochran, Bert. 1977. *Labor and Communism: The Conflict that Shaped American Unions.* Princeton: Princeton University Press.

Finegold, Kenneth, and Theda Skocpol. 1984. "State, Party, and Industry: From Business Recovery to the Wagner Act in America's New Deal." In *Statemaking and Social Movements: Essays in History and Theory,* edited by Charles Bright and Susan Harding, pp. 159-92. Ann Arbor, MI: University of Michigan Press.

Galambos, Louis. 1966. *Competition and Cooperation: The Emergence of a National Trade Association.* Baltimore: Johns Hopkins University Press.

Hawley, Ellis W. 1966. *The New Deal and the Problem of Monopoly.* Princeton: Princeton University Press.

Himmelberg, Robert F. 1976. *The Origins of the National Recovery Administration.* New York: Fordham University Press.

Howe, Carolyn, and Jess Gilbert. Unpublished (available in mimeograph). "State-Centered vs. Class-Struggle Theories of the State: The Case of New Deal Agricultural Policy."

Jessop, Bob. 1982. *The Capitalist State.* New York: New York University Press.

————. 1985. *Nicos Poulantzas: Marxist Theory and Political Strategy.* New York: St. Martin's Press.

Johnson, Hugh S. 1933. Letter to Louis Howe, November 17. Howe Papers, Box 86. FDR Library, Hyde Park, NY.

Kolko, Gabriel. 1976. *Main Currents in Modern American History.* New York: Harper & Row.

Leuchtenburg, William E. 1963. *Franklin D. Roosevelt and the New Deal, 1932-1940.* New York: Harper & Row.

Levine, Rhonda F. 1985. "Marxism, Sociology, and Neo-Marxist Theories of the State." In *Current Perspectives in Social Theory,* Vol. 6, edited by Scott G. McNall, pp. 149-67. Greenwich, CT: JAI.

————. 1987. *Class Struggle and the Capitalist State: Industrial Labor, Industrial Capital, and the New Deal.* Greenwich, CT: JAI.

Lund, Robert. 1933. Letter to Louis McHenry Howe, March 29. PPF 8246. FDR Library, Hyde Park, NY.

Miliband, Ralph. 1970. "The Capitalist State: A Reply to Nicos Poulantzas." *New Left Review* 59:53-60.

———. 1973a. *The State in Capitalist Society*. London: Quartet Books.

———. 1973b. "Poulantzas and the Capitalist State." *New Left Review* 82:83-92.

Milton, David. 1982. *The Politics of U.S. Labor: From the Great Depression to the New Deal*. New York: Monthly Review Press.

Nordlinger, Eric A. 1981. *On the Autonomy of the State*. Cambridge: Harvard University Press.

Poulantzas, Nicos. 1969. "The Problem of the Capitalist State." *New Left Review* 58:67-78.

———. 1975. *Classes in Contemporary Capitalism*. London: New Left Books.

———. 1976. "The Capitalist State: A Reply to Miliband and Laclau." *New Left Review* 95:63-83.

Quadagno, Jill. 1984. "Welfare Capitalism and the Social Security Act of 1935." *American Sociological Review* 49:632-47.

Radosh, Ronald. 1967. "The Development of the Corporate Ideology of American Labor Leaders, 1914-1933." Ph.D. dissertation, University of Wisconsin.

Roos, Charles. 1937. *NRA Economic Planning*. Bloomington: Principa Press.

Rosen, Elliot A. 1977. *Hoover, Roosevelt, and the Brains Trust*. New York: Columbia University Press.

Rubinow, Raymond S. N.d. "Section 7(a): Its History, Interpretation and Administration." Record Group 9, National Recovery Administration. National Archives, Washington, DC.

Schlesinger, Arthur M. 1959. *The Coming of the New Deal*. Boston: Houghton Mifflin.

Skocpol, Theda. 1980. "Political Response to Capitalist Crisis: New Marxist Theories of the State and the Case of the New Deal." *Politics and Society* 4:155-201.

———. 1985. "Bringing the State Back In: Strategies of Analysis in Current Research." In *Bringing the State Back In*, edited by Peter Evans, Dietrich Rueschemeyer, and Theda Skocpol, pp. 3-37. New York: Cambridge University Press.

Skocpol, Theda, and Edwin Amenta. 1985. "Did Capitalists Shape Social Security?" *American Sociological Review* 50:575-8.

Skocpol, Theda, and Kenneth Finegold. 1982. "State Capacity and Economic Intervention of the Early New Deal." *Political Science Quarterly* 97:255-78.

Sobel, Robert. 1972. *The Age of the Giant Corporations: A Microeconomic History of American Business, 1914-1970*. Westport, CT: Greenwood.

U.S. Bureau of the Census. 1975. *Historical Statistics of the United States, Colonial Times to 1970, Bicentennial Edition, Part I*. Washington, DC.

U.S. Congress, Senate. 1933. *Thirty-Hour Work Week*. Hearings before the Subcommittee on Judiciary, U.S. Senate, 72nd Congress, 2nd Session, on S. 5267, January.

Weir, Margaret, and Theda Skocpol. 1985. "State Structures and the Possibilities for 'Keynesian' Responses to the Great Depression in Sweden, Britain and the United States." In *Bringing the State Back In*, edited by Peter B. Evans, Dietrich Rueschemeyer, and Theda Skocpol, pp. 107-63. New York: Cambridge University Press.

5

The Limits of the World-System Perspective

Alex Dupuy and Barry Truchil

Beginning with the publication in 1974 of *The Modern World System*, the first volume of a proposed four-volume study of modern capitalism, the world-system perspective developed by Wallerstein has become an established new paradigm in the social sciences. In sociology it is recognized as a bona fide subsection of the American Sociological Association. Its multidisciplinary members hold annual meetings to explore old and new aspects of the theory, publish their findings through their Sage Publications series, and have their own periodical called *Review*. The popularity of this perspective is due to its descriptive and inductive character. It provides an alternative framework for scholars who became disenchanted with modernization theory, dependency theory, and/or classical Marxism, as it does not require agreement on certain premises, such as causal relationships in historical development. One can adopt a world-system perspective and still enjoy a great deal of flexibility in placing empirical research into the scheme. As with all other paradigms, however, the world-system perspective also has been subjected to a great deal of critical scrutiny across disciplines and from various theoretical perspectives. For the most part, though, most of the criticisms of the

We would like to thank Hubert J. O'Gorman for his comments. Part of the research for this paper was made possible by a summer fellowship from Rider College. Extracts from Immanuel Wallerstein, 1979, *The Capitalist World-Economy* (New York: Cambridge University Press), are reprinted with permission.

world-system perspective amount to a counterposition of paradigms rather than a demonstration of the internal inconsistencies of the world-system perspective or of its incompatibility with empirical reality.

Our paper aims to appraise critically the world-system perspective. We intend to demonstrate two propositions. The first is that the world-system perspective developed by Immanuel Wallerstein has made an original contribution to the analysis of capitalism as a social system. This contribution lies in its conception of capitalism as a world-system that can be understood only in its totality. The second claim is that the limits of the world-system perspective also stem from its very conception of capitalism as a world-system, that is, from the internal inconsistencies of the paradigm. We show that the world-system perspective cannot demonstrate theoretically the necessary conditions for the transformation of the capitalist world-system. We do this by focusing on how the proponents of the world-system perspective conceptualize the existing socialist societies and the transition from capitalism to socialism. These theoretical limitations have implications for empirical research on both the question of the "transition" to socialism, and on the nature of the existing socialist societies.

SUMMARY OF THE WORLD-SYSTEM PERSPECTIVE

The legitimacy of the world-system perspective as a distinct paradigm rests in its definition of capitalism as a world-system. Wallerstein's world-system theory is "based on the assumption, explicitly or implicitly, that the modern world comprises a single capitalist world-economy, which has emerged historically since the sixteenth century and which still exists today. It follows from such a premise that national states are not societies that have separate, parallel histories, but parts of a whole reflecting that whole" (Wallerstein 1979, p. 53).

The world-system perspective compares itself to two other pervasive paradigms which it explicitly rejects because of their focus on the nation-state as the unit of analysis: modernization theory and what Wallerstein refers to as "mechanical Marxism" (Wallerstein 1979, pp. 51–2). According to Wallerstein, modernization theory takes the advanced industrial societies of Western Europe as ideal types in contrast to which the "developing" countries of the Third World are viewed in order to identify the deficiencies blocking their progress toward industrialization. For Wallerstein, modernization theory cannot explain the problems of the underdeveloped countries because it fails to take into account the global forces that shaped and determined the internal characteristics of the so-called developing nations. Wallerstein rejects what he considers to be the static and ahistorical "developmentalist" approach of modernization theory which posits a unilinear pattern of social evolution for all nation-states culminating in modern industrial society. Drawing from the contributions of André Gunder Frank, who proposed an earlier version of the modern world-system perspective, Wallerstein seeks to explain the "development of underdevelopment" as an integral aspect of the emergence of capitalism as a world-system beginning in the sixteenth century.

Wallerstein also criticizes the so-called mechanical Marxists who argue that societies must evolve through successive historical stages, beginning with primitive communalism and arriving at capitalism, before reaching the final communist stage. The liberal modernization theory and this version of Marxist theory share a common concern with evolutionary stages of development by positing a universal unilinear pattern of national development abstracted from the Western European experience. Why Wallerstein chose this particular version of Marxist theory for his critique is unclear, given the emergence during the 1960s and 1970s of several Marxist perspectives that explicitly reject the "stagist" and unilinear interpretation of historical development advanced by the "monistic" Marxists (e.g., see Althusser and Balibar 1970; Therborn 1980; Poulantzas 1975; Laclau 1977). Furthermore, as Hobsbawm convincingly argued (1971, pp. 1-65), it is doubtful whether Marx himself advanced a unilinear conception of historical development. Moreover, the study of imperialism and its impacts on Third World societies has long been the focus and part of the *raison d'être* of Marxist scholarship since the writings of Lenin (e.g., see Lenin 1950; Baran 1957; Magdoff 1969; O'Connor 1971; Rey 1971, 1973). Marxists have also advanced theories that examine the global character of capitalism (e.g., see Bukharin 1929/1973). Despite these contributions, Wallerstein considers the nation-state to be the unit of analysis for Marxist theory.

Wallerstein proposes a world-system perspective with a different conception of a dialectical totality that seeks to explain the parts—that is, the nation-states—in terms of their functions within the global system. In Wallerstein's terms,

> What distinguishes the developmentalist and the world-system perspective is not liberalism versus Marxism nor evolutionism versus

something else (since both are essentially evolutionary). Rather I would locate the distinction in two places. One is in mode of thought. To put it in Hegelian terms, the developmentalist perspective is mechanical whereas the world-system perspective is dialectical. I mean by the latter term that at every point in the analysis, one asks not what is the formal structure but what is the consequence both for the whole and the parts of maintaining or changing a certain structure at that particular point in time, given the totality of particular positions of that moment in time [1979, p. 54].

The "totality" that Wallerstein speaks of refers to that of social systems. And there have only been two types of social systems, the minisystem and the world-system. A minisystem is a relatively small, autonomous subsistence economy that is not part of a larger tribute-extracting world-system. A minisystem is also culturally homogeneous and has an unrefined and limited division of labor (Wallerstein 1974, p. 348). By contrast, the world-system covers a wider geographic area, and it encompasses diverse cultures and political subsystems that are linked together by a well-developed and interdependent international division of labor. In the modern capitalist world-system there does not exist a single political system that administers all the territories that comprise it, in contrast to the preceding world empires.

For Wallerstein, therefore, "totality" means that analysis must be carried out at the level of the social system as a whole, the characteristic of which is "the existence within it of a division of labor, such that various sectors or areas within are dependent upon economic exchange with others for the smooth and continuous provisioning of the needs of the area. Such economic exchange can clearly exist without a common political structure and even more obvious without sharing the same culture" (1979, p. 5).

To clarify Wallerstein's meaning of "totality," it might be useful to contrast his with Marx's conception. Marx's method of analysis starts from the abstract to the empirical world. This means that the apprehension of the observable phenomena through theoretical categories is not given in empirical reality itself but is the product of a theoretical construction in which concepts are articulated and linked to one another. And as the analysis becomes more concrete, one must include in it many more theoretical determinations (Laclau 1977, p. 10). Thus in analyzing a concrete society, one must begin by making a distinction between the levels of analysis so as not to confuse theoretical categories with the concrete phenomena and their historical development.

In the reconstruction of the capitalist system and its historical development, Marx began not with its actual genesis, but with the theoretical specification of its properties in a constructed conceptual whole. This involved elaborating the specific combinations of social relations and forces of production characteristic of the capitalist mode of production. With these theoretical categories, Marx then depicted the dynamics of that mode of production and reconstructed its historical genesis and development in a concrete society, most notably England. As Mandel put it, "In its full richness and deployment, the concrete is always a combination of innumerable theoretical 'abstractions.' But the material concrete, that is, real bourgeois society, exists before the whole scientific endeavour, determines it in the last instance, and remains a constant practical point of reference to test the validity of the theory" (1977, p. 21).

For Marx, therefore, the unit of analysis is neither the nation-state nor the world economy, since neither of them determines the existence of social classes, their relations, their contradictions, their conflicts, and their effects. Rather, it is social classes, which through their relations, contradictions, and conflicts, create economic, political, ideological, and cultural practices. It is the institutionalization and reproduction of class practices in concrete geopolitically determined settings that we call societies. Moreover, focusing on social or class conflicts as the determinants of sociohistorical developments and of forms of society prevents a teleological understanding of history. That is, the outcomes of class conflicts cannot be predicted a priori. To posit such an outcome by appealing to the logical unfolding of successive modes of production violates the premise that the class struggle is the motive force of historical processes.

Wallerstein proceeds differently. In his perspective, a theoretical distinction is not made between the theoretical properties of capitalism and their actual manifestations. Put differently, the theoretical properties and dynamics of the capitalist world-system are identified and constructed through their concrete historical and territorial expressions. Thus, the world-system paradigm begins with the premise that there is an empirically observable capitalist world-economy commencing at a certain historical moment, regardless of how this world-economy is conceptualized. This approach is more inductive than Marx's.

The modern world-system emerged with the development of capitalism in Europe in the sixteenth century. Defining capitalism as a "mode of production for sale in a market in which the object is to realize the maximum profit," Wallerstein (1979, p. 15) argues that its existence does not presuppose the creation of wage-labor relations in all zones of the capitalist world-system. Quite the contrary, the capitalist world-system is characterized by the existence of a single international division of labor that comprises different "modes of labor control," such as slavery and coerced cash-crop labor, as well as free wage-labor. The world-economy comprises three distinct zones: the core, the semiperiphery, and the periphery. These three zones are linked together and coordinated by an international division of labor. The international division of labor determines the productive specialization of the different zones and the "modes of labor control" that will develop in each of them. It also guarantees the unequal relationships (i.e., exploitation) among the nations in the different zones, and the transfer of surplus wealth from periphery to core areas through the mechanisms of trade, capital flows, migration, and intervention of the strong state machineries of the core areas (Wallerstein 1979, p. 17).

The extent to which actors within the world-system use the machinery of the state to maximize their advantage in the world market plays a large role in assigning to a region a specialized function in the international division of labor. There thus exists a close relationship between economic and political power in the world-system perspective. In Wallerstein's terms,

> Once we get a difference in the strength of the state machineries, we get the operation of "unequal exchange," which is enforced by strong states on weak ones, by core states on peripheral areas. Thus capitalism involves not only appropriation of the surplus-value by an owner from a laborer, but an appropriation of surplus of the whole world-economy by core areas. And this was as true in the stage of agricultural capitalism as it is in the stage of industrial capitalism [1979, pp. 18-19].

It follows from this that the nation-state cannot be a unit of analysis, but must be studied as part of the larger modern world-system, as was previously noted. Nation-states are part of an unequal interstate system in which they compete against other nation-states for economic and political advantages (Chase-Dunn 1982b, p. 22; Hopkins 1982, p. 21).

Just as nation-states exist only insofar as they are functional parts of the world-economy, they cannot contain class relationships or patterns of development that differ from those that define the world-system as a whole. No matter what form the relationship between the owners of the means of production and the laboring classes might take, nation-states cannot transcend the defining characteristics of the capitalist world-system of which they are a part. Since the predominance of the capitalist world-system over the whole globe, any nation-state that participates in the modern world-system cannot be defined by another mode of production other than the capitalist mode. The world-system perspective therefore incorporates many Marxist concepts, such as exploitation, class, and imperialism, but it reconceptualizes them within a new paradigm.

This original definition of capitalism as a world-system made it possible for the proponents of that perspective to avoid many of the difficulties encountered by those who use the Marxist conception of mode of production in their analyses of underdeveloped societies. The difficulties are of two kinds. The first problem concerns how one characterizes those societies that came under the domination of the expanding capitalist societies of the "center." To say that they are capitalist violates the orthodox Marxist definition, which equates capitalism with the prevalence of wage-labor relations, since until very recently these societies did not exhibit such class relations.

The second difficulty pertains to the different dynamics of the central and peripheral societies. To argue that the underdeveloped societies are underdeveloped because of their incorporation in the world economy created by the expanding central capitalist economies is also to maintain that the capitalist mode of production has quite different laws of motion in the center than in the periphery. How does one explain this anomaly from an orthodox Marxist view of the so-called progressive nature of capitalism, namely, that capitalism causes the development of the productive forces, and hence of society as a whole?

Wallerstein explicitly rejects the equation of capitalism with progress. Capitalism, for him, is a tri-polar system—of core, semiperiphery, and periphery—wherein the development of the productive forces and material well-being, and the overall societal development are unequally distributed in favor of the core countries and at the expense of the peripheral ones, with the semiperipheries falling in between (see Wallerstein 1983). By thus defining capitalism as a world system of commodity production for exchange regardless of the system of labor relations existing in any one country, the proponents of the world-system perspective avoid having to explain why wage-labor relations exist here and not there, and why both may be called capitalist. Moreover, since the capitalist world-system presupposes developed core countries, and underdeveloped peripheries, one using that perspective need not account for the different modus operandi of the system in the different zones of the world-economy (Brewer 1980, p. 264).

THE WORLD-SYSTEM CONCEPTION OF
THE TRANSITION TO SOCIALISM

It is from this vantage point that the proponents of the world-system perspective have approached the study of the so-called socialist societies. According to them, socialism must be conceived of as a world-system characterized by a single world government and worldwide democratic state economic planning. Therefore, socialism cannot exist within a single nation-state because it is the larger world-system that defines the character of the mode of production in any given nation-state, and the current one is by definition capitalist (Chase-Dunn 1982c, pp. 282-3).

The proponents of the world-system perspective prefer to refer to the socialist states as countries in which "socialist movements" have conquered state power. Originally these socialist movements may have represented anti–world-systemic forces that sought to withdraw from the capitalist world-system. Eventually, however, these revolutionary societies became reintegrated as functional parts of the world-system, rather than forces for its transformation.

This is what happened to the Eastern European societies, as well as to China, Cuba, North Korea, and so forth. Their withdrawal from the capitalist world-system was temporary, and they even succeeded in establishing economic and political networks with each other. It was not long, however, before they became constrained by the geopolitical logic of the interstate system of capitalism. The socialist movements failed in their attempts to create an alternative socialist world-system because they never completely severed commodity production and trade with the world market, including dealings with capitalist multinational corporations. In some socialist states, foreign firms are allowed to invest in production, even if under controlled conditions (Chase-Dunn 1982b, pp. 41-2).

It is the incorporation of the socialist economies in the capitalist world-system that becomes the decisive criterion that determines their character, despite the qualitative transformations that occurred in them in terms of their social relations of production, ownership of the means of production, and wealth redistribution. Just as non-wage forms of labor relations and exploitation, such as slavery or coerced cash-crop labor, have been employed in peripheral zones for the purpose of capitalist production and accumulation, the non-market wage-labor form in the socialist states is not significant, except that it becomes the most heuristic means for these regimes to compete in the world-economy. Neither the nationalization of the means of production nor state economic planning abolishes the capitalist character of such societies, because

> [a] state which collectively owns all the means of production is merely a collective capitalist firm as long as it remains—as all states are, in fact, presently compelled to remain—a participant in the market of the capitalist world-economy. No doubt such a 'firm' may have different modalities of internal division of profit, but this does not change its essential economic role vis-à-vis others operating in the world-market [Wallerstein 1979, p. 68].

Thus, through their participation in the world market, these states retain the law of value as an operating principle, and their integration in the world-economy strengthens the interstate system of capitalism.

The collectivization of the means of production and the institutionalization of state economic planning allow these socialist regimes to pursue "mercantilist" strategies of "semi-withdrawal" to attain a stronger competitive position within the world-economy. Successful socialist movements occurred in semiperipheral and peripheral areas of the world system, and through their mercantilist strategies of semi-withdrawal they have been able to either prevent a further deterioration of their competitive position in the world market, or to reorganize their internal economies to achieve a more favorable position. Indeed, Wallerstein (1979, p. 33) sees the Russian Revolution as enabling the Soviet Union 50 years later to "enter the status of a core power in a *capitalist* world-economy."

However, one can question this assertion on several grounds. First, there is no empirical basis to sustain the interpretation that the goal of socialist movements is to achieve core status within the capitalist world-economy. To the contrary, any acquaintance with the writings of Lenin, Trotsky, Mao, and Ho Chi Minh reveals that the objectives of the socialist movements were to transform capitalist and imperialist relationships, regardless of their shifting positions within the capitalist world economy. This is not to suggest that one can determine the characteristics of a society by examining the intentions of its actors. It is to suggest that the economies erected following the successful revolutions led by the above revolutionaries

do not operate according to market principles, but rather to politically determined ones.

Second, within the world-system perspective, core powers exploit
peripheral areas. To be consistent with the premises of the theory, it
would have to follow that the Soviet Union, as a core power, enters
into exploitative relations with Third World peripheral societies. To
make their case convincingly, the proponents of the world-system
perspective need to demonstrate empirically that economic behavior
within the Soviet-type societies and between them and other societies conforms to the world-system proponents' definition of world
capitalism. Mere participation in trade with capitalist countries within the world economy is not a sufficient criterion to prove the
capitalist character of the Soviet-type societies or that trade with
Third World capitalist countries constitutes exploitation of them.
Exploitation would involve showing that the Soviet Union estab-
lishes or invests in productive enterprises in these societies to maximize profits, as is clearly the case with Western European, Japanese,
and U.S. multinational corporations.

Third, to demonstrate the capitalist character of the Soviet-type
societies, it would also have to be shown that the accumulation of
capital is the primary objective of the rulers of the socialist societies,
and that investment decisions and the allocation of resources among
enterprises and sectors of production within these societies are made
according to the laws of supply and demand—that is, the profit
motive—as is unambiguously the case in the so-called free market
economies. Thus far, the proponents of the world-system perspective
have not demonstrated empirically any of the above hypotheses.

There is, however, no lack of evidence to support the contrary
proposition, namely, that investment decisions and the allocation of
resources in Soviet-type societies are not determined by the profits
of enterprises, but by the priorities set by state planners, and that the
rulers of these societies do not seek to accumulate capital as an end
in itself, as is the case with their counterparts in the free market
economies.

The proponents of the world-system perspective shirk this problem by claiming that the internal organizational differences between
capitalist and socialist states are not critical. They simply represent
different strategies to compete in the world economy. What remains
paramount is the division of the capitalist world-system into core,
semiperipheral, and peripheral zones. Because the unit of analysis is
the world-system within which nation-states only play a functional
part, the character of that world-system becomes the defining

feature for all the participating nation-states. Hence, one can only speak of socialism within the framework of a socialist world-system that has replaced the capitalist world-system, and that includes a single world government and fully democratic worldwide state economic planning.

CRITIQUE

Wallerstein and the other proponents of the world-system perspective have received a great deal of criticism from a variety of perspectives, but most notably and predictably, from Marxists. Essentially, Marxists accuse the world-systemists of having committed three errors: (1) redefining capitalism by excluding wage-labor as a necessary criterion; (2) shifting the unit of analysis from the abstract concept of mode of production and its associated combination of relations and forces of production to the world-system; and (3) not differentiating among capitalist and noncapitalist forms of commodity production, surplus appropriation, and the modus operandi of different modes of production (e.g., see Brenner 1977; Navarro 1982; Worsley 1980).

Among the well-known criticisms of Wallerstein from a Marxist standpoint is that of Robert Brenner (1977). Essentially Brenner argues that because Wallerstein redefined capitalism to exclude the wage-labor relations as necessary for its existence, he cannot differentiate between the production of absolute surplus-value and relative surplus-value. Absolute surplus-value production refers to the lengthening of the working day to increase the surplus labor time during which the laborer produces additional surplus-value. This form of increasing surplus-value production does not imply any technological innovation or development of the means of production. Relative surplus-value production, however, pertains to shortening the necessary labor time, or increasing the surplus labor time, but without lengthening the working day. This can occur only by increasing the productivity of labor through technological innovation and the employment of skilled workers. Relative surplus-value production, therefore, implies the qualitative improvement and development of the means and techniques of production. Capitalist industrialization and technological development, argues Brenner, presuppose the transition from absolute surplus-value to relative surplus-value production, and this in turn presupposes an understanding of the role that wage-labor relations play in the capitalist process of production.

Brenner maintains that because he excludes wage-labor relations from his definition of capitalism, Wallerstein is unable to explain the dynamics of capitalism and hence cannot really differentiate between its earlier and later stages of development. According to Brenner, therefore, Wallerstein's view of capitalism is static. Moreover, he argues that Wallerstein cannot appreciate the qualitative differences between the capitalist and other modes of production characterized by different social relations of production.

This means, then, that unlike Wallerstein's model which collapses the differences among societies having different "modes of labor control," Brenner's approach makes it possible to argue that within the capitalist world economy there may exist societies that are characterized by different modes of production and exhibit different developmental tendencies and potentials while being linked to one another through the world market. It follows from this that the unequal development evident among the various nation-states within the world economy does not necessarily result because the core developed at the expense of the periphery, as Wallerstein maintains, but because the capitalist mode of production is more predominant in the core than in the periphery (Brenner 1977; see also Brewer 1980, pp. 170–1).

Along lines similar to those of Brenner, Peter Worsley (1980) offers a critique of Wallerstein's conceptualization of the socialist states. Starting from the premise that the social relations of production and forms of property ownership determine the characteristics of a society, Worsley accuses Wallerstein of overlooking the fundamental and qualitative differences between the capitalist and socialist societies. Unlike Wallerstein and the other world-system theorists who conceive of the socialist bloc as an integral part of the capitalist world-system, Worsley sees the socialist states as constituting a second world-system that competes with and differs from the capitalist world-system in several important ways. First, the socialist countries differ from capitalist countries in their systems of social stratification. In the socialist societies where the means of production are publicly owned, economic activities are politically regulated through the mechanisms of state planning. Under the dominance of an all powerful party that is self-recruiting and that monopolizes the means of communication and opinion making, the objective of the planning system is to provide a high level of social and material welfare to the population.

The socialist states are also integrated into their own trade and productive networks through COMECON and have their own socialist international division of labor dominated by the Soviet Union. Though initially the socialist world-system may have been under the strict control and hegemony of the Soviet Union, it is increasingly becoming polycentric, as exemplified by the rivalry between the Soviet Union and China, as well as by the resistance of the other Eastern European countries to Soviet pressure. Thus, according to Worsley, the integrated socialist bloc countries are not simply a part of the capitalist world-system, but constitute a second world-system that differs in kind from the first world-system of capitalism.

Both Brenner and Worsley raise important objections to Wallerstein's world-system perspective and offer insightful alternative explanations for the uneven development that is characteristic of the capitalist world-economy, and of the differences between capitalism and socialism as social systems. While these criticisms show how the world-system perspective differs from classical Marxism, they do not constitute a critique of the world-system paradigm per se. They amount to saying that Wallerstein and the other proponents of the world-system perspective are incorrect merely because they ignore the determining role of the social relations of production and of the mode of production in social analysis.

In our view these rejoinders do not constitute a critique but simply a counterposition of one set of premises for another. One cannot fault a paradigm for not recognizing and emphasizing what others see as important. The proponents of the world-system perspective are quite explicit in their rejection of the relations of production as the determining factor that characterizes a society as capitalist or socialist. The critical factor for the world-system theorists is not the existence of specifically capitalist or socialist relations of production, but rather that the nation-states characterized by particular social relations participate in the exchange networks of the larger capitalist world-economy, and, as such, remain functional parts of that system. Thus, a more convincing criticism of the world-system perspective would be to show either the internal inconsistencies of the paradigm or its inapplicability to empirical reality. We aim to show that the arguments of the world-system theorists are internally inconsistent in their attempt to justify the capitalist character of the socialist states, and in their view of the transition to a socialist world-system.

The first inconsistency concerns the contradictory methodology employed in defining capitalism and socialism as world-systems. When accounting for the origins of the capitalist world-system, the proponents of the world-system perspective did not set spatial criteria for its formation. The capitalist world-system emerged within the context of, and in conflict with, other existing world-systems—or world empires, in Wallerstein's terminology—that operated according to different criteria than those of the capitalist world-system. These were the Ottoman and Russian world empires, and the Indian Ocean proto–world-economy. Moreover, since the sixteenth century the emerging capitalist world-system entered into economic relationships with these other world-systems until the mid-eighteenth century when the former subsumed the latter and became the single global world-system (Wallerstein 1979, p. 26).

Thus we have one world-system based on capitalist principles co-existing and interacting during a certain time period with other world-systems based on noncapitalist principles. The nation-states that were part of the emerging capitalist world-system were said to be capitalist, while the other countries that belonged to the preexisting world empires were not characterized as capitalist even though they entered into trade relations with the capitalist world-system. These latter noncapitalist societies that were part of noncapitalist world-systems did not become capitalist until they were politically and economically subsumed by the expanding core countries of the capitalist world-system. When this occurred, they ceased to be world-systems *sui generis* and became parts of the single global capitalist world-system. Thus, the formation of a capitalist world-system did not require that it encompass the entire globe before it could exist, nor that capitalist commodity production and trade characterize the economies of *all* the areas with which it interacted. Indeed, the capitalist world-system is seen as having ubiquitously changing geo-political (spatial) boundaries over time (Hopkins 1978, p. 203).

Different criteria are set for the existence of socialism as a world-system. According to the world-system theorists, for socialism to exist it is not sufficient that socialist relations of production be established within a group of nation-states that develop their own economic and political networks that integrate them, such as the member countries of COMECON. Nor are socialist states allowed to trade with other world-systems. Rather, socialism must appear throughout the entire globe simultaneously, with a single world government and fully democratic global economic planning. Hence, maximum spatial and organizational criteria are set for the existence of a socialist world-system.

Socialism as a nascent world-system, therefore, cannot coexist with another world-system such as a capitalist world-system, as the capitalist world-system did in the period of its emergence. Likewise, socialist societies cannot subsume capitalist forms of labor relations, such as wage-labor, and commodity production to their own logic of state economic planning, as the emerging capitalist world-economy did with seemingly noncapitalist forms of labor relations—for example, landed rent, slavery, or coerced cash-crop labor. Thus, whereas a capitalist world-system does not need to be global in spatial and organizational forms to exist, socialism has to be global in spatial and organizational forms before it can begin to exist.

But why must this be the case? The answer cannot be that since the capitalist world-system now encompasses the whole globe no new world-system can emerge in a geographically delimited area of the world-economy without being incorporated into the dominant capitalist world-system. If the capitalist world-system could coexist with other world-systems during the period of its emergence, could have different spatial and geopolitical boundaries at various times in its history, and eventually could become global when its core countries became strong enough to expand the bounds of the system, why could not the capitalist world-system also retrench spatially as a consequence of emerging counter-systemic forces? These include socialist movements that are strong enough to create, maintain, and even gradually expand their own world-system. The proponents of the world-system perspective implicitly deny this possibility. Hence, this perspective adopts inconsistent theoretical and empirical criteria for the emergence of capitalist and socialist world-systems.

Another inconsistency concerns the nature of the transition toward the socialist world-system. As noted above, socialism can only exist as a worldwide system. Socialism is inconceivable as long as there is a world-economy dominated by capitalism. Since a socialist world-system cannot coexist with a capitalist world-system, the only way a socialist world-system could emerge would be after the collapse of the capitalist world-system due to a fatal economic and cultural crisis—perhaps like the so-called feudal crisis that paved the way for the emergence of capitalism in the sixteenth century. Indeed, Wallerstein argues that it is such a final crisis of the capitalist world-economy that will bring about its demise sometime during the twenty-first century, but which it is already beginning to experience (see Wallerstein 1983, pp. 75–93).

Another way a socialist world-system could emerge would be through a worldwide socialist revolution. Anything short of this compels the national revolutionary movements to reintegrate themselves and become functional parts of the capitalist world-economy. Given the existence of deep socioeconomic inequalities between core, semiperipheral, and peripheral nations, and the pervasiveness of nationalism, racism, and sexism that divide and pit social groups and classes of the different nation-states in the different zones against each other, it is difficult, if not impossible, to conceive of the possibility of such a worldwide revolution occurring simultaneously, or even near enough in time to create the preconditions for the establishment of a socialist world-system.

Such a worldwide revolutionary movement would require not only the overcoming of the nationalist, racist, and sexist sentiments of groups and classes in different nation-states, and in particular in the core countries. It would also require a universal *prise de conscience* about the desirability and possibility of creating a socialist world government. This outcome is unlikely, however, because according to the world-system perspective, racism, sexism, and nationalism are phenomena created or redefined by the global forces operating in the world-system to maintain the international, social, and gender divisions of labor among nation-states as well as among the different strata of the subordinated ethnic groups within the capitalist world-economy. Moreover, even when socialist movements succeed in gaining state power, they do not eliminate these divisions but rather tend to reinforce them (Wallerstein 1983, pp. 75–93 and passim).

Recognizing this difficulty, Wallerstein and Chase-Dunn, for example, concede the possibility of a gradual transition toward world socialism. While Wallerstein still sees the "states where socialist movements have come to power" as integral parts of the capitalist world-system, he now calls for a reassessment of how much "they have contributed to the world-wide struggle to ensure that the transition from capitalism is toward an egalitarian socialist world-order . . . [that is] one that meets the minimum defining characteristics of a historical system that maximizes equality and equity, one that increases humanity's control over its own life (democracy), and liberates the imagination" (Wallerstein 1983, pp. 108–10). This reassessment must involve a critical rejection of the so-called progressive and universalist claims of capitalism, and which until now have been unquestioningly accepted by the socialist movements (Wallerstein 1983, pp. 97–110).

For Chase-Dunn, the transition toward a socialist world-order could occur by expanding the opportunities for more direct democratic planning within the countries with socialist movements in power as well as within COMECON. This would involve the equal participation of these states in regional planning and the formation of a representative democratic regional quasi-state authority to replace the current Soviet-imposed policies. While these measures would not solve all the problems and remove all the obstacles toward the creation of a fully democratic socialist world government, they would mark an important step in that direction (Chase-Dunn 1982c, pp. 282-93).

However, such a formulation is entirely inconsistent with the premises of the world-system perspective. As already shown, the world-system perspective asserts that there is and can be only one world-system, and that all the existing socialist states are integral functional parts of the capitalist world-system that reinforce rather than counter the interstate system. Successful socialist movements take place in the peripheral and semiperipheral zones because those revolutions constitute strategies to secure a more competitive position within the world-economy rather than to transform it. The Soviet Union, as noted earlier, achieved core status via this route.

Moreover, since by definition the world-system must have core areas, one cannot expect a socialist movement to emerge in them because they already have core status and hence a beneficial position in the world-economy. Consequently, the emergence of a worldwide movement to create the possibilities for world socialism is theoretically inconceivable within the world-system perspective, in addition to being empirically unsustainable. The world-system perspective, therefore, is incapable of demonstrating theoretically (or empirically) the necessary conditions for the transformation of the capitalist world-system.

CONCLUSION

What we have, therefore, is a theoretical paradigm that cannot explain the transition from one social system to another. Whatever social change occurs can only be within the context of the existing social system. Countries that are part of the different zones of the world-system may be able to alter their respective positions and competitive advantages within it. But no country or set of countries is able to create an alternative social system to challenge and possibly even transform the dominant capitalist world-system. The limits of the world-system perspective as a paradigm that can explain social change and historical processes are self-evident and self-imposed. They stem from its own conception of what constitutes a "totality" and its understanding of the historical process. Moreover, our analysis raises important questions regarding not only the lack of empirical data to support many conclusions of the world-system perspective, but the presence of data that contradict some of their assumptions.

Our analysis thus raises questions regarding the usefulness of the world-system perspective for the study of revolutionary movements that seek to transform capitalism. As Kuhn (1970, p. 23) notes, "Paradigms gain their status because they are more successful than their competitors in solving a few problems that the group of practitioners has come to recognize as acute." The world-system paradigm may have gained popularity because it helped answer some questions regarding the subordinate nature of underdeveloped societies. However, it is unsatisfactory in accounting for the rise of revolutionary or socialist movements and the subsequent analysis of the transformations they generate.

REFERENCES

Althusser, Louis, and Etienne Balibar. 1970. *Reading Capital.* New York: Pantheon Books.

Baran, Paul. 1957. *The Political Economy of Growth.* New York: Monthly Review Press.

Brenner, Robert. 1977. "The Origins of Capitalist Development: A Critique of Neo-Smithian Marxism." *New Left Review*, no. 194:25–87.

Brewer, Anthony. 1980. *Marxist Theories of Imperialism: A Critical Survey.* London: Routledge & Kegan Paul.

Bukharin, Nikolai. 1973. *Imperialism and World-Economy.* New York: Monthly Review Press.

Chase-Dunn, Christopher, ed. 1982a. *Socialist States in the World-System.* Beverly Hills: Sage.

Chase-Dunn, Christopher. 1982b. "Socialist States in the Capitalist World-Economy." In *Socialist States in the World-System*, edited by Christopher Chase-Dunn.

———. 1982c. "The Transition to World-Socialism." In *Socialist States in the World-Economy*, edited by Christopher Chase-Dunn.

Hobsbawm, Eric. 1971. "Introduction." In Karl Marx, *Pre-Capitalist Economic Formations.* New York: International Publishers.

Hopkins, Terence K. 1978. "World-System Analysis: Methodological Issues." In *Social Change in the Capitalist World-Economy*, edited by Christopher Chase-Dunn. Beverly Hills: Sage.

———. 1982. "Patterns of Development of the Modern World-System." In *World-System Analysis: Theory and Methodology*, edited by Terence K. Hopkins, Immanuel Wallerstein, and associates. Beverly Hills: Sage.

Hopkins, Terence K., Immanuel Wallerstein, and associates. 1982. *World-System Analysis: Theory and Methodology.* Beverly Hills: Sage.

Kaplan, Barbara Hockey, ed. 1978. *Social Change in the Capitalist World-Economy.* Beverly Hills: Sage.

Kuhn, Thomas S. 1970. *The Structure of Scientific Revolutions.* Chicago: University of Chicago Press.

Laclau, Ernesto. 1977. *Politics and Ideology in Marxist Theory*. London: New Left Books.

Lenin, V. I. 1975. *Imperialism: The Highest Stage of Capitalism*. In *Selected Works*, Vol. 1. Moscow: Progress Publishers.

Magdoff, Harry. 1969. *The Age of Imperialism*. New York: Monthly Review Press.

Mandel, Ernest. 1977. "Introduction." In Karl Marx, *Capital: A Critique of Political Economy*. Vol. 1. New York: Vintage.

Navarro, Vincente. 1982. "The Limits of World-System Theory." In *Socialist States in the Capitalist World-Economy*, edited by Christopher Chase-Dunn, pp. 85–96. Beverly Hills: Sage.

O'Connor, James. 1971. "The Meaning of Economic Imperialism." In *Readings in U.S. Imperialism*, edited by K. T. Fann and Donald Hodges, pp. 23–68. Boston: Porter Sargent.

Poulantzas, Nicos. 1975. *Classes in Contemporary Capitalism*. London: New Left Books.

Rey, P.-P. 1971. *Colonialisme, néo-colonialisme et transition au capitalisme*. Paris: François Maspero.

———. 1973. *Les alliances de classes*. Paris: François Maspero.

Therborn, Goran. 1980. *Science, Class and Society*. London: New Left Books.

Wallerstein, Immanuel. 1974. *The Modern World-System: Capitalist Agriculture and the Origins of the European World-Economy in the Sixteenth Century*. New York: Academic Press.

———. 1979. *The Capitalist World-Economy*. Cambridge: Cambridge University Press.

———. 1983. *Historical Capitalism*. London: New Left Books.

Worsley, Peter. 1980. "One World or Three? A Critique of the Modern World-System Theory of Immanuel Wallerstein." *The Socialist Register*. Pp. 298–338.

6

Race, Ethnicity, and Class

James A. Geschwender

INTRODUCTION

Perhaps more sociological writing has focused on the analysis of race and ethnicity than on any other single set of social phenomena. The *assimilationist perspective* dominated U.S. sociology in the 1950s and 1960s. (For a critique of this perspective, see Geschwender 1978, pp. 39–69.) The assimilationists tended to view race and ethnicity as primordial categories with race being physiological and ethnicity cultural in nature. In their view, each minority group entered U.S. society in a disadvantaged position because of a lack of knowledge of U.S. culture and a deficiency of skills and competencies that would enable them to compete successfully in U.S. society. The "failure" of the assimilationist perspective to explain persistent racial inequality in the United States became all too evident as the struggle for racial equality swept through the United States in the mid- to late 1960s. The Civil Rights movement, Black Power movement, and numerous other social movements of the 1960s and early 1970s impacted on young sociologists who would soon provide a radical critique of mainstream U.S. sociology. It was clear to most of the

This paper tends to focus more on ethnicity than on race per se, although I firmly believe that race and ethnicity can be analyzed in similar, if not identical, fashion. For simplicity's sake, I shall use the terms "race" and "ethnicity," although I have argued elsewhere (Geschwender 1983) for their total exclusion from our discourse.

insurgents in the field that assimilationist theory was inadequate to account for the complexities surrounding race and ethnicity in the United States.

The traditional assimilationist perspective assumes that over time all minorities learn the dominant cultural perspectives and become integrated into U.S. society. It is not assumed that minorities would become identical to the dominant group, but that they would become a fully accepted part of a smoothly functioning social system. Most social scientists expect minorities to vary in their rate of assimilation as a consequence of variations in majority group resistance. Members of the majority group are expected to develop prejudice in response to various features of the minority group, with higher levels of hostility generated against groups that are racially or culturally different. Racial differences are thought to produce the most intense response. Majority group members are also expected to perceive large concentrations of minority group members as a threat. Each of these factors is expected to stimulate majority group prejudice leading to majority group resistance, which would retard but not entirely halt, the rate of minority group assimilation. All minorities are expected eventually to become acculturated and develop the skills and competencies necessary for effective competition in U.S. society. As a result, majority group prejudice would be reduced, and the minority would eventually be assimilated into U.S. society on a basis of total equality.

The assimilationist school does not give the concept of exploitation a central place in its analyses. It acknowledges that Afro-Americans were brought into U.S. society as slaves and that this had an impact upon the rate and progress of their assimilation. It does not raise questions as to whether this rate was deliberately retarded because it was profitable for the dominant economic class to have Afro-Americans in a less assimilated and more exploitable position. It also does not question the assumption that European immigration was a relatively free, voluntary search for a better life. There is no attempt to examine whether the immigrants were not also brought into U.S. society to fill a labor need and provide profits to the dominant economic class. Nor does this school question the extent to which racism may have developed as a rationalization for the exploitation of Afro-Americans or the extent to which prejudice may have been deliberately induced as a means to divide the working class and facilitate its exploitation.

Radical sociologists, touched by the social movements of the 1960s and early 1970s, could not understand how it was possible to analyze race and ethnicity without the key concepts of exploitation and oppression. They intuitively understood that the process of capitalist accumulation and its associated class struggle held the key to understanding race and ethnicity. They proposed a number of radical alternatives to assimilationist theory, each of which had its positive aspects ss well as its shortcomings. This paper will explore both the positive aspects and the shortcomings of *class reductionist theory*, *segmented labor market theory*, *split labor market theory*, and *global labor market theory* which has its roots in the *world-systems perspective*. This paper will conclude by proposing a theoretical approach that builds upon the positive aspects of each of the other radical alternatives and that locates the analysis of race and ethnicity in the class struggle that results from the twin contradictions of capitalism—that between capital and labor and that between the capitalist core and the periphery. Ironically, this theoretical perspective incorporates as an essential element a new theoretical perspective that emerged from mainstream sociology—and, in fact, from within assimilationist theory itself. *Ethnic emergence theory* provides the key element that was missing from the various radical alternatives.

CLASS REDUCTIONIST THEORY

Class reductionist approaches vary in degree of sophistication from the most simplistic to the relatively sophisticated innovations of Bonacich and Wallerstein. Despite the fact that Oliver Cox (1948) first formulated his thesis linking racism to capitalism in a book that concerned itself with the analysis of the growth and expansion of capitalism on a world scale, the typical scholar accepting a class reductionist perspective has primarily been concerned with the phenomena as observed within core geopolitical formations. The thesis (Baran and Sweezy 1966; Braverman 1974; Winston 1973; Castells 1975; Nikolinakos 1973, 1975; Legassick 1974a, 1974b; Wolpe 1970, 1972; Gabriel and Ben Tovim 1978) usually sees the members of the so-called "racial" or "ethnic" group as being an especially disadvantaged sector of the working class. This sector can serve as a "reserve army" and, when employed, can be more intensively exploited because of its relative powerlessness. Those who hold to this thesis tend to view capitalists as conscious and deliberate stimulators of racism within the working class in order to keep the class divided, weak, and exploitable.

It is usually sufficient to refute the more simplistic presentations of this thesis to note the extent to which all of the so-called "racial/ethnic" solidarities are class differentiated. Gabriel and Ben Tovim (1978) note that even in South Africa, where one finds a rather high concentration of Africans among the working class, there are Africans to be found among the bourgeoisie, while a significant number of Afrikaners are located in the working class. South Africa is probably the extreme case that exhibits the highest degree of correspondence between class and so-called racial/ethnic identity. In other societies we find an even higher degree of class differentiation among most other solidarities pertinent to our discussion. During the slavery era, Afro-Americans included in their numbers a few large plantation-operating slave owners and currently include owners of multimillion-dollar capitalist enterprises (Geschwender 1978). Paralleling this is the fact that European-Americans of Anglo-Saxon ancestry are included among both the working class and those permanently excluded from the labor force. It is simply not correct to reduce all of the myriad forms in which racism may be manifested to being simple expressions of the economic or political needs of capitalism.

Although we may still find examples of the cruder form of class reductionism described above, class reductionism today is much more likely to find expression in the more sophisticated version such as that embodied in the work of Edna Bonacich and Immanuel Wallerstein. Bonacich's work is multifaceted, and aspects of it will be discussed elsewhere in this paper. Nevertheless, she has made statements that suggest a belief that in the last analysis race and ethnicity may be reduced to class (Bonacich 1980a). She believes that ethnic movements are essentially political rather than primordial and that they have *material* roots in the relations of production. She further argues that nationalism, despite being argued in terms of primordial ties, grows out of the class relations and represents efforts to create alliances across class lines. At heart, she argues, nationalist movements are the product of class forces.

While Bonacich primarily manifested her tendency toward class reductionism in discussions of the situation of immigrant solidarities within the core, Wallerstein (1972, 1973a, 1973b, 1975; Arrighi et al. 1983) develops his argument in the context of a theoretical interpretation of Weber's classic discussion of class, status groups, and parties and the attempt to apply them to core/peripheral relations. Ethnicity is viewed as a status group category that serves as a mask concealing the realities of class differentials. Struggles may be generated and fueled using an ideology centering on ethnicity but

the fact remains that if the society were to become ethnically integrated, class antagonisms would not abate; rather they would intensify. And to the extent that class antagonisms might abate, status-
group antagonisms would also abate.

I share much of the sentiment expressed by Bonacich and Wallerstein, but, in part, I disagree. I think that they are absolutely right in
rejecting the primordial nature of race and ethnicity which are
correctly stressed as historical entities that emerge in a particular
sociohistorical context and have meaning only within that context.
Yet, by itself, this is not sufficient to convince me that the phenomena under examination may be fully and completely captured by
the concept of class.

Racism as an ideology exists within capitalist society and does
function to facilitate the exploitation of labor. Workers from minority ethnic solidarities may be shunted into poorly paid jobs that
would not exist without their presence. Surplus-value is created
where none might be otherwise. All labor is more easily controlled
because of its diversity. Yet racial domination extends beyond
simple exploitation. Systematic patterns of racial oppression impact
upon the ability of the members of an oppressed group to live in
ways consistent with their ability to earn a living. Their ability to
define for themselves their very life-styles is hampered. These restrictions appear in areas of life ranging from language, music, and art
to political self-determination. The ending of racial oppression does
mean the achievement of equality in the sphere of production—initially at least to the extent of equality in the job market but also ultimately in the destruction of that very market—but it also means
freedom in the realm of reproduction and cultural expression. Domination in these areas of life (racial oppression) clearly facilitates the
extraction of surplus, both of surplus-value from labor under capitalist production relations and of surplus from the periphery to the core
through unequal exchange. Yet racial oppression is not reducible to
class exploitation. Conversely, while freedom from oppression in
these realms may serve to inhibit the expanded reproduction of capital, it is not synonymous with its termination.

A further and even more telling defect in the class reductionist
approach is the fact that it overly simplifies the process of extraction of surplus. Bonacich's class reductionism fails to include the
fact that petty capitalist segments of the oppressed racial or ethnic
group operate to extract surplus from their co-ethnics and, in turn,
the major portion of that surplus is taken from them by larger
capitalist concerns located in the dominant community—a process

that she has analyzed so brilliantly in her writings on middlemen minorities (Bonacich 1973, 1978; Bonacich and Model 1980).

Wallerstein's reductionism also ignores the implications of his other writing that has elaborated upon the development of a three-tier format in which the middle tier (a comprador bourgeoisie) participates in the exploitation of a lower tier but, in turn, loses most of the fruits of its gains to capitalists in the core (Wallerstein 1975). Bonacich's analysis reduces racism to an ideological adjunct of class exploitation, while Wallerstein comes very close to eliminating the concept altogether. Both fail to appreciate fully the key role that racism plays in the process of capitalist accumulation.

DUAL OR SEGMENTED LABOR MARKET THEORY

Dual or segmented labor market theory was designed more to account for the position occupied by minorities (racial and ethnic) and gender in the economic order than it was to explain the origin and continued existence of such minorities. Nevertheless, it has much to offer that may prove useful in our quest. A number of authors (Gordon 1971, 1972; Doeringer and Piore 1971; Edwards 1975, 1979; Edwards, Reich, and Gordon 1975; Gordon, Edwards, and Reich 1982; Piore 1975; Wachtel and Betsy 1973; Vietorisz and Harrison 1973; Bluestone 1971) noted that the U.S. economy, and by implication all core economies, was segmented into monopoly (also called primary or core) and competitive (also called secondary or peripheral) sectors. Firms in the monopoly sector tended to be large, profitable, capital intensive, to produce durable goods, to be characterized by internal labor markets and bureaucratic control, and to be oligopolistic. Consequently, their labor force tends to be highly skilled, productive, unionized, earns high wages, and exhibits stable career patterns. Firms in the competitive sector tend to be small, marginally profitable, labor intensive, to be characterized by direct supervision and external labor markets, and to produce non-durable goods. Consequently, their labor force tends to be unskilled, unorganized, poorly paid, to exhibit low levels of productivity, and to be characterized by unstable employment patterns.

Much of the early writing in this tradition was descriptive in nature and did little to explain either the origin of the segmented labor market or the tendency for immigrant and minority workers to be concentrated in the competitive sector. Hodson (1978, p. 435) suggested that the high profit levels of monopoly sector firms enabled them to ignore the economic benefits of hiring cheaper labor and, instead, to buy labor power from preferred sources (presumably native, male, members of dominant racial/ethnic groups) at whatever cost is necessary. This argument appears to make employers' discrimination against women and minorities simply a matter of taste. Piore (1970, 1975) and Gordon (1972) went a bit beyond this in arguing that monopoly sector firms have a greater need for a stable work force in order to maintain high levels of productivity and profitability. Piore, although not Gordon, suggests, in a "culture-of-poverty" type argument, that minorities lack the requisite social and cultural characteristics and have not experienced sufficient security of regular employment in the past to become stable, reliable workers. Thus, in their writings, employer discrimination is simply a result of the rational application of a set of probabilistic expectation statements derived from observation and past experience.

The Piore and Gordon argument provides capital with a reason for its preference for discrimination but the explanation still seems somewhat ahistorical and static. All workers are made to appear as the passive recipients of action taken by an all-powerful capitalist class. Class struggle in any of its manifestations is totally absent from the picture. Edwards, Reich, and Gordon (1975; Gordon, Edwards, and Reich 1982) make a serious effort to include class struggle in their analysis of the origin and evolution of labor market segmentation. They locate their analysis in the nature of capitalism. They argue that the capitalist system is not stagnant. It constantly evolves and changes. Capitalist accumulation tends to expand the boundaries of the capitalist system and stimulates an increase in the size of firms; an increased concentration of the ownership and control of capital in fewer hands draws an increased proportion of the population into a wage-labor relation with capital. This leads to changes in the labor process including mechanization, introduction of new technologies, and changes in management systems of supervision and control. Workers defend themselves against the effects of capitalist accumulation through organization at the point of production, organized political action, and a host of less formal activities such as sabotage and slowdowns.

This abstract theoretical analysis was concretized by applying it to the evolution of a segmented labor market in the United States during three overlapping stages (Edwards, Reich, and Gordon 1975; Gordon, Edwards, and Reich 1982). The period of *initial proletarianization* ran from roughly 1820 to 1890, during which the labor process was not transformed to any significant extent and the labor market remained as numerous distinct pockets rather than forming a unified whole. The economic crisis of the 1870s and 1880s demonstrated to capital the inefficiency of its social organization of production so it began to experiment with steps leading toward *the homogenization of labor* and the institution of the drive system. The process, as it evolved, included mechanization, undercutting the power of skilled labor, decreased reliance upon craft labor, increased reliance upon lesser-skilled workers, increased capital-labor ratios, increased plant size, corporate consolidation, creation of a national labor market, increased labor reserves, and a vastly expanded potential labor supply.

During the 1930s labor rebelled against the combined impact of the Great Depression and homogenization. Numerous strikes brought recognition for industrial unions and various assorted benefits to workers that drove up the cost of production. It did not take capital long to respond to labor's victories, and it is in capital's counterattack that we see the origin of segmentation. Larger and more unionized firms began replacing direct supervision with bureaucratic control with emphasis upon impersonal rules and job definitions which were often incorporated into collective bargaining agreements. Internal labor markets developed in which benefits were tied to seniority, jobs were strung together to create career ladders, and artificial criteria (e.g., education) were employed in hiring. Workers who were excluded from entry-level jobs were denied the opportunity for the advancement and security that accompanied the development of internal labor markets. It became more costly for workers to change employers, and management got a more stable work force.

However, not all firms could follow this pattern. The general trend was for the larger, better capitalized firms to change in the manner described above while the smaller, less well capitalized firms had to continue to rely upon the older drive system. Thus there emerged a major structural segmentation in the U.S. economy between sectors that are commonly labelled "monopoly" and "competitive." However, the two sectors do not exist in isolation from one another. Rather, they have many intricate links including, but not limited to, franchising and subcontracting. The structural segmentation of the economy was accompanied by a segmentation of labor markets. Monopoly sector firms rely primarily upon internal labor markets, while competitive sector firms continue, as in most other regards, to resemble the typical firms of the homogenization era in relying upon external labor markets.

This provides us with a useful understanding of the historical process through which dual or segmented labor markets developed and how they operate in U.S. society. It does a fine job of demonstrating the important role of class struggle as both cause and consequence of the changes in the capitalist organization of production. Where it falls down is in explaining the process through which workers from racial/ethnic minority backgrounds come to be concentrated in the competitive sector while white males come to dominate the labor force in the primary sector. Bonacich (1980) argues that much of the writing in this tradition has the tendency to attribute the origin of manpower needs (i.e., labor market characteristics) to characteristics of the firms themselves when in fact the opposite is the case: the pattern of employment characteristic of the dual labor market is the direct result of split labor market dynamics. We cannot fully understand her specific argument in this regard without first considering the logic of split labor market theory.

SPLIT LABOR MARKET THEORY

Edna Bonacich developed the theoretical foundation for split labor market analysis in a series of articles (1972, 1975, 1976, 1977, 1979, 1980b). Three key classes or class fractions are involved in split labor markets: capital or individual capitalists, higher priced labor, and cheaper labor. The distinction between higher priced and cheaper labor often corresponds to that between native and immigrant populations or, put another way, to members of dominant and subordinate racial/ethnic solidarities, although it is clear that neither race, as a biological concept, nor ethnicity, referring to the cultural heritage of peoples, is the root cause of the differences. Immigrant populations frequently lack many of the resources available to native workers—often as a consequence of past core/peripheral relations—and consequently are in a disadvantaged position in the labor market. Subordinate racial/ethnic solidarities (i.e., earlier immigrant populations with a history in the core geopolitical formation) are similarly disadvantaged because of institutionalized patterns of discrimination.

Capitalists would prefer to hire the cheapest labor available and, left to their own devices, would entirely displace higher priced labor with cheaper labor. Naturally, higher priced labor (native labor or workers from the dominant racial/ethnic population) attempts to resist this to the best of its ability. While theoretically this resistance could take the form of class unity and a united working class struggle against capital, it quite frequently takes the form of attempts to restrict capital's ability to use cheap labor—often by attempting to exclude cheaper labor from the geopolitical formation, from the industry, or from certain occupations. One device for this has also included the attempt to isolate cheaper labor into caste-like social locations. Isolation may also include the attempt to exclude products produced elsewhere by cheap labor. Often this requires attempts to influence state policy (e.g., immigration laws, domestic content legislation, regulation of employment as in South Africa's "civilized labor policy") and at other times it involves direct action against the employer. In a paradoxical fashion, we may view these attacks by one segment of the proletariat against another as part of the class struggle in that they are indirect actions taken by labor against capital. Attempts to exclude cheap labor from the scene are, in effect, efforts to remove one weapon that capital may use against labor and thereby increase labor's relative power position. This may constitute a short-sighted strategy but it is, nevertheless, a strategy designed to strengthen labor and weaken capital. Class struggle is an interactive process. Not only does labor organize in response to capital's preference for cheaper immigrant labor, but capital's preference for cheaper immigrant labor is often a response to labor's earlier organizational successes.

Bonacich (1980b) uses the class-analytic approach embodied in split labor market theory to supplement and improve upon dual labor market theory. She fully accepts the description of the evolution of U.S. society into monopoly and competitive sectors and the fragmentation of the monopoly sector jobs into strata greatly differing in career opportunities and rewards. However, she sharply rejects the notion that the differential allocation of native and immigrant workers, or of majority and minority workers, may be explained by the automatic workings of the market or by differential needs of capital in the two sectors. Rather, she argues that the pattern of employment characteristic of the dual labor market is the direct result of split labor market dynamics. She argues that labor has often attempted to solidify its position by pressing the state for protective legislation. When it achieves this, capital counterattacks by attempting to create as many loopholes in the rules as it can. The tendency is for the protective laws to come to be applied in the monopoly sector and not in the competitive sector. Consequently, the competitive sector remains an area in which capital can continue to employ cheap, powerless, and readily exploitable workers who often come from minority racial/ethnic communities, while the more organized and powerful workers from the majority group dominate the jobs in the monopoly sector.

This approach is intuitively attractive because it locates the dual labor market in the nexus of class struggle which it acknowledges is carried on at the level of the state as well as at the point of production (Geschwender and Levine 1983, 1986; Levine and Geschwender 1981). Labor and capital constantly make moves and countermoves. Labor organizes, attempts to influence state policy, and succeeds in getting favorable protective legislation passed. Capital often cannot prevent passage of the legislation, so it helps to shape it into a form with which it can live (Levine 1980). It ensures that there are enough loopholes to allow it to continue to operate in a profitable manner, and it strives mightily to influence the manner of enforcement. All these actions generate renewed efforts on the part of labor. Nevertheless, this approach, however attractive for explaining certain features of the labor market, is not adequate unto itself to explain the origin of the dichotomy between monopoly and competitive sectors. It must be integrated into a structural analysis of capitalist development of the type presented by segmented labor market theorists.

That combination, while highly useful, still has some problems and leaves some questions unanswered. Sassen-Koob (1980) has demonstrated that immigrant and minority workers are not essential to the existence and operation of a dual labor market because this same bifurcation occurs in industrialized countries with a relatively homogeneous (in racial/ethnic terms) labor force. Portes and Bach (1985) also have noted that even in racially/ethnically heterogeneous geopolitical formations such as in the United States, a large proportion of the workers in the competitive sector are native and majority group workers. Thus, there is no identity between immigrant or minority status and location in the competitive sector despite a significant tendency for a disproportionate share of immigrant and minority workers (especially illegal immigrants) to be so employed. We must supplement the useful features of a combined segmented-split labor market theory with further analysis that explains the origin of race and ethnicity and the differential allocation of groups to sectors of the economy.

GLOBAL LABOR MIGRATION

Work done within the theoretical framework of world-systems theory pioneered by Wallerstein (1979, 1980b) has generated a large amount of research on labor migrations from the periphery to the core. Different scholars have tended to focus on different aspects of the process. Portes (1978) has laid out rather nicely for us the development of conditions in the periphery that are necessary preconditions for labor migrations. He notes that labor shortages in the core are never sufficient unto themselves to generate labor migrations. Rather, it is first necessary that political and economic institutions of the peripheral society be penetrated by the core society in such a manner as to create imbalances between sectors that lead eventually to labor displacement. This may take place in a variety of ways ranging from the total destruction of the preexisting noncapitalist economy to the development of parallel economies in the peripheral society. But whichever proves to be the case in any given peripheral society, there tends to be generated a proletarianized segment of the population—one that may or may not have had previous experience with wage labor but that now has no alternative but to offer its labor power for sale on the market. The labor market in the peripheral society generally proves to be incapable of utilizing anywhere near the available pool of labor, so a substantial portion of it must either migrate or starve.

Elizabeth Petras (1980, 1981), among others, tends to emphasize conditions in the core society that both attract immigrant workers and make immigrant workers attractive to core capital. She states that during the late stages of capitalist development, surplus or reserve labor is drawn across national barriers toward the core from nations located in the periphery or the semiperiphery. Immigrant labor appears to be particularly attractive to core capital for four basic types of reasons. First, immigrant labor is more powerless, may be hired for lower wages, and, consequently, the rate of exploitation may be intensified (Petras 1980, pp. 440-5; Castells 1975, p. 53; Portes 1978, pp. 31-3; Rosenblum 1983; Sassen-Koob 1980, 1981; Bach 1978). The major point is that immigrant workers are not citizens and thus lack some of the basic political resources that they need to protect themselves. Even when the resources are made available to them, they often lack the knowledge of how to take advantage of them. Immigrant workers can be treated differently from domestic workers. This enables employers both to pay them less at time of first entry, and also to keep their labor cheaper for a longer period of time. The tendency for migration to consist primarily of young, either unmarried or unaccompanied, males (and increasingly to include single women) eliminates any need for capital to pay a family wage. Illegal immigrants appear to be even more vulnerable and, consequently, even more desirable to capital (Portes 1978; Samora 1971).

Second, the social costs of reproduction of the working class may be transferred from core to peripheral societies (Petras 1980; Bonacich and Cheng 1984, p. 32; Castells 1975, p. 47; Gorz 1970, p. 29; Burawoy 1976; Sassen-Koob 1980, 1981). Often the costs of rearing and educating a child is borne by the periphery, only to have the person when adult migrate to the core for his/her productive years. All too frequently, the older worker returns to the periphery upon retirement, thus leaving the social costs of old age also to be borne by the peripheral society. The fact that core societies select the young and able-bodied to be admitted as immigrants also means that health and other costs borne by the receiving society are less for immigrant workers than for the more heterogeneous, domestic work force.

Third, extensive reliance by capital upon immigrant labor weakens all of labor in the class struggle (Petras 1980; Rosenblum 1973, pp. 39-40; Portes and Walton 1975, p. 57). Immigrant labor tends to be employed in low-wage occupations and is used to drive down wages for the entire working class. This creates resentment on the part of domestic workers that is usually directed (more correctly, it is usually misdirected) at the immigrant workers, thus fragmenting the working class. Even if domestic workers were eager to collaborate with immigrant workers in militant class action against capital, immigrant workers might still be reluctant. Immigrant labor that is too active in politics or in militant unions lacks the protection of citizenship and often fears that it may be readily expelled. It matters little whether these fears are real or imagined—they are real in their impact. The fears clearly have a reality base for illegal immigrants.

Fourth, the very process of draining off the surplus population of peripheral societies performs a service for those societies in removing an important potential source of political instability (Petras 1980, pp. 440-5; Portes 1979, p. 445; Bach 1984). Performance of this service and the potential threat to halt it combine with several other aspects of the relationship to continually reproduce the very relation of periphery to core that is at the heart of the entire process.

The major difference between these analysts who focus on conditions in the periphery and those who focus upon conditions in the core is simply one of emphasis. Most of them embed their analysis within a common set of assumptions that recognize the existence of a capitalist world-economy—something that was not recognized by the old "push-pull" theorists. Each recognizes the importance of conditions in both the core and the periphery, but they place different degrees of emphasis upon them. In fact, Portes (1978; see also Portes and Bach 1985, pp. 111-64) stresses the importance of the linkage in his discussion of migration networks in which he notes that regions of the world become closely linked so that labor migrations tend to follow established routes. Early immigrants communicate back to the kinsmen, friends, and neighbors, stimulating others to follow in their path. Consequently, large settlements develop within core societies that are almost entirely made up of individuals who can trace their origins back to the same tiny village and surrounding countryside. This may occur despite the fact that the immigrants themselves span several generations, having migrated at widely different times.

It should be noted that labor migrations historically have not been the simple result of workers simply evaluating their situation on a cost-benefit basis and opting to migrate in order to earn the higher wages available in the core (Portes and Bach 1985, pp. 5-7). The pull of higher wages paid in the United States often had to be supplemented by active recruiting efforts. This was particularly true during the 1820s and 1830s. However, even active recruiting efforts would not suffice in those areas not yet integrated into the capitalist world-system. In those cases, active coercion was required in order to achieve the needed supply of labor (see also Wallerstein 1986). However, a time is reached in the evolution of the capitalist world-system when sufficient capitalist penetration into the periphery has occurred so that neither coercion nor active recruiting is required to obtain the desired flow of workers (Portes and Bach 1985, p. 7).

The global labor migration school is not concerned with the analysis of race and ethnicity, per se, yet much of their work leans in that direction. The school makes a very positive contribution in locating the origin of diversity within core societies in the development of a capitalist world-system. It is not necessary to accept all of the assumptions of that school to recognize the importance of the world-wide spread of capitalism, the development of imperialism, the disruption and distortion of economies in peripheral societies, and the use of indigenous peoples as cheap labor either in their own societies or after transportation to the core.

Where this school tends to fall down is in its analysis of what happens to these peoples after their arrival in the core society. None of the authors cited herein address the question of the transformation of immigrants into racial or ethnic minorities. It is not sufficient simply to note physical or cultural differences as if they, in themselves, automatically give rise to racial or ethnic identity. The scholars in this school also fail to adequately explain why the native working class in the dominant society does not simply absorb the immigrants into a unified working class. The fact that capital can make profitable use of immigrant labor explains why they want immigrants to come to core societies, but it does not explain why labor tends to view these immigrants as enemies rather than as potential allies. We must turn to a perspective developed within mainstream sociology to help us understand this phenomenon—that presented by the ethnic emergence school. This approach will not be discussed separately but rather will be incorporated into the presentation of an integrated theoretical approach that builds upon all of the radical alternatives discussed herein.

TOWARD AN INTEGRATED THEORETICAL APPROACH

It seems clear that any adequate analysis of race and ethnicity must be rooted within a consideration of the interplay between the "twin contradictions of capitalism." The primary contradiction is between capital and labor. In its most fully developed form it involves a portion of the population that has been proletarianized and is forced to sell its labor power. Capital purchases labor power and uses it in the production of commodities. The value produced through the application of labor is greater than the price paid by capital and the remainder, after subtracting costs of equipment and raw materials, is surplus-value appropriated by capital.

A second key contradiction within capitalism is the relation of core to periphery. As the capitalist world-system expands from its centers of capital accumulation it incorporates new areas into the system and develops a global division of labor. The newly incorporated areas tend to become producers of primary products and/or suppliers of labor power, while the core areas become the centers for the most advanced technological applications to manufacturing processes. Exchange between core and peripheral areas tends to be unequal to the disadvantage of the periphery. Just as capital extracts surplus-value through the labor process, the core extracts surplus from the periphery through unequal exchange. Wages paid in the periphery tend to be much lower than those in the core.

These two contradictions are not unrelated. The struggle between capital and labor is the origin of the contradiction between core and periphery. The cost of labor in the core increases for a number of reasons, including the tendency toward full proletarianization of labor, the disappearance of the reserve army, the consequent competition among capitalists for labor, and the organization of workers into labor unions and/or political parties. Capital responds to this rising cost of labor both through imperialist expansion and through encouraging the migration of labor from periphery to core. Immigrants may differ from the native working class in terms of physical and/or cultural characteristics. However, they do not at this time constitute either a racial or an ethnic group. The key to understanding the process through which immigrant status is transformed into race or ethnicity is perhaps best described in the ethnic emergence and ethnic mobilization literature (Yancey et al. 1976; Nagel and Olzak 1982; Olzak 1983; Portes 1984; Portes et al. 1980; Bach 1986). This school sees ethnicity, or at least ethnic consciousness and ethnic solidarity, arising as a consequence of a group's structural location in society.

The position that immigrant populations come to occupy in core countries and the probability of their evolving into self-conscious ethnic groups is a function of the opportunity structure existing at the time of first immigration. Lieberson (1963, p. 63) notes that differences in destination between the "old immigration" to the United States (pre-1890) from Northern and Western Europe and the "new immigration" from Southern and Eastern Europe (the former into agriculture and the latter into the urban centers of the eastern seaboard) was largely a function of the fact that most of the good agricultural land had been settled by the time of the latter's migration.

Portes and Bach (1985, pp. 29–37) argue that by about 1890 the drive toward industrial consolidation and monopoly displaced agriculture as the dominant economic sector. Consequently, immigration ceased to be that of a settler-oriented people moving onto the land and became wage-oriented. Domestic labor and the older immigrants could still get enough cheap land so that they were not forced to depend upon the factories for their livelihood. Meanwhile, employers turned to Southern and Eastern Europe as their source of cheap labor. Thus, the source of immigrants changed at precisely the same time as did the use to which they were put in the United States.

Not only did the new immigrants primarily settle in the cities and in the industrial sector, but immigrants from the same part of the world tended to be concentrated by occupation, industrial sector, region, and part of the city. Regional concentration resulted from the tendency for migration to occur through networks as noted above. Yancey et al. (1976, pp. 393–5) and Golab (1973) noted that Polish immigrants tended to concentrate in the steel industry and Italian immigrants in construction precisely because these were then industrial sectors undergoing the most rapid expansion at the time of their arrival. Similarly, Jews tended to concentrate in the garment industry (Yancey et al. 1976, p. 393). This may have been partially a consequence of their previous background as tailors, but it resulted primarily from the emergence of the mass production of clothing at the end of the nineteenth century. The development of immigrant ghettos appears to be primarily a characteristic of the "new" immigration that took place between 1890 and 1940 and was brought about because industry evolved a factory system concentrating a large number of jobs into a single location at a time when the primitive nature of public transportation required that one live close to one's job. Part of it also resulted from the network of supportive institutions that grew up in the ghettos.

There is little question that this type of concentration lends itself to categorical labelling of immigrant populations by members of the host society. Stereotypes created earlier in the core/peripheral context may be reinforced or modified but they are unlikely to be abandoned. In those cases where there are no preexisting stereotypes, new ones may be created and normally are accompanied by prejudice and discrimination. Portes and Bach (1985, pp. 34-6) illustrate this with a discussion of the experiences of Italian immigrants to the United States—the largest immigrant group during this time period. They suggest that one cause for these developments was the desire of employers to keep Italian immigrants atomized and weak so that they might be more effective and more intensively exploited. But the actions of capital were only part of the explanation. Between the turn of the century and World War I, native workers and earlier immigrants came to view the new immigration as a threat because of its size and continued flow, the closing of the frontier, the decreasing numbers of opportunities outside the factory system, and the periodic use of immigrant strikebreakers in mines and factories. This stimulated active opposition (prejudice giving way to discrimination) against the immigrant groups, and it generated in response a protective increased solidarity and ethnic consciousness on their part. While it cannot be demonstrated with available data, it seems likely that it is during this period that ethnicity emerged—ethnic consciousness was created and ethnic mobilization took place—among the "older immigrants" (the peoples from Northern and Western Europe) in response to the perceived threat posed by the new immigrants from Southern and Eastern Europe (Nagel and Olzak 1982, p. 130; Olzak 1983, pp. 362-4).

There is abundant evidence that ethnicity among Southern and Eastern Europeans was created precisely as a consequence of the formation of communities that took place during labor migrations. Lieberson (1963) demonstrated that residential concentration leads to the creation and maintenance of ethnic solidarity. Ethnic solidarity is likely to increase concomitantly with increases in the degree of discrimination or hostility experienced by a given group (Sassen-Koob 1979; Portes et al. 1980; Schmitter 1980). Territorial concentration and ethnic solidarity tend to be accompanied by the development of a series of institutional structures (e.g., parochial schools) that serve to enhance and retain collective identity and to help establish territorial control over a portion of the city (Portes and Bach 1985, pp. 36-7).

It is not the case that this all-important sense of identity and ethnic consciousness emerges only among persons who came from a common origin and who previously had a common sense of identity (Yancey et al. 1976, p. 397). Numerous authors (e.g., Glazer 1954; Handlin 1961; Vecoli 1964) have pointed out that larger nationalistic groups developed in the United States out of coalitions of smaller groups that had only the most tenuous of cultural ties and no previous sense of collective identity. Nelli (1970) notes that Italian consciousness among immigrants from Italy was created in the United States, not in Europe. Killian (1970) says the same thing about the making of "Hillbillies" in Chicago out of a formerly highly differentiated set of white migrants from the South. Padilla (1982) suggests that a new ethnic group, Latinos, may be in the process of formation out of a loose federation of several national groups sharing somewhat of a common language. Greeley (1977, pp. 15–16) notes the same movement toward the formation of a Spanish-speaking ethnicity but suggests that it is occurring primarily in the Northeast and not the Southwest. He also notes similar movements toward emergent ethnicity among Native Americans. Nagel and Olzak (1982, pp. 128–30) cite several other examples of the creation of ethnic groups where none previously existed.

It is extremely important that we recognize that culture is not the primary, nor even an essential, ingredient in the emergence of ethnicity. I have already cited cases where external immigrants who previously possessed relatively little in terms of a common or shared heritage were forged into ethnic groups in the furnaces of U.S. society. However, most of them did, in fact, have cultural traditions that differed from those possessed by people already residing in the United States. But this was not the case for the Southerners who became Hillbillies in Chicago. Nor was it the case for the migrants who became Okies in California (Bonacich 1972, p. 557). Carey McWilliams (1945, pp. 82-3) described the process through which "dustbowl refugees" were shaped into a cohesive, self-conscious solidarity by the hostility and harsh treatment they received from indigenous residents of California. The newly created definition of ethnic group boundaries appeared to be shared by both those within and those without. Nor is cultural assimilation in any way a barrier to ethnic emergence. Portes et al. (1980, p. 220) note that it is precisely the most assimilated segment of the Cuban immigrant population (as measured by knowledge of U.S. society, ability to use the English language, and sharing of the dominant U.S. values) that exhibited the highest degree of ethnic consciousness and ethnic solidarity. It is precisely the most assimilated Cubans who recognized that they were in a subordinate economic and social position in U.S. society and, consequently, concluded that their common interests were best served through ethnic solidarity.

All of this suggests that it is hostility and discrimination generated by the fear of economic and social (but primarily economic) competition that generates the emergence of ethnicity. Geographic, sectoral, industrial, and occupational concentration provide the context in which experiences can be shared and a sense of common identity and common fate be created. The reality of that shared fate stimulates the creation of ethnic consciousness, but the fact must be re-emphasized that not all immigrant peoples become ethnic groups. Portes (1981, pp. 282-4) notes that recent immigrants coming into the United States under the "occupational skills" provision of immigration law are not the recipients of discrimination. They tend to enter the primary sector of the economy and experience a great deal of subsequent mobility. Nor do they become part of emergent ethnic communities. In contrast, we may note that Chinese immigrants were initially well received in the United States (Kitano 1974, pp. 193-211; Chen 1981). When they first arrived, they filled occupational niches left vacant by the shortage of women. They first experienced a significant degree of hostility when they moved into the gold mines and began competing with other miners for the valuable ore. However, the real crunch did not come until about 1870. A severe economic depression hit at the same time that 10,000 Chinese workers became unemployed because of the completion of the Central Pacific Railroad, and there was a significant increase in the number of white workers brought west by the new railroad. At this point, competition for jobs was intense, massive outbursts of hostility surfaced, and split labor market dynamics became evident. The Chinese were forced out of the numerous occupations and withdrew into Chinatowns for self-defense, but organized labor and other groups still made strenuous attempts to exclude them entirely from the United States.

It is evident that the class struggle is the motive force leading to the creation of race and ethnicity, the emergence of an ideology of racism, and the development of systems of racial/ethnic oppression. Class struggle within the core provides the motive force for the expansion of the capitalist world system. Class struggle and the victories of organized labor lead to the evolution of a segmented economy within core societies. Class struggle and labor victories also lead to capital's attempt to counteract labor's gains by importing workers from the periphery. The nature of the economy at the time of immigration and the point of entry into the economic order determines the probability of the immigrant population being transformed into a racial or ethnic group. If a racial or ethnic group does in fact emerge, then competition between immigrant and native labor is likely to generate the rise of racist ideology and split labor market dynamics through which native labor either attempts to exclude immigrant labor from the country, from the labor market, or simply from the monopoly sector, forcing them into the less desirable competitive sector of the economy. It is into this same competitive sector that most of the current labor immigration into the United States, both legal and illegal but predominantly illegal, is forced to move (Portes 1979; Portes and Bach 1985).

Thus, it is clear that we cannot understand the nature of race and ethnicity without locating it in a larger analysis of capitalist accumulation and the class struggle. We cannot reduce race and ethnicity to class, but at the same time we cannot understand them without the class concept. The radical scholars of the 1960s and the 1970s were absolutely correct in rejecting the mainstream assimilationist perspective. Each of the various radical alternatives that were proposed carried us a bit closer to the right perspective, but each was in itself less than fully adequate. The class reductionists made an important contribution in reminding us of the importance of class analysis, but they were mistaken in trying to reduce race and ethnicity to class because in so doing they failed to see the important role that racism plays in the capitalist accumulation process and in weakening labor in the class struggle. The segmented labor market theorists helped us to realize the importance of analyzing developments in the economic order and reminded us of the importance of class struggle, despite the fact that they totally failed to account for the emergence of race and ethnicity and the key role that they played. The split labor market school demonstrated the fact that working-class racism is, in fact, a tool that it uses in its struggle against capital, but it totally failed to account for the origin of race and ethnicity. It, like the segmented labor market school, tended to err in the opposite direction from the class reductionists, in that rather than reducing race/ethnicity to class, it tended to treat them as self-evident categories. The global labor migration school reminded us of the importance of the development of a capitalist world-system and the associated migration of labor from periphery to core. However, this school, like the others, failed to carry its analysis on to the point where one can understand the origin and role of race and ethnicity in the process of class struggle. Building upon the valuable contributions of each of these enables us to generate a theoretical perspective in which we see the origin of race and ethnicity in the twin contradictions of capitalism and helps us to understand the role that they play in the process of class struggle associated with them.

REFERENCES

Arrighi, Giovanni, Terence K. Hopkins, and Immanuel Wallerstein. 1983. "Rethinking the Concepts of Class and Status-Group in a World-System Perspective." *Review* 6:283-304.

Bach, Robert L. 1978. "Mexican Immigration and the American State." *International Migration Review* 12:536-58.

―――. 1984. "Political Frameworks for International Migration." In *The Americas in the New International Division of Labor*, edited by Steven Sanderson, pp. 95-124. New York: Holmes and Meier.

―――. 1986. "Immigration: Issues of Ethnicity, Class, and Public Policy in the United States." *Annals* 485:139-52.

Baran, Paul, and Paul M. Sweezy. 1966. *Monopoly Capital: An Essay on the American Economic and Social Order*. New York: Monthly Review Press.

Bluestone, Barry. 1970. "The Tripartite 'Economy' Labor Markets and the Working Poor." *Poverty and Human Resources* 5:15-36.

Bonacich, Edna. 1972. "A Theory of Ethnic Antagonism: The Split Labor Market." *American Sociological Review* 37:547-59.

―――. 1973. "A Theory of Middleman Minorities." *American Sociological Review* 38:583-94.

―――. 1975. "Abolition, the Extension of Slavery, and the Position of Free Blacks: A Study of Split Labor Markets in the United States, 1830-1863." *American Journal of Sociology* 81:601-28.

―――. 1976. "Advanced Capitalism and Black/White Race Relations in the United States: A Split Labor Market Interpretation." *American Sociological Review* 41:34-51.

―――. 1978. "U.S. Capitalism and Korean Immigrant Small Business." Paper presented at conference, "New Developments in the Labor Process," State University of New York at Binghamton.

―――. 1979. "The Past, Present, and Future of Split Labor Market Theory." In *Research in Race and Ethnic Relations*, Vol. 1, edited by Cora Bagley Marrett, pp. 17-64. Greenwich, CT: JAI.

―――. 1980a. "Class Approaches to Race and Ethnicity." *Insurgent Sociologist* 10:9-24.

————. 1980b. "The Creation of Dual Labor Markets." Paper presented at conference, "The Structure of Labor Markets," Athens, Georgia.

Bonacich, Edna, and Lucie Cheng. 1984. "Introduction: A Theoretical Orientation to International Labor Migration." In *Labor Immigration Under Capitalism: Asian Workers in the United States Before World War II*, edited by Lucie Cheng and Edna Bonacich, pp. 1-56. Berkeley: University of California Press.

Bonacich, Edna, and John Model. 1980. *The Economic Basis of Ethnic Solidarity: Small Business in the Japanese American Community*. Berkeley: University of California Press.

Braverman, Harry. 1974. *Labor and Monopoly Capital: The Degradation of Work in the Twentieth Century*. New York: Monthly Review Press.

Burawoy, Michael. 1976. "The Functions and Reproduction of Migrant Labor." *American Journal of Sociology* 81:1050-87.

Castells, Manuel. 1975. "Immigrant Workers and Class Struggles in Advanced Capitalism." *Politics and Society* 5:33-66.

Chen, Jack. 1981. *The Chinese of America*. San Francisco: Harper.

Cox, Oliver C. 1948. *Cast, Class and Race: A Study in Social Dynamics*. New York: Doubleday.

Doeringer, Peter B., and Michael J. Piore. 1971. *Internal Labor Markets and Manpower Analysis*. Lexington, MA: Lexington.

Edwards, Richard C. 1975. "The Social Relations of Production in the Firm and Labor Market Structure." In *Labor Market Segmentation*, edited by Richard C. Edwards, Michael Reich, and David M. Gordon, pp. 3-26. Lexington, MA: Lexington.

————. 1979. *Contested Terrain: The Transformation of the Workplace in the Twentieth Century*. Lexington, MA: Lexington.

Edwards, Richard C., Michael Reich, and David M. Gordon. 1975. *Labor Market Segmentation*. Lexington, MA: Lexington.

Gabriel, John, and Gideon Ben Tovim. 1978. "Marxism and the Concept of Racism." *Economy and Society* 7:118-54.

Geschwender, James A. 1978. *Racial Stratification in America*. Dubuque, IA: William C. Brown.

————. 1983. "Class, Race and Ethnicity." Unpublished (available in mimeograph).

Geschwender, James A., and Rhonda F. Levine. 1983. "Rationalization of Sugar Production in Hawaii, 1946-1960: A Dimension of the Class Struggle." *Social Problems* 30:352-68.

————. 1986. "Class Struggle and Political Transformations in Hawaii, 1946-1960." In *Research in Political Sociology*. Vol. 4, edited by Richard Braungart, pp. 241-68. Greenwich, CT: JAI.

Glazer, Nathan M. 1954. "Ethnic Groups in America: From National Culture to Ideology." In *Freedom and Control in Modern Society*, edited by Theodore Abel and Charles Page, pp. 158-72. New York: Van Nostrand.

Golab, Caroline. 1973. "The Immigrant and the City: Poles, Italians and Jews in Philadelphia, 1870-1920." In *The Peoples of Philadelphia*, edited by Allan F. Davis and Mark H. Haller, pp. 203-30. Philadelphia: University of Pennsylvania Press.

Gordon, David M. 1972. *Theories of Poverty and Underemployment*. Lexington, MA: Lexington.

Gordon, David M., Richard Edwards, and Michael Reich. 1982. *Segmented*

Work, Divided Workers: The Historical Transformation of Labor in the United States. Cambridge: Cambridge University Press.

Gorz, André. 1970. "Immigrant Labour." *New Left Review* 61:28–31.

Greeley, Andrew M. 1977. *The American Catholic: A Social Portrait.* New York: Basic Books.

Handlin, Oscar. 1961. "Historical Perspectives on the American Ethnic Group." *Daedalus* 90:220–32.

Hodson, Randy. 1978. "Labor in the Monopoly Competitive and State Sectors of Production." *Politics and Society* 8:429–80.

Killian, Lewis. 1970. *White Southerners.* New York: Random House.

Kitano, Harry H. L. 1974. *Race Relations.* Englewood Cliffs, NJ: Prentice-Hall.

Legassick, Martin. 1974a. "South Africa: Capital Accumulation and Violence." *Economy and Society* 3:253–91.

———. 1974b. "Legislation, Ideology and Economy in Post-1948 South Africa." *Journal of Southern African Studies* 1:5–35.

Levine, Rhonda F. 1980. "Class Struggle and the Capitalist State: The National Industrial Recovery Act and the New Deal." Unpublished Ph.D. dissertation, State University of New York at Binghamton.

Levine, Rhonda F., and James A. Geschwender. 1981. "Class Struggle, State Policy, and the Rationalization of Production: The Organization of Agriculture in Hawaii." In *Research in Social Movements, Conflict and Change.* Vol. 4, edited by Louis Kreisberg, pp. 123–50. Greenwich, CT: JAI.

Lieberson, Stanley. 1963. *Ethnic Patterns in American Cities.* New York: Free Press.

McWilliams, Carey. 1945. *Prejudice: Japanese Americans.* Boston: Little, Brown.

Nagel, Joane, and Susan Olzak. 1982. "Ethnic Mobilization in New and Old States: An Extension of the Competition Model." *Social Problems* 30:127–43.

Nelli, Humbert S. 1970. *The Italians in Chicago: 1880–1930.* New York: Oxford University Press.

Nikolinakos, Marios. 1973. "Notes on an Economic Theory of Racism." *Race* 13:365–81.

———. 1975. "Noted Towards a General Theory of Migration in Late Capitalism." *Race and Class* 17:5–17.

Olzak, Susan. 1983. "Contemporary Ethnic Mobilization." *Annual Review of Sociology* 9:355–74.

Petras, Elizabeth McLean. 1980. "Towards a Theory of International Migration: The New Division of Labor." In *Sourcebook on the New Immigration,* edited by Roy Bryce-LaPorte, pp. 439–49. New Brunswick, NJ: Transaction.

———. 1981. "The Global Labor Market in the Modern World Economy." In *Global Trends in Migration,* edited by Mary M. Katz, Charles B. Keely, and Silvano M. Tomasi, pp. 44–63. New York: CMS.

Piore, Michael J. 1970. "Jobs and Training." In *The State and the Poor,* edited by Samuel H. Beer and Richard E. Barringer, pp. 53–83. Cambridge, MA: Winthrop.

———. 1975. "Notes for a Theory of Labor Market Stratification." In *Labor Market Segmentation,* edited by Richard C. Edwards, Michael Reich, and David M. Gordon, pp. 125–50. Lexington, MA: Lexington.

Portes, Alejandro. 1978. "Migration and Underdevelopment." *Politics and Society* 8:1–48.

———. 1979. "Illegal Immigration and the International System: Lessons from

Recent Legal Mexican Immigrants to the United States." *Social Problems* 26:425-38.

———. 1981. "Modes of Structural Incorporation and Present Theories of Labor Immigration." In *Global Trends in Migration: Theory and Research on International Population Movements,* edited by Mary M. Kritz, Charles B. Keely, and Silvano M. Tomasi, pp. 279-97. New York: Center for Migration Studies.

———. 1984. "The Rise of Ethnicity: Determinants of Ethnic Perceptions Among Cuban Exiles in Miami." *American Sociological Review* 49:383-97.

Portes, Alejandro, and Robert L. Bach. 1985. *Latin Journey: Cuban and Mexican Immigrants in the United States.* Berkeley: University of California Press.

Portes, Alejandro, Robert N. Parker, and José A. Cobas. 1980. "Assimilation or Consciousness: Perceptions of U.S. Society Among Recent Latin American Immigrants to the United States." *Social Forces* 54:200-24.

Portes, Alejandro, and John Walton. 1981. *Labor, Class and the International System.* New York: Academic Press.

Reich, Michael, David M. Gordon, and Richard C. Edwards. 1973. "A Theory of Labor Market Segmentation." *American Economic Review* 63:359-65.

Rosenblum, Gerald. 1973. *Immigrant Workers: Their Impact Upon American Radicalism.* New York: Basic Books.

Samora, Julian. 1971. *Los Mojadas: The Wetback Story.* Notre Dame, IN: University of Notre Dame.

Sassen-Koob, Saskia. 1979. "Formal and Informal Associations: Dominicans and Colombians in New York." *International Migration Review* 14:179-92.

———. 1980. "Immigrant and Minority Workers in the Organization of the Labor Process." *Journal of Ethnic Studies* 1:1-34.

———. 1981. "Towards a Conceptualization of Immigrant Labor." *Social Problems* 24:65-85.

Schmitter, Barbara E. 1981. "Trade Unions and Immigration Politics in West Germany and Switzerland." *Politics and Society* 10:317-34.

Vecoli, Rudolph J. 1964. "Contadini in Chicago: A Critique of the Uprooted." *Journal of American History* 51:404-17.

Vietorisz, Thomas, and Bennett Harrison. 1973. "Labor Market Segmentation: Positive Feedback and Divergent Development." *American Economic Review* 63:366-76.

Wachtel, Howard, and Charles Betsey. 1972. "Employment at Low Wages." *Review of Economics and Statistics* 54:121-9.

Wallerstein, Immanuel. 1972. "Social Conflict in Post Independence Black Africa: The Concepts of Race and Ethnic Group Reconsidered." In *Racial Tensions and National Identity,* edited by Ernest Q. Campbell, pp. 206-26. Nashville: Vanderbilt University Press.

———. 1973a "The Two Modes of Ethnic Consciousness: Soviet Central Asia in Transition." In *The Nationality Question in Soviet Central Asia,* edited by Edward Allworth, pp. 168-75. New York: Praeger.

———. 1973b. "Class and Class Conflict in Contemporary Africa." *Canadian Journal of African Studies* 7:375-80.

———. 1974. *The Modern World-System: Capitalist Agriculture and the Origins of the European World-Economy in the Sixteenth Century.* New York: Academic Press.

———. 1975. "Class Formation in the Capitalist World-Economy." *Politics and Society* 5:367-75.

————. 1976. "American Slavery and the Capitalist World-Economy." *American Journal of Sociology* 812:1199-213.

————. 1980a. "The States in the Institutional Vortex of the Capitalist World-Economy." *International Social Science Journal* 32:743-51.

————. 1980b. *The Modern World-System II: Mercantilism, and the Consolidation of the European World-Economy, 1600-1750.* New York: Academic Press.

Winston, Henry. 1973. *Strategies for a Black Agenda: A Critique of New Theories of Liberation in the United States and Africa.* New York: International Publishers.

Wolpe, Harold. 1972. "Capitalism and Cheap Labour-Power in South Africa: From Segregation to Apartheid." *Economy and Society* 1:425-56.

————. 1975. "The Theory of Internal Colonialism: The South African Case." In *Beyond the Sociology of Development,* edited by Ivar Oxaal, Tony Barnett, and David Booth, pp. 229-52. London: Routledge, Kegan Paul.

Yancey, William L., Eugene P. Ericksen, and Richard N. Julian. 1976. "Emergent Ethnicity: A Review and Reformulation." *American Sociological Review* 41:391-403.

7

Recent Ideological Tendencies in Urban and Regional Research: Neo-Liberalism and Social Democracy

Richard Peet

At first sight, Marx's theory of ideology is simple indeed: "The ideas of the ruling class are in every epoch the ruling ideas: i.e. the class, which is the ruling *material* force of society, is at the same time its ruling *intellectual* force. The class which has the means of material production at its disposal, has control at the same time over the means of mental production" (Marx and Engels 1970, p. 64; emphasis added). This instrumental theory finds immediate supporting evidence in the sponsoring of research by foundations established by the leading entrepreneurial families of early advanced capitalism (Rockefeller, Carnegie, Mellon, Ford, etc.) and private ownership of the means of disseminating ideas—the so-called communications media, leading instruments of the ideological reproduction of capitalist culture. Evidence supporting this interpretation should not be dismissed merely because it is obvious. Yet it would be a mistake to limit the conception of ideology to the instrumental-manipulation level. Particularly since Althusser (1984; Benton 1984), ideology has been understood in broad, structural terms as the way a society thinks, as the system of understanding that makes society able to function. In this conception, even the fiercest critics of the existing social order must immediately support hegemonic ideology unless they do not care about people working and children getting fed. Capitalist ideology in particular has shown its ability to produce material security for a broad mass of humanity. There are very good reasons for broad social support for capitalism as the most successful mode of life thus far in the history of humanity. Yet because capitalism is also a contradictory form of society, run in the immediate interest of its ruling minority, its ideology must also be internally contradictory. In its technical form it is the nearest to science the mind has yet achieved. In its social and economic forms it serves more to disguise the essential causes of events than to reveal them.

In this latter sense, conventional social explanation assumes the form of "legitimation theory" (Peet 1985). Ideas formed during an honest search for truth *cannot* fully express fundamental, but contradictory and therefore crisis-ridden, social processes. Were such truths revealed as a normal part of popular education the result would be an intolerably critical understanding in partly-scientific minds. At times of crisis, such as during the Vietnam War, critical liberal and even radical ideas—nearly always disguised in safe clothing—begin to be widely discussed. But as crisis fades into normalcy they quickly become the embarrassment of a misspent youth in minds that soon forget in a system of meaningless experiences. In general, therefore, mainstream social explanation and understanding remain at the level of appearances or, where deeper, divert into noncritical, usually natural "causal" processes. By ignoring fundamental questions and disguising social processes as events of nature unchanging, ideology legitimates the existing social order.

The present conjuncture is characterized by an uneasy mass semiawareness that capitalism is again entering a period of crisis. There is little evidence, however, of mass belief in the need to restructure the existing social system, even though the suspicion arises that something may be fundamentally wrong. Economic recession in the 1980s is characterized ideologically by a sense of social discipline; this is, after all, an economic crisis characterized by automation, the migration of jobs, and unemployment that threaten livelihoods. This sense of being disciplined, and therefore exercising "self-discipline," is shared by students and intellectuals, and even characterizes "critical" research by members of the radical left, including Marxists. Since the 1960s, Marxist ideas have developed so rapidly and become so convincing that in many areas of social explanation they are necessary intellectual tools carried by competent analysts. Yet, because popular explanation must also function as legitimation theory, Marxist ideas cannot be applied in the manner for which they were intended—that is, for revolutionary purposes. Competent theorists therefore must be theoretically schizophrenic, paying some mental service to Marx but materially serving the existing social order.

THE SPATIO-ENVIRONMENTAL TRADITION

In what follows I explore certain dimensions of legitimation theory in the published work of the neo-Marxist–social democratic–neoliberal left, emphasizing two recent books in the urban and regional, spatial, and environmental tradition. Here we find the material events and ideological reactions of the present conjuncture interacting with a particular stream of thought from the past, organized in a number of academic fractions: geography, regional science, urban sociology, spatial economics, and so forth. Pursuing one of these, geography, in a little more detail, we find a discipline haunted by lingering memories of what was a severe case of academic inferiority complex. Between the middle 1920s when the theory of environmental determinism was institutionally abandoned, and the late 1950s when the "quantitative revolution" began, theoretical geography virtually collapsed. Explanation was derived through the sole of the field worker's boots rather than soul-full contemplation. When geography again entered the land of the intellectually living in the 1960s, geographers had an almost insatiable desire to be of social use. They, or more accurately we, would perform the most mundane research tasks to prove our functional utility. This naive quest to be of service proved to be contradictory, however, in that the very mundane nature of conventional "theoretical" geography—with its endless measurements of the centrality of places in space—was a powerful internal source of the alternative development and rapid spread of a radical geography movement in the late 1960s and 1970s (Peet 1977). This radical movement achieved considerable academic status. It had its own journals: in English, *Antipode: A Radical Journal of Geography; International Journal of Urban and Regional Research; Society and Space;* as well as several other radical journals in other languages. It formed its own organizations such as the Union of Socialist Geographers, that held meetings, and upheld a disciplinary reputation. Marxian articles appeared with increasing frequency in conventional journals, while histories of the discipline usually include (brief) sections on "the radicals." In the 1970s Marxism almost achieved the status of the latest fad in geography. But the 1980s saw a return to conventional number crunching, while parts of radical theory diverted into the endless rarifications of phenomenology and the mind-boggling trap of structuration (Giddens 1985). Here, as elsewhere under the discipline of economic recession, the critique of Althusser has been conveniently mistaken for the end of Marxist structuralism. A stream of post-Marxisms, each more abstruse than the last, shows every sign of turning into anti-Marxisms. The broad Marxist geography project finds itself at a turning point. Marxist spatial science must respond to the threat of resurgence of the conventional mind with a new critique and a further surge in analytical power, or it will be relegated to the obscure corners of a set of especially discourse-prone, and most obvious, mind-numbing pragmatism.

Thus, the critique that follows is not intended to be the pleasurable destruction of simple-minded, easy targets. The task of radical reconstruction is too important for that. Certain tendencies in economic and geopolitical relations, in the development and careless use of nuclear and chemical technology, and in both capitalist and Soviet relations with the environment, make essential a new Marxist understanding of society. At such times of ultimate contradiction, the possibility arises for mass transcendence of legitimation ideologies. For then fundamental criticism becomes functional, not only for the reproduction of the hegemonic social order, but also for human survival.

URBAN AND REGIONAL DIMENSIONS
OF GLOBAL ECONOMIC CRISIS

My critique of recent work in urban and regional studies is based on alternative sociospatial analysis developed primarily by Marxist geographers in the 1970s and 1980s (Harvey 1973, 1982; Peet 1977; Storper and Walker 1984). Here I give a brief summary of my own perspective, developed in detail elsewhere (Peet 1986, 1987), on certain dimensions of the accumulating economic crisis in global capitalism. The most effective reply to a critic is, "What explanation would *you* prefer?" So I should get my own analysis out front.

Capitalism is a spontaneous economy, the efficient operation of which requires competition between privately owned units of production. One significant dimension of competition is the location of production at geographically efficient places—efficient, that is, in terms of costs to the individual firm. In the eighteenth and nineteenth centuries, when the forces of production and the technical capacity to traverse space were relatively undeveloped, the locational capability of producers was also limited, usually to resource deposits and existing markets. As the nineteenth century progressed these relatively few places became the sites of large industrial cities in a manufacturing belt that stretched from northern Italy through Western Europe, on to the northern United States, and to the U.S.

and Canadian middlewest. At a low level of development of the mechanical productive forces, capital was also forced to rely on the industrial skills of the workers amassed in the same cities. Concentrated into powerful masses, workers took advantage of capital's (temporary) reliance on it by organizing and demanding an increasing share of the value that their labor so obviously created. This concentrated process of class struggle created a new geography of demand focused on the markets of what was becoming a highly-paid, organized working class in the capitalist core of the global system. In this paradoxical way, the urban centers of organized working-class resistance to capital also became the centers of mass consumption essential to rapid capital accumulation.

Paradox, however, is merely contradiction in drag. Individual capitals must compete to reduce wage costs and lower labor resistance. They develop the forces of production, communication, and transport as tools to further competition and class struggle. Hence automation is not the neutral result of autonomous technological change but is biased toward eliminating labor by capitalist social relations. Likewise new institutional forms, like the multinational corporation, emerge and develop in the struggle to survive in a spatially-widening capitalist environment. Since the 1960s automation and global sourcing by multinational corporations have been used to attack the jobs of organized labor. This has reduced labor costs to the individual corporation but also has created massive unemployment in many national societies. The newly industrializing countries of the semiperiphery of the global economy have gained 6.3 million low-paid manufacturing jobs in the last decade while the old industrial countries of the center have lost 7.5 million high-paid jobs. Unemployment rates in the center now range from 7 percent in the United States to 13 to 14 percent in several countries of Western Europe. Real wages in the seven largest OECD countries, which grew at annual rates of 3 to 4 percent in the 1960s, grew at 1.6 percent per year in 1974–79 and stopped growing in the 1980s. This ended the post-war period of rapid increase in working-class demands. The center's organized labor no longer provides the demand push behind modern capitalist development. Capitalism has an underconsumption crisis of growing dimensions stemming, like the other causes of present crises, from developments in the system's essential structure—that is, the social relations of capitalist production. This economic crisis persists because it is the intractable result of tendencies inherent in capitalist development The transcendence of crisis involves the transcendence of capitalism.

Against such a systemic critique we shall compare other forms of radical and left liberal critical work in the field.

SILICON LANDSCAPES

Publications explaining how to succeed in difficult times are among the few growth industries in the contemporary United States. Their authors include liberals and leftists. *Silicon Landscapes* (Hall and Markusen 1985), co-edited by the unlikely combination of Ann Markusen [who elsewhere describes her recent work as building on Marxist analysis (Markusen 1985, p. 2)] and Peter Hall [originator of the "enterprise zone" concept (Goldsmith 1984, p. 342)] is an example of this work. The main ideology of the collection is a somewhat dated Atari democratism, but my critique deals more broadly with the replication of material contradiction in neo-liberal ideology of this kind.

For Hall, regions achieve economic success by following the French example ("to make the country a living showplace of technology, to serve as a base for export orders . . . it seems to be working") or the Japanese miracle ["the systematic and ruthless partnership between the government, in the form of the Ministry of International Trade and Industry (MITI), and private industry"] (Hall 1985, p. 5). Regional economic success depends on achieving technological or organizational breakthroughs that work and finding products that sell—"find a need and fill it." Hall relates this to a geographic version of the Kondratieff/Schumpeter long-cycle theories, in which new industrial traditions become rooted in different places. Selective growth in a relatively small industrial base, especially the development of innovative high-technology industries and associated producer services, stimulated by the spatial bunching of innovations, creates income and employment multiplier effects in areas of high-quality environments, the classic example being Silicon Valley next door to Stanford University in California. Old industrial cities, by comparison, are "just as repellent to the new industries as could be imagined" (Hall 1985, p. 14). Hall advocates regional policy as an R&D strategy—government funding of inner-city universities of excellence, coupled with a scheme to provide venture capital for graduates to set up local enterprises. Generally Hall is for research, high technology, selective intervention by the capitalist state, and finding things that will sell, which he sees as the fountains of future regional economic growth.

Sixty pages later in the same book, Marc Weiss examines the effects of high-tech industries on the future of employment—in effect, a case study of Hall's recommendations. Weiss argues that high-tech industries may achieve rapid growth in employment. But the problem is that,

> even assuming fantastic growth levels, these industries cannot possibly absorb all the surplus labour from other sectors nor accommodate all the new entries into the labour force each year. If every level of government everywhere pursues high-tech development strategies, most of them will surely be doomed to failure. . . . New technology producers go through product and profit cycles just like any other industry, and some areas of electronics production are already facing world overcapacity with employment stagnating or even declining. Further, in addition to layoffs and cutbacks due to competition and excess capacity, many firms which are still experiencing growth in output and sales are reducing the size of their labour force due to automation [Weiss 1985, p. 83].

For Weiss this raises the question of social control over technology. Workers and communities, he says, need to develop tools for collective bargaining with private employers and public institutions over the introduction of new technologies. Without this a "government policy of investing heavily in high-tech may bring economic chaos, not salvation" (Weiss 1985, p. 92).

Finally, in their conclusion to the book, Hall and Markusen return to the question of high technology and urban-regional policy. Failing positive state intervention, "a relatively few favoured places will generate a modest number of high-technology jobs and a much larger number of service jobs dependent on them" (Hall and Markusen 1985, p. 144). Even so, government policy should be directed at helping old industrial areas acquire high-tech bases, "anchor sets" for regional rejuvenation (which, indeed, might be preferred over "enterprise" zones). This intervention, they admit, would require a major upheaval in ingrained decision-making structures. But as the fifth Kondratieff long wave begins, the critical question is, "What combination of policies will shape the location of the even newer technologies. . . . And here, the possibilities are still quite open" (Hall and Markusen 1985, p. 151).

Let us focus on just these three statements from a book that obviously contains many more. Hall opens by advocating high-tech growth and modest state intervention. Weiss then destroys this argument, pointing to the limited nature of high-tech growth even in "successful" areas and the impossibility of solving unemployment problems through this type of development. Hall and Markusen concede this, saying that it is the best that can be done anyway, yet they manage optimism about nebulous future possibilities. Such contradictions in the neo-liberal argument replicate the contradictory nature of this form of capitalist development. The very purpose of high technology under capitalism is to replace human brain and muscle with computers and machines. It cannot solve unemployment problems because it creates them—at least under capitalism. Hall and Markusen's argument cannot conclude this because they do not set technological development in the context of the relations of production—under capitalism, private ownership of the means of producing technology and antagonistic relations between producers give technology the appearance of autonomous, almost natural development, which Hall takes as his analytic starting point. Such relations between privately owned machines and living labor necessarily structure the mechanization and automation processes toward the reduction of class antagonism by eliminating the working subject. Control over both technology and the location of its application thus varies between social forms, for example between capitalism and socialism (Kaplinsky 1984). Weiss realizes this but makes social control over technology a matter of liberal wishful thinking rather than systematic socialist politics. Altogether, the neo-liberal argument lacks an analysis of the social-structural origins of technological development that would direct "policy" at the cause of the problem, that is, to be effective, policy must involve the transformation of the social relations of production.

At least one of the editors (Markusen) should be familiar with this argument. But an open-minded alliance between her neo-Marxism and the neo-liberalism of Hall causes social relations to be conveniently ignored in this joint effort. Why such a bias toward neglecting the most basic category of Marxist analysis? Here we have an economic activity, high-tech industry, that is the only apparent economic salvation in a capitalist future plagued by massive unemployment. Massive financial and research resources are therefore expended on examining its potential. For the most part this yields the expected research product, a flattering portrait of the technological fix. Critical work of the type exemplified by Hall and Markusen is rare indeed. However, if such work were to plunge further into unbridled criticism, grants would go elsewhere, toward those researchers willing to pretend eternal optimism. Yet some serious students of society, like Hall and Markusen, cannot totally ignore the contradictions of high-tech growth. An aversion to pushing arguments to their logical conclusion, and the impossibility in general of tracing technology to social relations are thus inherent in funded neo-liberal research. Capitalism cannot escape its inherent contradictions in part because it cannot understand them!

THE DEINDUSTRIALIZATION OF AMERICA

Bluestone and Harrison's (1982) book is widely acclaimed as a radical analysis of the other side of regional development, the persistent tendency toward deindustrialization in the capitalist center. Their work achieved broad popularity for several years in the early 1980s, and they serve as left spokesmen on a range of related topics in the capitalist media. *The Deindustrialization of America* is a fine piece of empirical research. This writer has learned much from various readings of it. But I also find that it typifies a left liberal-social democratic analysis that is counterproductive to the development of a truly radical analysis. To illustrate this, I summarize the main arguments and proposals of Bluestone and Harrison's book before presenting my critique (see also Peet 1982; Harrison 1982).

In the post-war expansion, Bluestone and Harrison argue, U.S. investment abroad generated its own future competition. The results of this were declining market shares and shrinking profits for U.S. corporations in the 1970s. The corporations reacted in two ways. First, conglomerates closed even profitable plants as they shifted capital in pursuit of high price/earnings ratios: capital diverted from productive investment to unproductive speculation, mergers, and foreign ventures; the domestic capital stock aged; and manufacturing jobs were lost. Second, corporate capital used greater spatial mobility to break the social contract reached with organized labor in the 1950s. The main consequence of both is deindustrialization—systematic disinvestment in the nation's productive capacity. Traditional liberal policy proved inadequate to deal with this: Government regulation is ineffective under conditions of the hypermobility of capital. Neo-liberal proposals for state investment in sunset industries (Rohatyn) or, maybe, sunrise industries (Thorow), are similarly ineffective. Instead, Bluestone and Harrison advocate radical change. Holes in the social safety net should be repaired immediately by reallocating government funds from existing military budgets and by taxing corporations. Legislation would be needed to address the whole range of problems created by plant closings, such as legislation requiring advance warning of plant closures. For the longer term, Bluestone and Harrison tentatively outline a radical industrialization policy involving partnerships between state and private enterprise, public enterprises, some worker control, and public research. Right now they advocate people's monitoring of corporate activities, with popular information campaigns to demand the redefinition of private management's prerogatives.

Bluestone and Harrison's explanation is strongest at the institutional level of the actual corporative forms assumed by capital flight. They recognize that corporations act in the context of competitive struggle and class antagonism. Their analysis, however, refers only occasionally to structural determinants. For the most part the discourse is in terms of individual case histories and lists of immediate causes, laced with graphic accounts of horrendous social consequences. Thus the crucial decade of the 1960s, when corporate profits began to fall precipitating the deindustrialization process, is explained in terms of the collapse of the Bretton Woods accord, the onset of stagflation and failure of Keynesian policy, and increasing international competition as Germany and Japan recovered from World War II. The analysis then quickly moves to the details of corporate response and resulting plant shutdowns. The detail in which the latter kinds of effects are discussed contrasts sharply with the perfunctory mentioning of underlying causal pressures coming from movements in global capitalism. Hence the analysis appears as a kind of left-liberal, muck-raking exposé of the reprehensible activities of multinational corporations, which really need taming.

The counter-argument usually made at this point is that it is better to make such a case, one that has an immediate effect, that is "taken seriously," and that "influences policy makers" than to present a radical analysis that is ignored by "movers and shakers." Certainly there is little point in publishing "politically correct" books that few people read, even when this is possible given the preferences of the capitalist media. But I want to illustrate the use of "pragmatic" analyses for achieving the reverse of what Bluestone and Harrison clearly intended to do—that is, reach a mass audience with a radical message. As an example of media attention, take the case of the review of the Bluestone and Harrison book in the Boston *Globe*. The (sympathetic) reviewer emphasizes the effects of capital flight on the fabric of industrial communities and unemployed workers. The villains of the piece are a mixture of technology, tax laws, and greedy conglomerates. The reviewer details the "acceptable" solutions offered by Bluestone and Harrison—plant closing legislation, retraining workers, and worker participation. "Much thought is needed on these issues" he concludes, for they are not radical but as "American as the town meeting and the small business. . . . The rebuilding of

American enterprise with due regard for workers and communities would be a truly American triumph" (Scharfenberg 1982).

Bluestone and Harrison's social democratic analysis is picked through, ideologically sieved, so to speak, to yield a moral critique of the big and therefore bad multinational corporation. The Bluestone and Harrison proposal that the (existing capitalist) state should intervene is not mentioned, nor are their social democratic proposals for worker control. Furthermore, the review finds enough nationalism in the book to call for a renewed, wartime-style Americanism— "radical reindustrialization" becomes as American as apple pie. The effect of the media's "noticing and communicating" Bluestone and Harrison's book is thus a reinforcement of the existing structures of liberal and nationalist prejudice. At best, Bluestone and Harrison provide a good excuse for liberal hearts to really bleed before Sunday lunch. At worst, they merely provide ideologically neutralized filler for pages mainly carrying advertising.

How does this happen? We must assume the predilection of the capitalist media to sanitize any analysis they widely disseminate. We must expect mass media reports to conclude with "more thought is necessary," "no one knows what the future will bring," and "every cloud has a silver lining, so let's end on an upbeat note ready for the following words from our sponsors." This being the case, can radical analysts avoid providing grist for the media mill—or even worse, gathering an audience for advertisements for the very corporations they criticize?

The social uses to which Bluestone and Harrison's book was put follow not only from the media's ability to make ideology, but also from the structure and presentation of their original analysis. Theirs is a critique of specific multinational conglomerates rather than of the capitalist system as a whole. This level of critique is suited to a capitalist system characterized by corporate infighting, which may include criticism of production corporations by service (media) corporations "acting on behalf of the consumer." Similarly, Bluestone and Harrison's "solutions" would leave intact the very mechanism of corporate profit making, an internal analytical contradiction that *allows* safe policies to be extracted by the capitalist media. In short, because Bluestone and Harrison do not carry out a radical analysis linking social problems to structural causes and consistently advocating structure-transforming policies, they allow the conversion of their "critical" analysis into safe ideology. In this way, intellectuals are immediately responsible for their words, but also for the long-term political uses to which their analyses are put.

CONCLUSION: MARXISM AND ACADEMIC PRACTICE

For those convinced that Marxism is the foundation of radical understanding there is a corollary: revolutionary politics follows not as matter of choice but as the logical conclusion. Marxism finds the basic causes of events in the social relations of production. Change in any aspect of society requires change in the relations that constitute the economic structure. Fundamental social change in capitalism requires transforming social relations so that the working masses own and control the means of production. To repeat, if Marxist theory is accurately understood, a revolutionary politics *necessarily* emerges. The idea of revolutionary change cannot sometimes be included in political practice guided by Marxism and sometimes not. It is *always* a component in research, teaching, organizing, mode of living, and self presentation.

This does not mean that Marxism precludes sponsored research, policy prescription, or active political engagement within the existing capitalist society. Marxism is only valid when it accurately guides social and political practices such as these. Practice confirms (and sometimes denies) Marxism's emerging scientific accuracy: logical deduction alone cannot develop a theory of human society. Practice within the existing social order is necessary to mitigate what are indeed the horrendous results of everyday capitalist life. Practical intervention in the existing politics is necessary to prevent an outmoded species of social existence from destroying the very possibility of its own transcendence. Particular academic practices, like research and policy prescription, necessarily occur within this sociopolitical context. But Marxism demands that research consistently and immediately refer to the social relations of production for the causes of economic, social, and cultural events. It demands that policies formulated within the existing social order also prescribe fundamental change of that order. This task can be done openly or subtly depending on the particular political situation. But a revolutionary intent has to lie behind all practice consistent with a Marxist understanding of the world.

Against the logic of Marxist analysis is the consistent illogic of the hegemonic society, with all its powers of compulsion, persuasion, and incorporation. More basically there is a sincere reluctance to abandon a system that has proven its ability to resolve its problems in the past. At every level and in a thousand ways, therefore, the experiences of capitalist society expose the intellectual to crisis but divert consciousness from fundamental criticism and serious intellectual consideration of social alternatives. In this chapter I have looked at two such diversions by left, or at least critical, thinkers: the neo-liberalism of *Silicon Landscapes* and the social democracy of *The Deindustrialization of America*. My conclusion is that both involve critical reactions to ongoing crises and are affected by Marxism, yet both fail to provide consistently a fundamental analysis or solution to the problem of regional underdevelopment under capitalism. Hall and Markusen advocate extending high-tech forms of development, which their own book shows destroys the employment base of advanced capitalist societies. Their failure to understand development in terms of the social relations of production implies that they view technology as an autonomously developing process that has workers and policy advocates as its captives. The contradictions of material process are here replicated in the contradictions of mental structure—the ideology of neo-liberal theory. This is a case of social pragmatism (getting a popular book out fast on a hot topic) yielding a premature view that simply *avoids* fundamental analysis. The Bluestone and Harrison book is more a case of insufficient penetration. Bluestone and Harrison achieve only an institutional analysis and reformist social democratic politics. This allows their analysis and proposals to be subverted into nationalistic support of the very capitalist system they only begin to criticize. Diversion into unthreatening ideology in both cases stems from continued adherence to the existing social order. The result, again in both cases, is an unscientific, contradictory social theory and muddle-headed, liberal, or quasi-socialist politics.

I am not advocating Marxist purism or correct lineism, nor do I think that Marxists should abstain from short-term policy recommendations. Marxism is a way of thinking that individuals must be free to use and combine with other theories in their own ways. Marxism must continue to form the basis of various kinds of radical thinking. However, the freedom of thought that characterizes Western Marxism cannot provide an excuse for abandoning the fundamentals of Marxist analysis. Nor should policy prescription be the occasion for failing to push for social transformation; ameliorative policies must obviously and consistently be set in system-transforming politics. These simple guidelines allow the creative burst of radical imagination that the maturation of capitalist contradiction makes imminently necessary. But they also structure theoretical and political ideas that point toward a single coherent conclusion—the necessity of destroying capitalism and replacing it with democratic socialism.

REFERENCES

Althusser, Louis. 1984. *Essays on Ideology*. London: Verso.

Benton, Ted. 1984. *The Rise and Fall of Structural Marxism: Althusser and His Influence*. New York: St. Martin's Press.

Bluestone, B., and B. Harrison. 1982. *The Deindustrialization of America*. New York: Basic Books.

Giddens, Anthony. 1985. "Time, Space, and Regionalisation." In *Social Relations and Spatial Structures*, edited by D. Gregory and J. Urry, pp. 265-95. New York: St. Martin's Press.

Goldsmith, William. 1984. "Bringing the Third World Home: Enterprise Zones for America?" In *Sunbelt/Snowbelt*, edited by L. Sawers and William Tabb, pp. 339-50. New York: Oxford University Press.

Hall, Peter, and Ann Markusen, eds. 1985. *Silicon Landscapes*. Boston: Allen and Unwin.

Harrison, Ben. 1982. "Reply." *Antipode* 14, 2:51-2.

Harvey, David. 1973. *Social Justice and the City*. Baltimore: The Johns Hopkins University Press.

Harvey, David. 1982. *The Limits to Capital*. Chicago: The University of Chicago Press.

Kaplinsky, R. 1984. *Automation: The Technology and Society*. Harlow: Longman.

Markusen, Ann R. 1985. *Profit Cycles, Oligopoly, and Regional Development*. Cambridge: MIT Press.

Marx, K., and F. Engels. 1970. *The German Ideology*. New York: International Publishers.

Peet, Richard. 1977. *Radical Geography*. Chicago: Maaroufa Press.

―――. 1982. "The Deindustrialization of America" and "Response." *Antipode* 14, 2:47-50, 53.

―――. 1985. "The Social Origins of Environmental Determinism." *Annals*. Association of American Geographers. 75, 3:309-33.

―――. 1986. "Industrial Devolution and the Crisis of International Capitalism." *Antipode* 18, 1 (April):78-95.

―――. 1987. *Industrial Capitalism and Industrial Restructuring*. London: Allen and Unwin.

Scharfenberg, K. 1982. "Review of the Deindustrialization of America." Boston *Globe* November 7, p. B11.

Storper, Michael, and Richard Walker. 1984. "The Spatial Division of Labor: Labor and the Location of Industries." In *Sunbelt/Snowbelt*, edited by L. Sawers and William Tabb, pp. 19-47. New York: Oxford University Press.

Weiss, Marc. 1985. "High Technology Industries and the Future of Employment." In *Silicon Landscapes*, edited by Hall and Markusen, pp. 80-93. Boston: Allen and Unwin.

8

Behind the Veil of Neutrality: Hegemony in the Academic Marketplace

Peter Seybold

In the 1980s the business of the United States is business. For academic institutions this is equally true as the scramble for research dollars from the Pentagon and big corporations threatens to compromise the integrity of universities and colleges.

To be sure, the corporatization of higher education has drawn fire from social critics, but with little effect and scarcely any discussion of its political implications. Instead, social scientists have learned to adjust to the current social climate and accept as given the larger social context in which they work. As in the larger economy, the invisible hand of the "free marketplace" of ideas is said to sort out good work from bad and magically restore balance to academic institutions reputedly under the sway of left-wing influences.

The institutionalization of ideas, however, is only partially explained by even the most sophisticated market models. To examine only market forces necessarily places arbitrary limits on the scope of inquiry by ignoring the larger social, political, and economic context in which ideas are developed. Applied to academe, the free marketplace argument falls short in two critical problem areas. First, how is power exercised in the college and university system, and what effect does it have on the development of ideas? Second, by what means are power relations in the academic world mystified to intellectual workers? This chapter attempts to shed some light on both problems.

THE CONCEPT OF HEGEMONY

The framework for such an analysis is provided by the notion of hegemony, formulated by classical Marxists—notably Antonio Gramsci—and developed by more recent research (Gramsci 1979; Boggs 1976; Anderson 1977; Williams 1977; Gitlin 1980; Mintz and Schwartz 1985). In Gramsci's usage, hegemony refers to the permeation of "a way of life" or "social organization" into every sphere of society and constitutes the crucial mechanism by which the ruling class dominates subordinate classes. When this occurs, current institutional arrangements appear to be unalterable and constitute a "natural order of things." When this perception of the social order becomes "common sense", challenges to the stability and legitimacy of social institutions do not occur. Hegemony "is the saturation of the whole process of living, to such a depth that the pressures and limits of what can ultimately be seen as a specific economic, political, and cultural system seem to most of us the pressures and limits of simple experience and common sense" (Williams 1977).

In Gramsci's view hegemony is the main form of domination found in advanced capitalist societies. People so internalize the fundamental mechanisms of social control that the real alternatives and/or choices are unrecognized. Subordinate classes may be unable to articulate grievances or identify conflicts of interest. Institutional arrangements become "givens"; no other "realistic" mode of organization can be perceived. Even (or, perhaps, especially) the ruling class adopts this stance; the process pervades their lives and thoughts as completely as it dominates the activities and perceptions of subordinate classes.

While Gramsci argued that hegemonic processes are crucial to an analysis of capitalist society, he saw them as dependent upon the availability of repression and coercion, should subtle means of domination collapse. In Gramsci's scheme, class rule is an unfolding process ranging from overt forms of control (the use of force) to almost unrecognizable shaping of alternatives (hegemony). If institutional arrangements remain unchallenged they continue to exert influence on people's perceptions and alternatives as a lived presence. If challenges are issued to the legitimacy of the social institutions, their grasp upon people may weaken and coercion may be employed as a means of social control.

The hegemonic perspective avoids some of the pitfalls that other views have stumbled into when analyzing power. It looks beyond both the direct means of control which pluralists study, and the covert exercise of power which power elite theorists stress. At the same time it implies the possibility of less-than-complete domination, since institutional hegemony can be perceived and challenged, at least periodically. Institutional legitimacy is not always unquestioned, and on many occasions it may have to be created or recreated. While supporting the notion that a ruling class can impose a way of life upon subordinate classes by controlling institutions and socializing individuals into the dominant value system, it also points to the pervasive contradictions between the established value system and the concrete experiences and deprivations in everyday life. These experiences generate discontent, alternative value systems, and protest which, in a fragmented and incomplete way, challenge the legitimacy of the social order. On most occasions this conflict is muted, disunified, and unfocused. The underlying conflict of interest is therefore difficult to identify (both for participant and observers), and the social order remains unchallenged. On some occasions, however, the legitimacy of the social order might be brought into question and the subordinate class or sections of it might perceive self-interests substantially different from ruling-class interests. For the most part the ongoing process produces different patterns simultaneously—coercion/consent, domination/hegemony, compliance/resistance, and dominant value system/subordinate value systems all coexisting within the social system. The preservation of the existing order and the maintenance of its legitimacy and effectiveness is then an ongoing process.

KNOWLEDGE AND THE STRUGGLE FOR HEGEMONY

Maintenance of class hegemony is therefore a complicated process that involves a variety of institutions within society. The production of knowledge and management of the general flow of information become key issues for the ruling class; and in the post–World War II period changes in these realms involve a microcosmic replication of the most general processes involved in the establishment and maintenance of hegemonic domination in the society as a whole. There is a curious "play within a play" aspect to the power structure debate. Hegemonic structures have operated to nurture pluralist ideas and research and exclude analyses that investigate the nature of capitalist hegemony. Capitalist domination of society as a whole includes capitalist domination of the knowledge-producing sector and thus has led to the ascendancy of scientific theories that deny capitalist ascendancy in the society as a whole.

Even theories that oppose the mainstream are shaped by the existing mobilization of class bias. The form and content of opposing theories is constructed in response to the dominant perspective, and thus the terms of debate reflect the prevailing way of seeing. Challenges to the dominant framework generally occur within existing paradigms. Examples of the structuring of opposing theories abound within U.S. social science where a behavioralist framework has been assumed since the 1950s.

Pluralist theory in sociology and political science, for example, is opposed by elite theory instead of by a Marxist class analysis. Social class itself is conceptualized within an individualist framework and is opposed within the field of social stratification by theories that seek to demonstrate that Marxist categories explain more variance than mainstream categories. The notion of socioeconomic status is not counterposed to a Marxist notion of social class. Rather, socioeconomic status as a concept is refined by the application of Marxist categories.

In short, as a result of hegemonic structures, a class-based analysis of social problems remains relatively undeveloped within U.S. social science. Class as a concept in mainstream social science has been stripped of its analytical power and has become just the sum of a number of indicators. The struggle to create a social science that offers an alternative perspective (counter hegemony) has been sidetracked in a hollow academic debate. More importantly, the connection between left political theory and left political praxis has been severed so that social movements increasingly find left academic theories to be irrelevant to their concerns.

Scholar/activists who seek to bridge the gap between theory and praxis work both within academia and in the larger society. But their efforts are often constrained by bureaucratic procedures and academic norms that enforce political neutrality. In the area of teaching, for example, a distinction is often made between educating and politicizing students. However, an effective teacher is open to the experiences and class background of his or her students and uses this information as raw material to connect abstract theories to concrete situations. In some instances students become politicized by examining their own experiences and those of their families. Good teachers who seek to involve their students in the educational process and validate their experiences may run the risk of being charged with promoting a political agenda.

Similarly, if community activists or professors suggest that a university address issues relevant to poor and working people or minorities and women, administrators often express concern that an academic institution should not take sides. Yet, when universities or colleges work in conjunction with the powers that be to preserve existing institutional arrangements, they are not seen as taking sides. Instead, service to business and political elites is regarded as apolitical and good for public relations. The definition of the boundaries of accepted practice in teaching, research, and service in academia are thus developed within the larger context of the mobilization of class bias.

Scholar/activists who persist in teaching and living according to the anti-war, anti-corporate, anti-racist, anti-sexist, and populist principles of the Vietnam War era have seen their teaching positions eliminated under the guise of fiscal austerity, retrenchment in their academic departments, or simply because they refuse to compromise their integrity and be silent about the corporate invasion of the university. Political repression in academia is thus carried out behind a veil of neutrality and a denial of politicality.

The authors of *Guarding the Ivory Tower* contend that a counter-offensive against left-wing professors in U.S. universities and colleges has been waged in the 1970s and 1980s (Meranto, Meranto, and Lippman 1985). In contrast to the relative openness of higher education in the late 1960s and early 1970s, a repressive climate has returned to campus. Violations of academic freedom are routinely sanctioned by university administrators, particularly if it is the rights of dissident professors that are left unprotected.

Systematic data on cases of political repression in academia is not easily obtained. This is due in part because of the hold that the free market model has on intellectual workers as well as the unstated prohibitions on investigating academic repression. Despite evidence to the contrary, higher education is generally thought to be meritocratic in structure and insulated from the influence of economic and political elites.

In reality, a political struggle has been evident in U.S. higher education since its expansion following World War II. Sometimes the conflict between right and left has been visible and at other times it is submerged. As Piliawsky reports, the ideological position of the complainant in academia has been the most crucial ground for dismissal since 1945 and the number of contested dismissals has been increasing over time (Piliawsky 1982). Certainly, the number of visible cases of academic repression has increased in the last ten years. Meranto, Meranto, and Lippman offer the following partial list of lesser known cases as documentation of the dimensions of academic repression (Meranto, Meranto, and Lippman 1985; used with permission).

Stolberg was terminated for writing a letter protesting the suspension of students at a nearby university and offering the mediation services of the AAUP [Association of American University Professors]. *Southern Connecticut State College* (1973).

Rozeman was terminated for sitting in at a ROTC building, asking the university to make a stronger statement on the Cambodian invasion and the Kent State incident and for helping students negotiate with the university administration. *University of Nebraska* (1975).

Adamian, a tenured associate professor, was dismissed for protesting the Cambodian invasion and the Kent State incident by shouting at ROTC cadets during Governor's Day Ceremony, making loud noises and joining a demonstration on the stadium field during the ROTC drills. *University of Nevada* (Reno) (1975).

Duke, a teaching assistant, was terminated from her position for using "profane" language during a talk to freshmen; for bringing a "subculture group" into the university orientation program; and for organizing a meeting held in violation of university rules. *North Texas State* (1972).

Keddie was terminated for criticizing United States involvement in Vietnam, social policies with respect to poor people, organizing protest activities, being faculty advisor for SDS [Students for a Democratic Society], and counseling students charged with disciplinary violations. *Penn State* (1976).

Markwell was fired for protesting that class time was being reduced by 20 percent for chemistry students; 50 percent of students were required to receive a C or better; and the new chair of the chemistry department was not qualified in Markwell's view. *San Antonio College* (1975).

Mabey was fired for objecting, in a speech to the faculty senate, to the college president's characterization in the *Los Angeles Times* of younger faculty as "punks" and as "jerks." *Fresno State* (1973).

Lindsey was questioned by the police and then fired for compiling and mailing a questionnaire to faculty concerning various aspects of faculty morale and administrative practices. *University of Georgia* (1979).

Kaprelian was dismissed for criticizing the existing curriculum as "behind the times" and "inferior." *Texas Women's University* (1975).

Starsky was fired for protesting the arrest of students at the University of Arizona; canceling a scheduled class to speak at a rally;

handing out leaflets on campus; insulting other faculty; and encouraging students to occupy a campus building. *Arizona State* (1972).

Megill was fired for combining his course with another instructor's; calling the university authoritarian; criticizing a colleague's termination; and for interrupting a panel on student dissent at the Yale Club. *University of Florida* (1976).

Carr was fired for protesting the coercing of graduate students to participate in religious activities; protesting the prescribed textbooks used in introductory courses; and for presenting Marxist points of view in class. *University of Akron* (1979).

Hostrop was fired for circulating a proposal among his administrative staff, which was made public, proposing changes in the college's ethnic studies program. He was asked to resign, refused and was fired. *Prairie State Junior College* (1972).

Bradford was fired for protesting the dismissal of several faculty members to the college president during a faculty meeting. The chair of her department characterized her behavior, in public, as "unprofessional." She threatened to sue and was terminated. *Tarrant County Junior College* (1974).

Roseman was fired for alleging that the acting chair had suppressed a candidate's application. She expressed these views, at the invitation of the dean, at a faculty meeting. *Indiana University of Pennsylvania* (1975).

Lyman, a tenured professor, was dismissed for refusing to cooperate with a special university evaluation of his professional and personal conduct. No charges were made of any impropriety. He wrote a public letter of protest and was fired. *Idaho State University* (1980).

Hillis was ordered by his department chair to give a "B" to a female student whose work he had never evaluated and who never attended class. He was terminated. *Stephen F. Austin State University* (1980).

Stewart, a faculty member, was fired for refusing to submit to a psychiatric exam, was assigned to work in the library, did so for six weeks, stopped and was fired. *San Mateo College* (1973).

Hander was terminated for refusing to shave off his beard. *San Jacinto Junior College* (1975).

Stasny, a tenured professor, was fired for insubordination when he presented a paper in Israel without the permission of the dean. *Western Washington State College* (1979-80).

Goss was dismissed for campaigning on behalf of her husband for a seat on the local Junior College Board of Regents. *San Jacinto Junior College* (1979).

Smith was terminated for supporting a Democratic candidate in a state senatorial election and criticizing, in conjunction with the College Young Democrats, the record of the Republican candidate. *Dixie Junior College* (1973).

Chaw and Winn, tenured faculty, boycotted graduation and a faculty workshop to protest the college's refusal to recognize a faculty union. They did not submit the required letter of apology implicitly recognizing their misconduct and were terminated. *Frederick Community College* (1975).

Jackson, a teaching assistant, was fired without a hearing based upon the allegation of the state attorney general that he purchased 27 boxes of ammunition and delivered them to members of the Black community. *University of Kansas* (1979).

Hetrick was dismissed for emphasizing "student responsibility and freedom" rather than teaching "fundamentals" and following "conventional teaching patterns." *Eastern Kentucky University* (1973).

Clark was fired for emphasizing sex education in a health class (although students requested this information), counseling an excessive number of students instead of referring them to a professional counselor and for criticizing other faculty in front of students. *Northern Illinois University* (1972).

Cooper was fired for his membership in the Progressive Labor Party; stating that he was a Marxist in class; and for distributing a handout on Marx to his class. *University of Arkansas* (Little Rock) (1979).

In the current political climate untenured professors who go beyond simply publishing radical analyses in professional journals by becoming politically active in labor and community struggles are finding it difficult to retain their teaching positions. To publish theories critical of the status quo is one thing, but to put theory into practice on an everyday basis in the university and in the community is to risk political repression. The form that this repression takes however, has changed since the end of the McCarthy era, when only one Marxist economist, Paul Baran at Stanford, held a tenured faculty position in a U.S. university. Political repression today also differs from the 1960s. During that era, challenges to the most basic tenets of higher education were met directly by university presidents who took overt measures to retain control and stem the tide of protest. Students and faculty who would not abide by the rules of the game were abruptly terminated, and if all else failed, the university temporarily closed or the National Guard was called in for a deadly reminder that the state could use force with impunity.

By the 1980s, political repression within higher education had been institutionalized. That is, it had been built into the organizational routines of universities and colleges. On most occasions, it was no longer necessary for academic departments or administrators to intervene with a heavy hand to screen out political dissidents. Political repression had been routinized. The mobilization of class bias was embedded in a set of bureaucratic procedures that had the seemingly unintended consequence of weeding out political activists, or at least those political activists who had not succumbed to the professionalization of radicalism. As Ken Geiser has noted, "there is an important distinction between those who practice Marxist scholarship in the confines of the library, and those who attack. . . . If you're a good, solid Marxist, write well, and publish in the right journals, you're probably all right" (Fordon 1983). In fact, it is likely that administrators will point to such nonactivist leftists as evidence of the openness of the academy. Thus, academic leftists unwittingly contribute to maintaining the status quo in higher education by blunting social criticism.

To fail to adjust to the rules of the academic game is to risk marginalization. In recent years, activist scholars have witnessed the growing utilization of part-time instructors and the creation of a more or less permanent academic underclass. Those who have challenged the rules of the game may face years on the periphery of academic life bouncing from one temporary appointment to another or teaching part time, if at all. Lacking institutional legitimacy and resources, and working other jobs to support themselves, these marginalized academics have little opportunity to publish enough to work their way back into a full-time academic position.

The stories of these increasingly invisible second-class citizens of academia rarely are included in discussions of social control in higher education (Seybold 1985; Ryan and Sachrey 1984; Ollman 1984). The implicit assumption is that if you did not make the grade, then you must not be fit. Just as unemployed people are blamed for their circumstances, those on the margins of academia are said to have sealed their own fate.

The political nature of renewal and tenure decisions is often shielded from public scrutiny, especially when departmental faculty, using what appear to be professional criteria, pass judgement on activist professors. To raise questions concerning social control within academia and social control over the production of knowledge in the United States is to challenge the legitimacy of social science at its core. Consequently, those who broach such issues encounter resistance not only from political opponents but also from virtually everyone in academia who benefits from the present set of institutional arrangements. For this reason, questions relating to social control are branded as politically inspired and the suggestion that political repression is a regular feature of academia is met with astonishment.

LEGITIMACY AND THE FREE MARKETPLACE OF IDEAS

To fully comprehend the reluctance of social scientists to study the political economy of knowledge in the United States, we need to further probe the institutionalized thought structure in academia. Among the foremost explanations for the failure of social scientists to subject academia to the same scrutiny as other institutions is that such investigations may weaken the legitimacy of the social sciences.

While historically social science in the United States stands on stronger ground than it does in some other countries, periodically it has had to defend itself from conservative attacks. Such attacks are grounded in charges that social science is unscientific and merely elaborates the obvious. Investigations that make explicit the social structuring of social science research and of promotion and tenure decisions may well undermine social scientists' claims of neutrality and objectivity. If research findings are in some sense socially "determined," social scientists might have difficulty finding support for their work, and the value of their research might be diminished by the attacks of skeptics. If the political content in departmental personnel decisions is examined, claims of universality begin to erode. Why be involved in potentially weakening the legitimacy of your own profession?

Closely related to the issue of legitimacy is the idea that critical examinations of the production of social science research might challenge the professional identities of social scientists. Crucial to their image is the argument that social scientists deal exclusively in facts and weigh evidence as do any other scientists. A demonstration that social scientists are influenced, even in a subtle manner, by social, political, and economic forces would call into question the professional self image, an image carefully nurtured and defended from the time social science research began to grow in the United States.

Moreover, considerable fear exists within the social science community that social scientists will be criticized for studying themselves rather than examining other more important social phenomena. However, if social scientists do not study the production of knowledge, that area intimately involved in their occupation, then who will study this process? Again, many complicated and subtle processes are involved that discourage such work including the lack of professional rewards and the reign of a narrow empirical outlook. And there exists a substantial fear of what might be discovered through such study. Tensions that develop between the desire to know more about the occupation one has selected and anxiety about what implications might be drawn from that knowledge have often been resolved by avoiding such a study or by sharply limiting the scope of such an investigation. For example, many social scientists involved in studies in the sociology of science confine their analysis to social forces within their discipline and therefore necessarily exclude the connections between academia and the larger political economy.

The notion that U.S. academic life operates as a free marketplace of ideas is deeply entrenched in the popular consciousness and is implicitly assumed by professional social scientists. The argument for this view, though rarely articulated, is a familiar one: the merit of all products, economic or intellectual, in a free society is determined by the invisible hand of the marketplace. If the U.S. public needs or likes a commercial product, it purchases it in preference to others; and these "dollar votes" ensure the products success. If the product does not fulfill a specific need, or if people do not like it, they will not buy it and it ultimately will be removed from the market. In the last analysis it is the consumer who determines the fate of commercial ventures, and insofar as consumers are sensible, intelligent, and thoughtful, competition will eliminate bad products and preserve good ones. A dynamic of progress is basic to the operation of the system. This simple but compelling argument is so ingrained in the U.S. consciousness that any challenge to its validity seems almost unnatural.

A similar free-enterprise argument permeates our understanding of intellectual life, and it has corresponding resiliency. The merits of an intellectual product, like that of any other product, is determined by competition in a marketplace of ideas. A good idea or set of ideas is ultimately adopted by its audience—the general public, educated lay people, or professionals. If it can remain current despite the attempts by other scholars to forward their own competing viewpoints, it becomes established as an accurate description of reality and will be utilized until a better idea replaces it. An idea or theory with little merit will meet a fate similar to that of an inferior product; it will not be adopted by enough people to survive. It may exist as an unrespected alternative for a time, but eventually it will die out and be replaced by more useful and accurate viewpoints.

In this free-enterprise model of the world of ideas, questions about social control are inappropriate since the consumer enjoys ultimate control. The good arguments ultimately win adherents and the weak arguments eventually die out. Imperfections in the marketplace can slow down or modify the process, but they do not fundamentally alter its dynamics.

This simple model for understanding which ideas gain prominence has been modified to some extent by sociologists of science. The sociologists apply resource mobilization arguments and studies of the institutionalization of ideas to qualify the operation of the free market (Oberschall 1972; Shils 1970). The best example of this approach is the work of Anthony Oberschall. Oberschall argues that the most significant factors enabling sociology to be institutionalized in the United States were: (1) the wide resource base and competitive nature of education, (2) the sponsorship of sociology by respectable reformist groups, and (3) the aspirations and drive of upwardly mobile academics and the sheer number of universities that started sociology programs (Oberschall 1972).

Clearly, Oberschall's argument rests on the application of a modified free-market model. As an example of the institutional approach to the development of ideas, this view has the advantage of being sensitive to the impact of extradisciplinary influences on sociology but it fails to carry the analysis far enough in this direction. At the end, we return inexorably and almost by habit to the same relatively uncontested assumption. This assumption leads us to believe that the marketplace analogy provides an accurate, if not elegant, explanation of the way ideas (theories) are sorted out in U.S. society. But this is also its major weakness, for in this perspective the market mechanism is taken for granted and the social and political forces that shape the supply and demand for a specific discipline remain unexamined.

When applied to an intellectual debate, the marketplace argument suggests the existence of a natural course of a debate, somewhat analogous to a life cycle, in which the more plausible explanation gains adherents and eventually becomes dominant in a field. An example directly relevant to our discussion can be found in the debate over the structure of power in the United States.

In the late 1940s, behavioral political science, which argued that social policy emerged from the contradictory pressures of myriad social groups on policy-making bodies, won a great many adherents among social scientists. In a relatively short time, it displaced traditional institutional analysis, which argued that individuals developed independent political positions and cast votes for politicians representing their viewpoints (Truman 1951; Berelson, Lazarsfeld, and McPhee 1954; Eulau, Eldersveld, and Janowitz 1956). During the late 1950s and 1960s, power elite theorists challenged this view, positing undemocratic control by a tightly coordinated elite, but their challenge resulted only in a modification of pluralism to incorporate the idea that elites were the active agency of group pressures. It could not displace the fundamental notion that popular will, mediated by the formation of interest groups, determined political policy (Keller 1963; Rose 1967).

The underlying dynamics for the rise and reign of pluralism very plausibly could be its superiority in explaining and predicting the actual events in U.S. political life, and such an explanation is often implicitly assumed by social scientists and popular opinion. However, this interpretation is, at best, premature unless certain crucial issues are addressed and subjected to empirical tests. Just as giant multinational corporations are capable, in some circumstances, of imposing substantial restrictions on the level of competition in the economy, major institutions in the knowledge-producing sector are capable of restricting competition in the realm of ideas. A few large powerful universities and research institutes often dominate an area of inquiry and are linked to essential financial sources, especially to the government and large foundations. Individual researchers no longer have free reign over the development of their ideas, insofar as they require large monetary and other resources to carry on their work. Increasingly, research is undertaken in the context of huge bureaucratic organizations in which the individual researcher is a part of a research apparatus.

Though this bureaucratization of the production of knowledge appears to raise important questions about the viability of the free marketplace of ideas model, social scientists have usually avoided confronting these issues. Bureaucratic forms of organization in the knowledge-producing sector are simply accepted as an inescapable consequence of advancing industrialization and increasing societal complexity. This thinking implicitly assumes that the extension of bureaucratic forms (in the workplace, and in government, as well as in the knowledge-producing sphere) is depoliticized and has no significant influence on the content of the commodity produced.

It is imperative that the process of bureaucratization be examined directly. What social forces produced it? What is the relationship between bureaucratization of academia and the parallel development of bureaucracy in other areas of U.S. society? How was the specific hierarchy of organizations in the knowledge-producing sector established? Who has benefitted from this form of organization and who has lost prominence or power? To what extent can the network of bureaucratic organizations that have developed after World War II coordinate their activities to a common purpose, and who can accomplish this coordination? These questions are difficult to answer, but our understanding of the rise (and fall) of scientific ideas depends upon investigating them.

In contrast to the market model, which envisages a community of scholars interacting through a marketplace of ideas, I contend that the knowledge-producing sector is a complex network of bureaucratic organizations—most significantly, private foundations, governmental agencies, policy planning institutes, research institutes, think tanks, and universities. This network has constituted the research environment in the United States since World War II, and its institutional dynamics and biases must be taken into account if we are to study seriously the development of ideas and theories in modern society (Seybold 1980).

The very existence of this network introduces a number of analytic issues that are alien to the marketplace of ideas portrait of the research process. The formation of a research agenda by an institute at least partially structures the research environment for that discipline by providing opportunities for some researchers, thereby implicitly obstructing the work of others. No overt act is needed for this influence to operate: Once a foundation or government agency indicates an interest in a particular area, scientists who are seeking researchable issues will gravitate toward it. Other organizations may also explore this area, since the initial support provided by the original institution allows them to pursue this work with a much less encompassing commitment of resources. These initial involvements may result in personal commitments, the development of expertise, and the creation of physical and institutional apparatus that produce a long-term commitment to the line of research. Thus, the establishment of research agendas by major institutions can constitute a decision over which direction a subfield will explore, which subfields will survive, and where the broader resources—monetary and personnel—of the scientific community will ultimately flow.

This institutional decision making is frequently a useful mechanism, since dispersed, uncoordinated, and contradictory research programs may be inefficient; coordinated, concentrated effort may be necessary to produce scientific advance and useful results.

Inevitably, however, this a priori decision making by funding agencies and dominant institutions favors one set of ideas over another. In the social sciences this selectivity is especially dangerous, since it almost inevitably involves the risk of some forms of ideological favoritism. Some ideas will correspond more closely to the preexisting priorities of the research network; others will simply not fit into this agenda. For example, research proposals on urban problems that adopt a narrow framework to address these questions and emphasize the search for "practical" reforms are more likely to be favorably reviewed than other proposals that adopt a broader political-economic perspective and recommend more fundamental structural changes (Warren, Rose, and Bergunder 1974).

The process of setting an agenda does not eliminate controversy, since the individual researchers who take up the issues may find much to dispute and many contrary hypotheses to test. This controversy contributes to the sense that the marketplace of ideas exists, especially since the excluded lines of research may remain undeveloped and therefore invisible.

No coercion is applied in these situations, and for the most part the influence of bureaucratic agenda setting is invisible both to participants and observers of the research process, even those who set the agenda itself. This invisibility creates a sense of a natural order of things undistorted by the exercise of institutional power. This sense of voluntary, autonomous action by individual researchers is the hallmark of hegemonic domination. Schattschneider succinctly summarized the broad implications of this phenomena in the political realm: "Organization is the mobilization of bias. Some issues are organized into politics while others are organized out" (Schattschneider 1960). In the knowledge-producing sector some ideas are organized into the research agenda and others are organized out. Concretely this operates as an ancillary process to the final deliberations on the quality of a grant proposal. The prospectus must first fit into the areas the agency is seeking to nurture. Only after it is judged relevant is the scientific merit evaluated.

The degree to which this agenda setting discriminates against certain social scientific viewpoints is, of course, an empirical question. The institutionally encouraged range of topics in a discipline could be representative of the collective scientific judgements of the discipline's practitioners, or it could massively discriminate against certain theories or viewpoints.

Even if massive institutional bias exists, it appears possible that independent researchers could choose to carry out research individually, without trying to acquire funding for a proposal and/or without working inside a research institute. Such a result would appear to rescue science from the institutional coercion of modern bureaucracy, but only under circumscribed conditions. Many scientific fields require resources that universities cannot supply for *all* lines of research; the maverick may not be able to finance his/her work. Nontenured researchers must convince senior colleagues of the viability of their work within five to six years; unusual, unfunded, or controversial lines of research are likely to be risky, to take longer, and to be less clearly established when tenure review arrives. Each subfield has an established universe of discourse which changes very slowly; nonconformist research must address itself to this vocabulary, even when this makes the argument seem strained and unconvincing. Finally, the maverick researcher usually works alone and is therefore deprived of the advantages of collective endeavor, informed interchange, and collegial support, which are often essential for quality work.

Even when the institutional agenda allows for an acceptable range of research, mobilization of bias operates to exclude newcomers and include those already tied into the research community. Consider two neophyte social scientists with ideas for research projects. One has worked with already established beneficiaries of granting institutions, while the other has no connections to the research establishment. Holding career factors like age and previous publications constant, it is apparent that even prior to the proposal writing stage, the first individual enjoys distinct advantages. He or she has or can obtain through colleagues a clearer, more complete idea of the interests of private foundations, governmental agencies, and research institutes, and he or she may be acquainted with previously funded proposals and/or people with contacts in prestigious organizations. As a result, proposals can be tailored to fit the on-going institutional emphasis. A social scientist's proximity to the research establishment increases the changes of grasping the "natural order of things" and making adjustments to that order even when no overt political bias is operating.

Thus, we must attend to those factors, other than quality of research, that influence scientific success. Some ideas may be eliminated because they are not on the institutional research agenda. Others die because their authors do not conceptualize problems in a way that is congenial to the mobilization of bias because they possess very little experience with the research establishment, or are insufficiently integrated into the network. Others are regularly funded and may become the consultants of various agencies, thus influencing the next round of research.

It is evident that the range of possibilities is enormous. The official refereeing of grants and publications—the exclusive focus for most sociology and social science—is actually the last stage in a long and complex process and includes only the survivors of the prevailing mobilization of bias.

CONCLUSION

It is simply untrue that competition between ideas in academia is relatively unencumbered by institutional interference. Power is exercised at all points in the process and that power is probably exercised to the fullest extent before the marketplace of ideas is entered. The impact of this process is enhanced by its hegemonic nature, which may conceal its presence and mask its underpinnings in the political economy. The misplaced emphasis on the concept of "control" has up until now worked against a careful investigation of these processes.

In political and organizational sociology, the notion of control has usually been conceptualized within an individualized framework that focuses on the overt behavior of one or more people. While behavioral notions of control clarify some dimensions of the exercise of power, they often imply too much agency and thus are insensitive to subtle, unobtrusive, institutionalized forms of domination. Behavioral notions of power can often be boiled down to a simple idea: If we are unable to measure the exercise of power, it does not exist.

But the exercise of power in its most insidious form involves the denial that power is exercised at all. In this case, the existing mode of organization is taken for granted and is, in effect, declared the only "way of seeing." In order to see something else, one must be aware that power can be exercised with devastating results at precisely the point when a method of comprehending reality is defined.

The ability of giant corporations, for instance, to define the universe of discourse on economic issues guarantees that competition as well as knowledge upon which decisions are based will be imperfect. Shaped by the necessity for corporations to turn a sizeable profit, mass transit systems do not constitute a viable option within the present institutional framework. Solar energy alternatives, developed within the context of monopoly capitalism, leave decentralized community-controlled solar energy systems relatively undeveloped. If corporate needs are able to shape the range of alternatives outside academia, why should their influence stop at the campus gates?

This chapter has sketched the broad outlines of a theory of hegemony within academia. It has raised more questions than it has answered. But to ask the right questions is the beginning of an alternative path for research. To address the issues raised in this chapter requires an extensive examination of the social structure in which knowledge is produced in the United States. The starting point for the present chapter is the concept of hegemony which brings into focus social processes that fall outside the scope of inquiry of mainstream perspectives.

As in the larger political economy, analyzing the marketplace yields some valuable insights but it does not tell the whole story. A series of prior questions concerning the exercise of power in academia must be examined to understand clearly how an idea eventually reaches the academic marketplace. The path to this competitive arena is more convoluted than one might expect. On the way, individual scholars encounter an interorganizational network which stamps some theories with a seal of approval and buries others. Throughout the process there is rarely a hint that political criteria enter into consideration. Individual academics learn that a network of individuals and organizations constitute the natural order in higher education. By applying the notion of hegemony to the structure of academia we can demystify the operation of the academic marketplace and thus see behind the veil of neutrality.

REFERENCES

Anderson, Perry. 1976-77. "The Antinomies of Antonio Gramsci." *New Left Review* 100 (Nov. 1976–Jan. 1977):5-78.

Berelson, Bernard, Paul Lazarsfeld, and William McPhee. 1954. *Voting.* Chicago: University of Chicago Press.

Boggs, Carl. 1976. *Gramsci's Marxism.* London: Pluto Press.

Eulau, Heinz, Samuel Eldersveld, and Morris Janowitz, eds. 1956. *Political Behavior: A Reader in Theory and Research.* New York: Free Press.

Gitlin, Todd. 1980. *The Whole World Is Watching: Mass Media in the Making and Unmaking of the New Left.* Berkeley: University of California Press.

Gordon, Suzanne. 1983. "Impaired Faculties—Revolution 101 Will Not Be Offered This Semester." *The Progressive* 47, 2:18-21.

Gramsci, Antonio. 1971. *Prison Notebooks.* New York: International Publishers.

Keller, Suzanne. 1963. *Beyond the Ruling Class.* New York: Random House.

Meranto, Phillip, Oneida Meranto, and Mathew Lippman. 1985. *Guarding the*

Ivory Tower: Repression and Rebellion in Higher Education. Denver: Lucha Publications.

Mintz, Beth, and Michael Schwartz. 1985. *The Structure of Power in American Business.* Chicago: University of Chicago Press.

Oberschall, Anthony. 1972. *The Establishment of Empirical Sociology: Studies in Continuity, Discontinuity, and Institutionalization.* New York: Harper & Row.

Ollman, Bertell. 1984. "Academic Freedom in America Today: A Marxist View." *Monthly Review* 10.

Piliawsky, Monte. 1982. *Exit 13—Oppression and Racism in Academia.* Boston: South End.

Rose, Arnold. 1967. *The Power Structure.* New York: Oxford University Press.

Ryan, Jake, and Charles Sachrey. 1984. *Strangers in Paradise: Academics From the Working Class.* Boston: South End.

Schattschneider, E. E. 1960. *The Semi-Sovereign People.* New York: Holt, Rinehart and Winston.

Seybold, Peter. 1985. "Working Class Professor-Middle Class Institution: The Persistence of Academic Repression in the 1980s." In *Guarding the Ivory Tower: Repression and Rebellion in Higher Education,* edited by Meranto, Meranto, and Lippman. Denver: Lucha Publications.

―――. 1980. "The Ford Foundation and the Triumph of Behavioralism in American Political Science." In *Philanthropy and Cultural Imperialism: The Foundations at Home and Abroad,* edited by Robert F. Arnove. Boston: G. K. Hall.

Shils, Edward. 1970. "Tradition, Ecology, and Institution in the History of Sociology." *Daedalus* 99:760–825.

Truman, David. 1951. *The Governmental Process.* New York: Knopf.

Warren, Roland L., Stephen M. Rose, and Ann F. Bergunder. *The Structure of Urban Reform.* Lexington: D. C. Heath.

Williams, Raymond. 1977. *Marxism and Literature.* New York: Oxford University Press.

9

Feminism:
A Marxist Critique

Albert Szymanski

The purpose of this critique is to challenge the current dominant tendency within the women's movement and thereby encourage the development of a Marxist-informed movement for the liberation of women—a movement that can accomplish both their general and special liberation. While developing a critique of both feminism and what has become the hegemonic tendency within it, the fundamental validity of the central premises of the women's movement—that there is a specific oppression of women and that the left must make the liberation of women a priority—are reaffirmed.

In order to explain the specific oppression of women, many feminist scholars have attempted to develop a theory of patriarchy that does not in the last analysis reduce to either biological or historical materialist factors. These various theories are examined and an attempt is made to show that in fact only historical materialist explanations of patriarchy are substantiable. A general class-specific theory of the oppression of women in capitalist society is outlined. The social basis of the various trends within the women's movement are examined, and the various tendencies in, and the rightward thrust of, the mainstream of the women's movement are explained in terms of its shifting base. Finally, the essential politics of a socialist movement for the liberation of women are outlined.

THE RIGHTWARD DRIFT OF FEMINIST THEORY

In the late 1960s most attempts to offer an explanation of male chauvinism and patriarchal structures within the mainstream of the women's movement attempted to relate "sexism" to the logic of capitalism. Thus, such classical articles as those by Margaret Benston (1969), and the Rowntrees (1970) were most influential. But by the late 1970s the (sometimes crude) insights into the nature of sexism, which the women's movement understood at its birth, had largely been lost and was replaced by a combination of moralism, anti-male sentiments, and incomplete theories of patriarchy. The rejection of explanations in terms of the logic of capitalism was a necessary corollary of the rightward drift of the feminist movement, made all the more necessary by the desire of its social basis "to deal with our own oppression" and to "make the personal political." The substitution of rather superficial articles for the insightful pieces by Goldberg and by Reich and Davies in the second edition of *The Capitalist System* (Edwards et al. 1972) is illustrative of the general trend.

As Marxian modes of analysis and concepts declined in the women's movement, they were replaced by concepts, methods, and modes of analysis reminiscent of both subjectivism/moralism and of traditional academic (bourgeois) social science. When theoretical analyses and research has increasingly been done, it has been done largely within the categories and framework of traditional academic social science. A whole new field of social science centered within sociology, the sociology of women/women's studies, developed with its own journals, professional organizations, and "old boy" network to facilitate getting jobs, recommendations, grants, promotions, articles published, and so forth. An examination of the extensive literature generated by academic women in this area since the early 1970s demonstrates: (1) a rather crude moralism, for example, this or that theory or individual or concept is a sexist mode of argument; (2) the use of traditional methods of survey research supplemented by some field work, if there is any hard data at all; (3) the increasing use of traditional academic and idealist concepts such as "roles," "socialization," and "norms," together with the declining usage of concepts such as "class," "imperialism," and "capitalism" as the vocabulary of analysis; and (4) incomplete theoretical arguments, such as the various cases for a "nonreductionist" theory of patriarchy, which sometimes become transparent as justifications for an autonomous women's movement. A distinct set of institutions and a literature designed to advance the careers of professional women have been created.

THEORIES OF PATRIARCHY

The 1970s saw many feminist theorists attempt to develop a theory of patriarchy that was neither reducible to genetic differences or to the logic of the mode of production. All of these failed, either by explaining patriarchy, in the last instance, in terms of the logic of the mode of production, or biology, or by simply leaving patriarchy unexplained.

Zillah Eisenstein (1979) argues that patriarchy is rooted in the sexist stereotypes men put on the biological differences between the sexes which then become institutionalized in the family and in female socialization. But she does not give an autonomous reason why men are in a position that enables them to define women's role. She argues that patriarchy performs a number of important functions for capitalism: it provides cheap labor, facilitates consumption, reproduces labor power, and so forth. Thus her argument reduces to the historical materialist premise that the logic of the mode of production produces patriarchal structures.

Christine Delphy (1977) argues that the "family mode of production" is autonomous of, and equal in importance to, the "capitalist mode of production." While the latter operates by appropriating the labor of the working class, the former operates by men appropriating the labor of women. Her basing of patriarchy in a separate and parallel mode of production ignores the strong historical relations between the general mode of production and housework/family relations. It also generalizes the separation of the capitalist family from economy to all modes of production. In feudal and tribal societies there was no distinction between the economic processes that occurred among family members and those that occurred outside. Such a sharp dichotomization into two spheres (housework and wage labor) is a distinctive mark of only the contemporary mode of production.

Heidi Hartmann (1976) bases her analysis of patriarchy in men's control over women's labor which results in women being denied access to economic resources as well as to restrictions on sexuality. Unlike Delphy, Hartmann does not see patriarchy as a universal structure, nor does she emphasize the family at the expense of women's wage work. But her theory is based on the subjectivist notion of a conspiracy among men being responsible for patriarchy. It is men's conscious actions and decisions to exclude family women from high-paying jobs in order to ensure their dependence within the family that is the heart of patriarchy. Such a subjective account fails to account for patriarchal structures, just as explanations of capitalism in terms of greedy or evil businessmen fails to account for capitalist structures. Her categorization of a conspiratorial alliance between male workers and male capitalists in the nineteenth century being behind the attempt to exclude women from many industrial occupations so that working-class men could themselves exploit women is a fiction. The movement for a family wage and for protective legislation was supported by and benefitted women of the working class (Humphries, 1977).

Both Hartmann's and Delphy's explanations of patriarchy are ahistorical and static and tend to reify the patriarchal relations existent in the mid-twentieth century Western family to all societies through all times, while ignoring the immense historical variations in the relationship between the sexes. Their insistence that husbands' control over the labor power of their wives is equal to that of the capitalists' over the workers, and persists through time, is untenable. First, working women have considerably more economic independence, manifested in real independence from their husbands, than do long-time housewives. Housework, and with it individual male control over individual women, is declining as women are increasingly pulled into full-time wage labor. Second, the notion is not credible that while capitalist logic undermines the master-slave relation, peasantry, serfdom, tribal societies, and so forth, transforming all labor into wage-labor relations between capital and labor, it does not undermine the separate family mode of production. Capitalism at various points entered into an alliance with slave owners (in fact it was responsible for their recreation), with feudal lords (in fact east of the Elbe it was responsible for serfdom's generation), and with tribal chiefs in Africa, all in order to increase profits. But in all cases, increasing profits and reducing costs eventually implied the destruction of all noncapitalist modes of production. It was also true that at one point capitalism required (and in fact reproduced) the patriarchal family with the wife as a full-time housewife as the most profitable and cheapest way of reproducing labor power. However, it is clear that the rapid mechanization and socialization of housework and childcare, which has resulted in a radical reduction in the socially necessary labor time to reproduce labor power together with the great demand of the corporations for cheap and relatively docile female labor, has radically transformed women's economic role. From being firmly ensconsed in the "household mode of production," she has been placed firmly (along with men of the working class) directly in the capitalist mode of production. Delphy and Hartmann thus base their case for an autonomous patriarchy on a myth.

Whether one examines the historically specific role of housework prior to mid-twentieth century capitalist society or the rapid decline of its role in determining women's position since the mid-twentieth century, one would seem to be led to historical materialist accounts which bring the analysis back to the logic of the mode of production (and the contradictions and transformations of that logic).

Roisin McDonough and Rachel Harrison (1978) attempt to argue that patriarchy is based on the control of female fertility and sexuality by men. They argue that in the bourgeois family such control is maintained through differential access to property, while in the proletarian family it is maintained through differential access to the wage. In the former class, male dominance is shaped by the need for legitimate male heirs, and in the latter, by the process of reproducing labor power. Claude Meillassoux (1975) makes a similar argument in maintaining that the origins of patriarchy lie in the control that male elders had over the regulation of the fertility of women, itself required by the necessity of social control over the reproduction of labor power. Both these arguments fail to provide an answer to how it is that men came to be the controllers of women's reproductive power, that is, it leaves the ultimate cause of patriarchy unexplained. Either men came to be in such a position because they control property, bring home the wage and so forth (i.e., the argument reduces to that of historical materialism), or it simply hangs in the air.

Juliett Mitchell (1974), adopting the ideas of the non-Marxist structuralist Levi-Straus, argues that the symbolic exchange of women by men, the fundamental principle of kinship organization, is the basis for the subordination of women within the relationships of human reproduction—patriarchy. Mitchell also adapts the classical Freudian notions of Electra and Oedipal complexes to account for the reproduction of the subordination of women. The incorporation of the ahistorical Levi-Strausian and Freudian notions as the basis for patriarchy has the fatal flaw of implying that patriarchy is universal and unchanging over time, without significant variation among nations and classes. She also shares with the theories of Meillassoux and McDonough and Harrison the problem of accounting for how it came to be that men exchange women and not vice-versa, or why girls feel "penis envy" rather than little boys "vagina" or "womb envy." Mitchell's account of patriarchy runs against the comparative evidence. Further, like most attempts to establish an autonomous basis for patriarchy, it is theoretically inadequate in that it never really does offer an explanation for male dominance. It merely pushes the question back a step or two.

All attempts fail to establish an autonomous basis for patriarchy that is based neither in genetic factors nor in the logic of the mode of production within which the family occurs. In spite of considerable intelligence and even genius applied in the attempt to develop a theory for feminist politics, feminist theorists have failed. The attempt to root patriarchy and male chauvinism in biology has two insuperable problems: it is incompatible with the evidence of comparative, national, and class variation in these phenomena, and it offers radical lesbian separatism (a not very realistic alternative) as the only consistent politics. Aware of the problems of attempting to establish patriarchy on a biological basis and recoiling from classical historical materialist explanations, the theorists of an autonomous patriarchy are left with incomplete arguments and hence present inadequate theoretical accounts. The inability of biological reductionist arguments to account for the tremendous variation in patriarchal structures suggests that historical materialist arguments are the best candidate for the correct accounts of patriarchy. But this cannot be conclusively demonstrated until other nonbiologically reductionist accounts, such as that of Marvin Harris (1977), are refuted *and* sufficient positive evidence is presented in favor of a specific historical materialist account.

Marvin Harris (1977) suggests that patriarchy is a result of primitive peoples' need to reduce population to keep in equilibrium with their environment in order to secure a reasonably high living standard. He argues that warfare among primitives is a principal way in which population is kept down. Warfare accomplishes its purpose, not by producing high casualty rates, but rather in producing a high social evaluation of men as soldiers and a low evaluation of women as nonsoldiers. On the one hand a high evaluation of soldiers results in boy babies getting special and preferential care, and in female babies being subjected to either conscious or unconscious female infanticide; on the other hand, it results in women being given as rewards for male soldiers' heroic deeds in battle. The reduction in the number of girls resulting from this process lowers the reproductive rate of the society.

Harris's theory has some serious empirical problems. First, it is based on the notion that warfare is a central part of the life of primitive peoples. Such is not the case. Most all hunting and gathering peoples before the intrusion of imperialism were peaceful. If such simple peoples came up against a more advanced and warlike society, their typical response was to leave (see Lenski and Lenski 1978). Second, the differential female/male ratios that he reports from recorded primitive societies (something like 50 percent more young men than women) are insufficient to significantly slow down the rate of population increase of a society to keep it in harmony with its environment. The implicit step in Harris's logic is that tribes that fail to reduce the number of females through overevaluating males as soldiers would have faced Malthusian pressures from the scarcity of resources and thus apparently be so weakened that they would perish through starvation, disease, or military conquest or be so burdened with tedious labor as to modify their institutions. It seems unlikely that primitive societies generally hit on the institution of unconscious female infanticide (which merely reduced the female/male ratio slightly) as the primary way to maintain a high living standard. It would seem that more likely courses of action would have been migration or intensification. In any event, the evidence that unconscious female infanticide really did play an important role in keeping up a high living standard is shaky. Third, the bulk of contemporary anthropological evidence shows that women's position in hunting and gathering and simple horticultural societies was generally qualitatively better than in class societies. Thus the amount of patriarchy that a theory like that of Harris's, which traces patriarchy back to the logic of primitive social life, fails to account for the greater bulk of patriarchal structures that came into being with the decline of primitive societies. Finally, Harris offers no substantial argument as to why patriarchal institutions that came into being thousands of years ago in order to secure ecological balance in very different conditions of both availability of resources and warfare have continued to be reproduced. In sum, although it is a brilliant attempt to offer a nonhistorical materialist, but formally complete, theory of patriarchy that does not resort to biological reductionism, Harris's theory fails.

It is difficult to conceive of what a solid theory of patriarchy that at least roughly corresponds to the presently available evidence would look like if it did not in the last instance resort to historical materialist explanations. The most logical candidate would seem to be a theory that argued that there was some inherent logic of the family or sexual relations that varies over time and among different populations. While it is true that there is a certain "relative autonomy" of the family from the logic of the mode of production, this logic is ahistorical, not a variable like that of the mode of production. Regardless of the logic of the mode of production, women bear children; only women can breast feed, and a considerable amount of time and love are necessary to rear healthy children; certain socialization techniques are more effective in producing given results, and so forth. Such factors operate autonomously from the logic of the mode of production and are not reducible to its logic. However, their actual effect on specific institutions and the degree of their effectiveness are very much a product of the variable logic of the mode of production. In this sense, they are very much like the legitimation functions of the state, or the demands that an ideology be logically consistent. However, all a constant can explain is another constant. While such factors, in interaction with the variables of productive relations, may well predict the concrete structures of patriarchy and relations between the sexes, they can have no effect on the tremendous variation in such structures. Only a variable, such as the mode of production, can in the last instance actually account for variation.

AN OUTLINE OF A HISTORICAL MATERIALIST THEORY OF PATRIARCHY

Regardless of whether or not the question of the origins of patriarchy is addressed or whether or not the historical development of the structures of patriarchy is considered to be an important problem, an adequate historical materialist theory of patriarchy must: (1) account for the reproduction of patriarchal structures in terms of their role in the contemporary mode of production, both in terms of their functions for that mode, and why the particular forms of patriarchy best, or most conveniently, fulfill those functions; (2) account for the contemporary variations in the structures of patriarchy in terms of class factors and position within the world capitalist system; (3) account for the changes in patriarchal structures in terms of the underlying logic and transformations in the capitalist mode of production; and (4) be sensitive to the possibility of contradictions between the inherent logic of the family and the requirements of the mode of production. Negative action from patriarchal structures on the capitalist mode of production perhaps could be a source of destabilization or even revolutionary energy.

During the early period of capitalism, women predominantly performed the role of housewives/mothers whose contribution to the capitalist mode of production varied qualitatively by class. In the working class, even if women worked in a mill before they were married, or if they were widowed or never married, most women were full-time housewives, working perhaps 90 to 100 hours a week tending a garden, canning food, chopping wood, washing clothes, cleaning the house, looking after the children, making and mending clothes, cooking, washing up, providing emotional support to children and the working man, and so forth.

Working-class women functioned to reproduce the labor power of their husbands who sold their labor power directly to the capitalists, as well as to bring up another generation of male workers and female wife-mothers. Her labor power *was* paid for by the capitalist. It was incorporated into the value of the labor power of her husband and sons. But it was paid for in the form of a wage paid to them, not to her. There was nothing inherently more demeaning, menial, or brutal about doing housework in comparison to working 12 hours a day in the mills or mines as a manual laborer. However the fact that the male got the family wage, and not the wife, gave the working-class man a position of power over the woman, a position that was used to secure a degree of subordination.

In the capitalist class, women were considerably better off—they had servants and nursemaids to do the housework and child care, that is, working-class women performed these functions in the capitalist-class family. Such women were largely excluded from economic functions, being restricted to performing social functions and engaging in leisure, in good part as conspicuous consumption by capitalist-class men. But such women traditionally were clearly subordinate to their men, that is, before women had the right to own or inherit property.

Conditions in the classical petty bourgeois family were very much like those in the capitalist-class family (only at a substantially lower standard of living). Such families typically had a live-in servant who did the bulk of the housework and much of the child care, largely releasing the petty bourgeois woman for social and leisure activities, or in the case of shopkeepers and farmers, to assist the husband in the small family business.

The course of the twentieth century, especially in the post-1950 period, saw the radical transformation of the position of women in all classes, especially in the working class. As the socially necessary labor time to reproduce labor power of husbands and children radically decreased, women for the first time became available for wage labor outside the home. At the same time, the demand of the corporations for more cheap and docile white-collar and service workers greatly increased. Wives/mothers were pulled out of the home and pulled into the offices and salesrooms. This process, which is not yet completed, has meant the undermining of the traditional economic position of the working-class husband who no longer exclusively brings home the wage. Working-class women's economic security is considerable. Hence dependence on a man is considerably reduced and the material basis for more egalitarian nonpatriarchal relationships in the family is laid.

In the course of the late nineteenth century, upper- and middle-class women came to acquire most of the legal rights (other than the vote) that their husbands had. Women were granted the right to own and inherit property and barriers to their admission into professional schools came down. Even before the franchise, these two classes of women were largely granted formally equal status and equality of opportunity with the men of their class. Such rights as the right to inherit property or entry into professional schools meant nothing to working-class women whose relatives had no property to pass on to them, nor the education and money to attend professional schools. Women of the capitalist class, who were now able to own property on their own, utilized this right to equalize in good part their economic power with the men of their class, even though they continued to be excluded from most managerial positions. As the traditional petty bourgeois went bankrupt and family businesses in which the woman worked were replaced by the salaried professions and administration as the primary economic base of the middle class, petty bourgeois women found themselves without a direct relationship to the economy. At the same time the cost of servants and housing went up, and most middle-class women could no longer afford to hire a live-in servant to do the bulk of the housework/childcare unless they themselves worked. Both the number of children going to college and the costs of higher education increased, further putting pressure on petty bourgeois women to work. A bit later the divorce rate increased and the prevalence of single professional women increased. The increasing need for a second (or independent) income in this class provided the pressure to bring down the barriers to petty bourgeois careers. Women thus increasingly entered the professions. It should be noted that the petty bourgeois women's entry into salaried labor followed that of the working-class women's entry into wage labor (at first mostly young unmarried women, widows, and the most economically desperate of married working-class women).

A far higher percentage of married women in the working class engage in wage labor than women in the petty bourgeoisie, indicating that the motivation for work outside of the home is primarily economic need. Even though working women continue to do the bulk of the housework (the total time spent by women who work full time on housework, commuting, and wage labor averages about five hours more a week than does her husband's), distinctively "sexist" oppression is probably greatest for petty bourgeois house-wives. Without the means to secure a middle-class livelihood on their own, moreover, separation from their husbands would probably plunge them quickly into the working class with a drastic decline in their living standards. Thus, their economic security and, hence, dependence on and subordination to their husbands is greater than in the working class where wives mostly work and where, if the husband leaves, women generally suffer rather less of a decline in living standards than would middle-class women.

The fact that most working-class women work at clerical, sales, and service jobs, thereby establishing an economic basis for relatively egalitarian relationships in the family, by no means results in the undermining of sexist relationships. Working-class women overwhelmingly go into occupations in which stereotypically "feminine" as opposed to "masculine" behavior is sought. Traditional sex roles are thus reproduced on the job. The last half of the twentieth century is thus experiencing a socialization of patriarchal structures, with the reproduction of women's traditional subordinate and "feminine" roles increasingly occurring within the corporations, rather than in the patriarchal family.

Working-class women have been rapidly drawn into wage labor in the post–World War II period because: (a) the corporations radically increased their need for cheap and docile white collar (clerical and sales) labor; (b) the socially necessary labor time required to reproduce male labor power in the home was radically reduced due to the mechanization of housework, the increasing production of goods formerly produced by women in the home as commodities outside of the home, and the significant reduction in the number of years devoted to child bearing and rearing; and (c) it became increasingly difficult to meet the socially defined minimum living standard with just one wage.

Women are preferred in the rapidly expanding white collar sector because: (a) their socialization in the patriarchal family tends to make them more docile workers and tends to orient them to the role of housewife/mother even while they work full time, thus making them more amenable to manipulation and less likely to organize; (b) they generally will work for less than the value of their labor power, because part of the costs of the reproduction of their labor power is typically borne either by their husbands if married, or by their parent if they are single. Because women's wage is set on this basis, unmarried working-class women living alone are typically reduced to poverty. Women's greater docility and noncareer orientation makes them especially useful in occupations that are being "de-skilled" and subject to qualitatively greater management control. In good part their introduction to office work is a result of the process of the evolution of management (male) and clerical work (female) occupations out of the traditional eighteenth and nineteenth century male head clerks and accountants. The mechanization and reorganization of office work was made far easier by bringing in young women than it would have been had the men who had traditionally been the highly-skilled clerks been forcibly reduced to the new office proletariat. Native-born women were, of course, preferable to the new working class of European immigrants (female or male), who were flooding into manual jobs at the same time as the office proletariat was created, because they were literate in English (a requisite of office labor, but not of physical labor).

Petty bourgeois women with professional or managerial careers have benefitted enormously from the affirmative action programs of the 1970s, even though they have not yet caught up with men. It appears that the bulk of remaining discrimination here is a result of past practices as well as the voluntary decision of many women to take time off from their careers to have children, rather than a result of contemporary discrimination in either admissions to schools, hiring, or promotion policies of the state or private corporations.

Thus the two forms of patriarchy that are felt as the most oppressive tend to be the oppression experienced by petty bourgeois housewives as housewives and the oppression of working-class women primarily as wage workers. It would be very difficult to make a case that the women in the capitalist class, most of whom own significant amounts of property and who employ working-class women both to do their household labor and to generate the fortunes on which they base their life of luxury, are in any important sense oppressed, or are in any meaningful sense the "sisters" of those they exploit. Petty bourgeois women in the professions have for the most part both very good and rather well paying jobs, and for the most part enjoy promotional opportunities that are equivalent to men's. They seem to have become pretty much full participants in the relative privileges of the salaried petty bourgeois. While they have not yet achieved full equality with the men of their class, they would seem to be significantly less oppressed than petty bourgeois housewives and qualitatively less oppressed than either working-class housewives or working-class wage working women. The most oppressed section of women would appear to be working-class women. It would still seem to be the case that petty bourgeois housewives and perhaps unmarried white collar women still suffer more from the patriarchal structures of the family (or the lack of security the family provides) and from the male chauvinism of individual men.

Patriarchal structures are both the essential way women are especially oppressed *and* the cause of the other manifestations of women's special oppression—male chauvinism and sexist ideology. While women of the capitalist class are not oppressed in any significant sense by patriarchal structures, and while there are qualitative differences between the petty bourgeoisie and the working class, and between women who are primarily housewives (in both of these classes) and women who primarily work outside of the home, male chauvinism and sexist ideology would seem to be pretty much constant.

Sexist ideology is propagated in the schools, in the mass media, in military training, and in virtually all the central institutions of capitalist society *because of* the role of patriarchy in capitalism. Sexist ideology is the theoretical justification for the patriarchal family which reproduces male labor power, provides female workers who work for less than the value of their labor because part of the costs of the reproduction of their labor is borne by their family and assists in the reproduction of traditional "feminine" sex role characteristics that the corporations find so convenient in their service and clerical workers. Sexist ideology also operates to legitimate the lower pay and greater docility of the female labor force. Sexist ideology also has other functions for monopoly capitalism, not the least of which is to reinforce authoritarian and militaristic sentiments, especially in soldiers, as well as to promote consumption of such goods as cosmetics, sports cars, clothing, and stereos.

Although all women are equally caricatured by sexist ideology, not all women suffer equally from its effects. The women most oppressed by it are those who internalize the ideal of being a "good mother" and "good wife" and who thus desires to provide her family with all the conveniences and support the ideal family requires. For a working-class or lower petty bourgeois woman to accomplish this ideal, two things are necessary: (1) that she work more or less full time outside of the house to secure enough money to buy the appliances, goods, services, and education that the ideal dictates; and (2) that she strive also to be the full-time mother and wife the ideal requires. The impossibility of doing both well puts incredible pressure on women of these classes, a pressure that can well lead to emotional breakdowns, alcoholism, and so forth, as well as be the energy that can be mobilized by the women's liberation movement.

Male chauvinism, the behavior of individual men in their relationships with women, is a product of both men's position within patriarchal structures (as fathers, husbands, supervisors, owners, etc.) and a result of the internalization of sexist ideology (in the family, on the job, in the military, from the media, in school). Even in the absence of the reproduction of such behavior in patriarchal structures and exposure to sexist ideology, male chauvinism is *reproduced* because of its role in giving men, especially men of the working class, a feeling of solidarity and false dignity.

A similar effect operates within both the working-class and the petty bourgeois family, especially where the woman is performing the unwaged labor of housewife. Wives are often brutalized, much more often in subtle ways than through actual physical battering, as a consequence of the oppressive conditions of the husband, either as a manual laborer or as a small businessman. The aggression built up on the job, which cannot be directly taken out on the boss or on customers, suppliers, or competitors, can relatively safely be taken out against an economically dependent wife. It would seem that such manifestations of male chauvinism are most characteristic of traditional petty bourgeois and working-class families, rather than of new petty bourgeois families with working wives or of capitalist-class families. Capitalist-class men, for example, have many subordinates (both men and women) on which to take out their aggression. Further, their work is inherently more enjoyable than that of other classes of men, and their wives are more often not economically dependent on them. Thus, they have less aggression to displace onto their wives, and the wives are less likely to put up with it. Working-class women (in the office or factory), rather than the wives of men of the capitalist class, are more likely to bear the brunt of male chauvinism. It must be emphasized that the cause of all forms of male chauvinism is ultimately to be located within the logic of capitalism— either in its generation of patriarchal structures, in the internalization of its sexist ideology, or as a compensation for the daily oppression of working-class or petty bourgeois life.

THE SOCIAL BASIS OF THE WOMEN'S MOVEMENT

The very different experiences of the women of different classes means that women experience different forms and degrees of oppression. Furthermore, the degree and form of oppression varies both over time and by position within the world capitalist economy as a result of the logic of the capitalist mode of production. The different degrees and forms of oppression in turn tend to result in very different issues being raised by various classes of women. The class and national variations in women's oppression have too little in common, and the women of various classes have too much in common with the men in the same position in comparison to the women of other classes for a unified women's movement to exist unless it has a specific class orientation.

As Marxist women's critiques (see for example, Kollentai 1977, pp. 58-73) of the original feminist movement pointed out, there is not a single "woman question," but rather at least four separate "women's questions." The attempt of narrow feminism to appropriate the legitimacy of speaking for all women is based on their false claim that all women share an essentially common oppression. This false claim that there is really only one women's question is a generalization of the felt oppression of only one set of women—white middle-class women—that has been the primary social basis of the narrow feminist tendency in the women's movement.

The separate women's questions are: (1) the condition of capitalist-class women; (2) the condition of petty bourgeois housewives, ex-housewife nonprofessionals, and petty bourgeois professionals; (3) the condition of working-class women; and (4) the condition of women especially oppressed by their national or ethnic group status. Each of these four groups puts forth *different* demands reflecting their qualitatively different social structural position. Capitalist-class women, as fully integrated members of their class, put forth demands of that class: increased exploitation, increased productivity, support for imperialist wars, cutbacks in social welfare programs for the poor and minorities, and so forth. It cannot be forgotten that the extreme wealth and privilege of these women is a result of the exploitation and oppression of their working-class sisters. Petty bourgeois professional women have tended to stress affirmative action for petty bourgeois women, which facilitates their entry into professional schools, the professions, and management as well as their promotion within these fields. Petty bourgeois housewives (and ex-housewives) tend to stress issues of power and "exploitation" within the family. Younger unmarried professionals and preprofessionals (as well as many younger white collar single women) tend to stress the issues that most oppress them: the threat of rape, sexual exploitation by individual men, the lack of emotional security within relationships, and a woman's right to control her body. Working-class women tend to stress issues of improving working conditions, higher pay, job safety, the availability of high-quality, convenient, and reliable day care, control over their jobs, unionization, equal pay for equal work, access to better paying jobs, and so forth.

Petty bourgeois professional women tend to demand their full share in the privileges of the petty bourgeoisie rather than the equalization of the condition of working-class and middle-class women. They in fact defend the privileges of the petty bourgeoisie against equalization. The limited number of petty bourgeois positions, and the individual nature of petty bourgeois work and promotional prospects dictate that there will be stiff competition with men for scarce resources. If a woman gets a tenured job or an executive advancement, this means that a man does not. Thus the special conditions of the competitive nature of the petty bourgeoisie tends to generate an anti-male consciousness and anti-male ideology among the upwardly striving women, and a counter antifeminist sentiment among the petty bourgeois men attempting to hang on to increasingly scarce privileges.

Middle-class housewives, ex-housewives/nonprofessionals, and young unmarried preprofessionals, professionals, and many young unmarried white collar workers tend to stress psychological oppression by individual men, while downplaying both patriarchal structures outside the family and economic exploitation. Such women have been brutalized more by individual men than they have suffered hunger, racism, or severe economic exploitation. Such women have generated the slogans of "organize around your own oppression," and "the personal is the political." Their emphasis on male chauvinism rather than on exploitation results in privatizing what are really structural contradictions, instead of the politicalization of them as part of the general struggle against the capitalist system and the patriarchal structures it generates.

The condition of working-class women is very different. Women who work cannot get ahead, as can women of the petty bourgeoisie, over the backs of their brothers and husbands. Both white and minority women in this class are oppressed primarily as workers. Thus their brothers and husbands of the same class and ethnic group, who share their most essential oppression, are their natural allies. "Equal rights" for such women mostly means equality in domination and exploitation with their men. The daily experience of such women on the job *tends* to make it clear, especially to blue collar women and perhaps to women in the larger offices, that it is the boss/capitalist, not their husbands and brothers, who are the enemy. The working-class women's movement, unlike either segment of the petty bourgeois women's movement, thus tends to focus on exploitation and related issues that are class specific to their condition, including racism and national oppression. The anti-male, antifamily sentiments of so much of the petty bourgeois women's movement make no sense in this class. Not only are working-class men the natural allies of working women, but the working-class family, even with all of its problems, is, and is strongly perceived to be, a source of at least minimal economic and emotional security. Being a single mother working in the office or mill is not looked on favorably by many women of this class as the ideal. The demand for not only equal pay for equal work but for equal access to higher paying jobs is important, especially to establish the basis for economic equality and hence personal equality in the working-class family. But it should be noted that if equal pay with working-class men results in a pay reduction for male workers to pay for a raise for female workers, then the average income of the working family, and hence the living standards of working-class women, remain unchanged.

The most important impact that the demand for equal pay could have for most working-class women is that the funding for equal pay come out of profits, not out of men's paychecks. That women could succeed in such a demand would seem to depend on their working together with men in a solidified class movement against capitalism. Further, a misdirected attempt to achieve equal pay with working-class men at the expense of the decline in make wages would undoubtedly result in: (1) many housewives and working wives opposing such a divisive demand because it would mean their living standards would go down, and (2) driving male workers into opposition to the women's demands for the same reason. The struggle against patriarchal structures in the working class must be part of the overall struggle for improvement in working-class conditions and eventually the achievement of socialism. Because men are, and are generally perceived by working-class women to be, allies of women in this struggle, manifestations of male chauvinism among men must be dealt with in a comradely and educational manner appropriate to consolidating and mobilizing friends. In the middle class, in contrast, the struggle against male chauvinism can be and usually is treated as an antagonistic contradiction, and the tactics developed for dealing with it become weapons in the general battle for scarce privilege against the men of this class.

The appropriation of "feminism" by professional women allows them facilely to use the charge of sexism to advance their own careers and positions, to substitute moralistic criticism of male chauvinism for the theory and analysis so desperately needed, and to ignore or downplay the worldwide anti-imperialist, antiracist and working-class struggles to advance their own narrow interests. The appropriation of feminism and the opportunist charge of sexism legitimates their narrow self-interested and careerist politics and neglect of the far more serious oppression of women (and men) of other class positions and nationalities, while at the same time intimidating and confusing both women and men who do not accept their claims.

Narrow feminism offers nothing to the vast majority of the women in the world. This is underlined again and again by its lack of appeal to the women of the oppressed nations, to minority women in the United States, or for that matter to most white working-class women in the United States. It is not surprising that each International Women's Conference ends up in a split between North American/ Western European women and women from the rest of the world, or that there is a growing pro-family movement among working-class women in the United States. For the vast majority it is patently obvious that their hopes for improvement in their lives lie in solidarity with the men of their class and nationality, not in attacking them, and that problems within male-female relationships must be worked out in the process of both sexes struggling *together* against a far greater enemy. This reflects the fact that working-class, minority, and most women in the less developed countries are oppressed primarily by their class position, by their minority status, or by the imperial domination of their countries, *not* because they are women.

The strategy of narrow feminism based among white professional women is, however, by no means irrational from the point of view of its social base. Their targeting of men as the primary enemies (rather than capitalism or imperialism), or in the case of "socialist-feminism" men as co-equal enemies along with capitalism (but it seems still the primary enemy in practice), makes considerable sense. With limited privileged jobs (in management, university positions, tenure), especially in a contracting economy, what middle-class men do not get, women will. In a typically petty bourgeois fight over scarce resources, fully analogous to the competitive struggle among small shopkeepers over limited customers, success is only obtained by destroying one's competitors. Solidarity here does not make sense.

THE POLITICS OF FEMINISM

The mainstream of the feminist movement over the course of the 1970s has evolved from being part of the left to becoming essentially part of the New Right. This development parallels the course of the earlier feminist movement in the last half of the nineteenth century. Both movements were spin-offs of the support movement for the liberation of black people. The first movement originated as part of the abolitionist movement in the pre-Civil War period, and the second originated in good part as a part of the civil rights movement of the 1960s. In both cases, white female participants in these movements began to see parallels between the condition of blacks and their own situation, and as a result began to put increasing energy into fighting their own battles rather than those of blacks. Because of the class basis of both movements, the increasingly compelling argument that women were as oppressed as blacks justified a gradual reorientation away from the issues that primarily concerned minority and poorer women toward the issues of primary concern to the middle and upper middle classes.

Before the 1880s an important mainstream of the early women's movement (the National Woman Suffrage Association) did involve itself in issues of central concern to minority and working-class women. But in the 1880s the feminist movement came to focus exclusively on middle- and upper-class white women's concerns. The depoliticization of the women's movement was represented by a new united organization formed in 1890, the National American Woman Suffrage Association (NAWSA) (with Elizabeth Cady Stanton as president) and the new dedication to a sole issue—gaining the right to vote. From the mid-1880s the rhetoric of the feminist movement became racist (both against blacks *and* the new European immigrants), antiworking-class and antisocialist. The general middle- and upper-class fear of the new immigrants and the revolutionary potential they brought with them became very much a part of the feminist movement—its origins in the support of the abolition of slavery were totally forgotten. Black women were explicitly excluded from participation in the movement and working-class women were discouraged. The movement accepted the prevailing racism of the era that black women should be permanently confined to agricultural and domestic work because of their biological inferiority. It also shared in the prevalent racist views about the inherent intellectual inferiority of the new Jewish, Italian, and Slavic immigrants. After 1890 one of the principal arguments of the NAWSA was that granting the native born white women the vote together with a literacy requirement to preclude male and female foreign born from voting would protect the United States against the dangerous influence of the new working class. The organization opposed the Homestead Steel Strike of 1892 (its leaders asked, "Why didn't the workers go out and start their own business if they objected to working conditions?") and opposed doing anything about the new Jim Crow system in the South. A resolution passed at the 1893 convention of the NAWSA read:

we call attention to the significant facts that in every state there are more women who can read and write than all negro voters; more American women who can read and write than all foreign voters, so that the enfranchisement of such women would settle the vexed question of rule by illiteracy, whether of homegrown or foreign born production [cited in Sachs 1976].

Emma Goldman, a prominent U.S. anarchist, said of the feminist movement, "valiant fighters for a wretched little bill which will benefit a handful of propertied ladies, with absolutely no provision for the vast majority of working women" (cited in Sachs 1976).

In spite of their total adherence to mainstream conservative and capitalist values, the NAWSA was unable to convince upper-class men to grant them the franchise until the post–World War I red scare. In face of the Bolshevik Revolution and unrest in the United States in the wake of World War I, the Nineteenth Amendment granting women the right to vote was rushed through Congress and ratified within a year. Compare this schedule to what has happened to the Equal Rights Amendment. The rush to give white native born women the vote occurred in the midst of the worst political repression the United States has ever seen. The notorious Palmer raids occurred on January 2, 1920. Thousands of socialists and communists were given lengthy jail terms. The presidential candidate of the Socialist party, Eugene Debs, received a million votes for president in November 1920 while in the federal penitentiary in Atlanta. With their goal, the franchise, achieved, the feminist movement collapsed, not to be awakened again until the revival of the black movement in the 1960s.

It should be noted that the dominant feminist tendency in the 1880s through 1920 period was not the only trend in the women's movement—there were others, for example, the working-class women's movement that focused on organizing trade unions, increasing wages, and improving working conditions (especially in fighting for protective legislation); and the black women's movement that focused on combating Jim Crow and the lynching of blacks. Women were in the forefront and leadership of the trade union movement since the 1840s. From the 1850s immigrant women were employed in large numbers in unskilled and labor-intensive industries, especially textiles and garment. Unlike the mainstream feminist movement, the working-class women's movement saw the employers (rather than the liquor interests) as their enemy. In 1903 a group of middle-class women formed the National Women's Trade Union League to support the struggles of working-class women. In the 1909–12 period there was a tremendous surge of working-class women's activity, the most famous strike of which has been commemorated throughout the world on March 8 as International Women's Day. The mainstream feminist movement had nothing to do with such events. Unlike the middle-class women's movement, the working-class women's movement did not die in 1920, but continued in the 1920s and 1930s in the campaigns to organize women textile and tobacco workers (see Sachs 1976).

The contrast between the middle/upper-class mainstream feminist movement and the Marxist working-class women's movement in the pre–World War I period was stronger in Europe than in the United States. Clara Zetkin in Germany and Alexandra Kollentai in Russia carried on a relentless battle against what Marxist women sometimes referred to as "the enemy sisters." Kollentai wrote a 400-page polemic, *On the Social Basis of the Women's Movement*, arguing that working-class and middle-class women had nothing in common. Kollentai argued,

> The feminists see men as the main enemy, for men have unjustly seized all rights and privileges for themselves, leaving women only chains and duties. For them a victory is won when a prerogative previously enjoyed exclusively by the male sex is conceded to the "fair sex." Proletarian women have a different attitude. They do not see men as the enemy and the oppressor; on the contrary, they think of men as their comrades, who share with them the drudgery of the daily round and fight with them for a better future.... Where, then, is that general "woman question?" Where is that unity of tasks and aspirations about which the feminists have so much to say? A sober glance at reality shows that such unity does not and cannot exist. In vain the feminists try to assure themselves that the "woman question" has nothing to do with that of the political party and that "its solution is possible only with the participation of all parties and all women." . . . once the barrier is down and the bourgeois women have received access to political activity, the recent defenders of the "rights of all women" become enthusiastic defenders of the privileges of their class, content to leave their younger sisters with no rights at all. Thus, when the feminists talk to working women about the need for a common struggle to realize some "general women's" principle, women of the working class are naturally distrustful [Kollentai 1977, 58–73].

Reflecting their middle-class basis, the principal issues raised by the hegemonic tendency within the mainstream feminist movement of the early 1980s are virtually indistinguishable from those raised by the Moral Majority, the Libertarian party, or other segments of the New Right. The mainstream of the women's movement has thus moved from its late-1960s association with radical critiques of capitalism, as well as support for anti-imperialist and antiracist struggles. It has been caught up in the general right drift of U.S. politics. Freed of its original ties to movements of the oppressed at home and abroad, the distinctively middle-class social basis of narrow feminism has produced politics parallel to those produced in much of the rest of the middle class.

Increasingly the antirape, antibattering, antipornography, and sexual harassment issues have become central and taken the form of traditional law-and-order politics with which people like Ronald Reagan and the local police are quite happy. Professional women concerned about their careers and professional advancement have increasingly appropriated the legitimacy of the women's movement to advance their narrow careerist interest at the expense of working-class and minority women. Charges of sexism are increasingly used in defense of both traditional law-and-order politics and to advance professional careers. Further, the emphasis on a woman's absolute right to control her body without transcending social obligations is a manifestation of classical liberalism. The progressive socialists' orientation of the women's movement of the late 1960s and early 1970s is virtually dead.

In fact, the outstanding differences between the hegemonic feminist tendency and groups like the Moral Majority are issues in which the hegemonic feminist tendency defends classical liberal positions against preliberal protraditional family notions of the Moral Majority. Issues of socialism do not enter in; the battle between them is in terms of eighteenth century politics. The hegemonic feminist tendency vehemently insists on the right of the individual woman to control her body. The Moral Majority, on the other hand, opposes such rights. It argues that the rights of the unborn infant are superior to the right of a woman to terminate a pregnancy. Further, it argues against the right to premarital or extramarital sex, to have lesbian relationships, and perhaps even the right to practice contraception. The Libertarian party, which takes classical liberalism to its economic and moral extremes, is in 100 percent concurrence with the mainstream of the feminist movement on all moral questions of reproductive rights and sexual preference. The politics of the mainstream of the feminist movement by 1980 became an amalgam of the two principal tendencies of the New Right: the traditionalist anticrime pro-law and order, antipornography Moral Majority and the extreme individualism of the Libertarian party.

Libertarians, further, would have no difficulty supporting women's equal access to all occupations, although they, unlike the traditionalists around groups like the Moral Majority, would have difficulty with state-enforced programs designed to accomplish this end. While Moral Majority people oppose affirmative action it is not on the grounds that they oppose strong state intervention (e.g., they support a ban on abortions, for example, and tougher laws against muggers and rapists). It is rather because they support traditional patriarchal structures and want to use state power in their defense, rather than to break them down.

A distinctively socialist women's movement takes a very different approach to the oppression of women than do the dominant tendencies within feminism in either the 1970s or the 1980s. The middle-class liberalism, careerism, and law-and-order politics which have been hegemonic since the decline of the New Left (and its associated anti-racist and anti-imperialist) movements have nothing in common with a socialist analysis or program.

CONCLUSION: A SOCIALIST MOVEMENT FOR THE LIBERATION OF WOMEN

The "narrow feminist" tendency of the women's movement claims to be the legitimate representation of the entire women's liberation movement. It claims to speak for all women of all classes, nations, and ethnic groups. But there are in fact other tendencies within women's liberation. There is a wide range of positions that are equally opposed to patriarchal structures, male chauvinist behavior, and sexist ideas, but that differ fundamentally on their analysis of the basis of the oppression of women and in their programs for dealing with it. The leadership of narrow feminism has brought the mainstream of the movement into the right wing of U.S. politics, while increasingly isolating it from the concerns of minority and working-class women. It has increasingly come to express the bitterness and anti-male sentiments of sociologically rather marginal groups of women, rather than the concerns of the vast majority. The hope for the women's movement lies in reasserting its progressive roots in an effective socialist challenge to the current law-and-order and anti-male tendencies.

What should a distinctively socialist program for the liberation of women look like? How would it contrast with the hegemonic narrow feminism?

(1) A socialist women's movement would *not* reject what have become the primary concerns of narrow feminism: rape and battering, women's right to control their bodies, and affirmative action for professional women. But it would put these in perspective as well as provide an analysis and strategy that could really effect a radical decrease in violence against women as well as consolidate women's rights over their own bodies. It is most oppressive not to be able to walk the streets at night, to be battered by one's husband or lover, just as it is most oppressive to be subject to mugging and other forms of violent crime that are not sex specific. But a materialist, non-moralistic analysis dictates that an effective strategy to reduce violence requires the elimination of the social conditions that generate it. Therefore, the movement for women's liberation must take the issue of socialism seriously, for it is capitalism with its corollaries of racism and imperialism that is responsible for the urban decay, massive unemployment, racial oppression, and individualization that generate rape and other violent crimes.

Likewise, women's rights to choose her sexual partners and whether or not to conceive and give birth are valid rights that any socialist movement must support. It has in fact been the socialist left over the years that has been the most consistent supporter of the right to love, the right to contraception, and the right to abortion.

The right of women to equal access to the professions and to promotion within them is also an issue socialists must support. However, the right to enter management and be promoted into higher executive positions raises a question of advancement of those serving the function of exploiters of the working class. Managerial women are truly "enemy sisters" and their demands for equal access to exploiting working women should be treated as equivalent to the demands of female career military or prison officers or officials to be promoted to generals or wardens on an equal basis with men. These are not issues that a truly socialist movement would be concerned about. Further, affirmative action for professionals largely operates to allow the female children of the petty bourgeois equal access to the relative privileges of that class. Even to the extent that it facilitates the upward mobility of working-class daughters, it does nothing for working-class women as a whole. Thus while a socialist women's movement has to endorse the right of petty bourgeois women to have careers equal to those of the men of their class, and for working-class daughters to have equal opportunities with middle-class sons and daughters, this is not a socialist issue and should not be a matter of priority. Priority must be given to matters that have the potential of advancing the *whole* class and not changing individual occupants of class positions.

(2) Unlike the dominant tendency of narrow feminism, a socialist movement for the liberation of women would not be anti-male, nor would it give the appearance of being antifamily. It would accept men as well as women as full participants in the movement, even while recognizing the usefulness of all-women organizations, study groups, consciousness raising groups, and so forth. Rather than holding out an anti-male and antifamily ideal, which tends to dictate a standard "feminist" life style, it would hold out the ideal of the right to choose one's own life style. The goals of a socialist women's movement would be to abolish the patriarchal structures of both the family and jobs so that, freed of the determination of those structures, women would be truly free to decide how much time and energy they wanted to give to children, to the home, to "career," to men, to themselves, and to other women.

Lesbianism is a right that a socialist women's movement must of course endorse, but it must be understood that this life style (unlike bisexuality) is in part based in the bitter experiences of women in their relationships with men. Whether or not women choose men as lovers, men are in fact not the real enemy. Further, alliance between the women's movement and working-class men is an essential precondition for the abolition of the patriarchal structures generated by capitalism. Therefore, the anti-male tendencies of the lesbian movement must be considered to be counterproductive and not progressive. A socialist movement must support one's *right* to one's own sexual preference, but it should not *celebrate* lesbianism, anti-male sentiments, or antifamily attitudes, especially in a world in which the vast majority of working-class women cannot relate to such issues.

(3) A socialist women's movement must focus on capitalism and its corollaries of imperialism and racism as the *primary* ways in which most women are oppressed. The vast majority of the world's women are most oppressed by being in subordinate ethnic groups that are the subject of racist humiliations, living in semicolonized countries brutalized by imperialism, or are subject to the daily oppression and humiliation of the working class, or in the case of many single mothers, subproletarian life. The primary goal of a socialist women's movement is then to carry the anticapitalist (and antiracist and antiimperialist) struggle to these women.

To raise the question of antagonism toward men of their class, nation, and ethnic group to the level of oppression by capitalism, racism, or imperialism, is to be divisive as well as scientifically inaccurate and politically incorrect. For narrow feminists going to minority or white working-class women with an essentially anti-male, antifamily program is to do the work of the bourgeoisie in hindering the development of a socialist (and antiracist) movement that unites oppressed women and men in an effective struggle against their common oppressor. Male Chauvinism within the working class and among minority men must be fought in a manner appropriate to contradictions among the people and effectively resolved in ways that strengthen the overall primary struggle (the classical film *Salt of the Earth* presents a good socialist model for dealing with such contradictions).

(4) A socialist women's movement must also raise the issues of the special oppression of women, especially of working-class and minority women. It must have as one of its primary focuses the organization and mobilization of women as part of the overall struggle against capitalism. It must continually be emphasized that women's special oppression (real sexism) as well as most of women's general oppression is a product of capitalism, and thus that the transformation of capitalism is a necessary condition for ending real sexism. To be effective in this task, it must pay special attention to the actual problems of women. Following in the footsteps of the traditional Marxist women's movements (such as those led by Clara Zetkin in Germany and Alexandra Kollentai in Russia), a socialist women's movement would *stress* such working-class issues as unionization of white collar, service, and textile workers (occupations that are predominantly female); equal pay for equal work; jobs for all that want to work; improvement in working conditions (including special protective legislation, which might well serve as the model for later advances by male workers); higher pay (which should come from profits rather than from male workers' wages); free, readily available, and quality day care (especially at the work place); support for the rights and improvement in the conditions of welfare mothers (40 percent of black families do not have an adult man present); and support for improvement in medical care for women and children.

It is a standard narrow feminist parody of Marxism to argue that Marxists feel that the "woman question" need not be given any special attention, either before or after the socialist revolution; since, the argument goes, capitalism produces the oppression of women, it will automatically disappear with capitalism. First, Marxists have always given considerable attention to the oppression of women. Women's associations were central institutions in the Chinese and Vietnamese Revolutions, both before and after the seizure of power. Kollentai's Women's Association played a leading role in winning support for the revolution among the peasants and minorities after 1917. The Leninist tradition throughout the West, including the United States, has consistently emphasized the special problems of women workers as well as stressed the importance of combating patriarchal structures and male chauvinism. No Marxist would ever argue that anything would automatically disappear or be resolved after a socialist revolution. What distinguishes Marxists from anarchists is the theory of the dictatorship of the proletariat. Marxists, unlike anarchists who have a much more romantic view of transformation, insist that wiping out the "muck of the ages" is a long, slow, hard process that perhaps will take generations to accomplish after the working class seizes power. The creation of a new type of person, without selfishness, white chauvinism, and male chauvinism, who relates to everyone as brothers and sisters and who feels quite comfortable about operating according to the principle "from each according to their ability, to each according to their needs," takes the active intervention of the proletarian state quite a time to create. Of course, male chauvinism will not automatically disappear with a socialist revolution, but the abolition of capitalism and its corollary of patriarchal structures is the necessary *precondition* for the abolition of male chauvinism. Without the abolition of the structures that continually reproduce male chauvinism, "fighting sexism" is like plowing the sea. All this is not to argue that nothing should be done about patriarchy or male chauvinism until after the revolution, no more than to argue that capitalism generates racism, poverty, or war instructs Marxists not to do anything about these until after the revolution. The revolutionary premise is that Marxists must take up the oppression of all segments of the people, put forth their demands, and lead their struggles in the here and now. Although small gains (minor reforms) can be won through solidarity, fundamental change is impossible without a revolution. Thus while a specific war might be ended (e.g., Vietnam), concrete improvements made in the condition of blacks (e.g., the Civil Rights Act of 1965, the integration of public accommodations), the living standards of the working class raised (as through the Social Security and Wagner Acts of the late 1930s), capitalism will continue to generate more wars, more racism, and more unemployment, poverty, and oppression of the working class. Likewise, minor reforms that improve the condition of women can be won, and should be fought for, in the here and now (affirmative action for professional women, the Equal Rights Amendment, abortion rights), but patriarchal structures and male chauvinist attitudes will continue to be reproduced (even if the locus of their reproduction is displaced from the family to the office) as long as capitalism exists.

What differentiates the reformist tradition from revolutionary Marxism is not whether to fight for reforms, or even whether or not it is felt that some progress can be made without a revolution, but the question of whether or not problems can be *fundamentally solved* piecemeal *within* the logic of the capitalist mode of production. To the extent that it addresses the question of long-term strategy at all (which, given its prevailing moralism, is seldom), the dominant tendency of narrow feminism seems to answer with the reformist tradition that sexism can in fact be overcome piecemeal within the capitalist mode of production. The Marxist women's movement, on the other hand, answers, no. A revolution is the necessary condition for the full liberation of women. And further, the commitment to making this revolution is not an abstract principle to be taken out for a parade on May Day, but rather the reality that Marxists must take to working-class and minority women as the answer to their daily felt oppressions.

REFERENCES

Beechey, Veronica. 1977. "Some Notes on Female Wage Labor in Capitalist Production." *Capital and Class* no. 3.

Benston, Margaret. 1969. "Towards a Political Economy of Women's Liberation." *Monthly Review* 21, 4:13-27.

Blumberg, Rae Lesser. 1979. *Stratification*. Dubuque, IA: William C. Brown.

Burris, Val. 1980. "The Dialectic of Women's Oppression: Notes on the Relation between Capitalism and Patriarchy." University of Oregon, mimeograph.

David, Margery, and M. Reich. 1972. "The Relationship between Sexism and Capitalism." In *The Capitalist System*, edited by Richard Edwards et al. Englewood Cliffs, NJ: Prentice Hall.

Delphy, Christine. 1977. *The Main Enemy: A Materialist Analysis of Women's Oppression*. London: WRRC Publications.

Dixon, Marlene. 1971. "Public Ideology and the Class Composition of the Women's Movement." *Berkeley Journal of Sociology* 16:149-67.

Draper, Hal, and A. Lipow. 1976. "Marxist Women vs. Bourgeois Feminism." *The Socialist Register*.

Edwards, Richard, M. Reich, and T. Weisskopf. 1972. *The Capitalist System*. Englewood Cliffs, NJ: Prentice Hall.

Eisenstein, Zillah, ed. 1979. *Capitalist Patriarchy and the Case of Socialist Feminism*. New York: Monthly Review Press.

Goldberg, Marilyn. 1972. "The Economic Exploitation of Women." In *The Capitalist System*, edited by R. Edwards et al. Englewood Cliffs, NJ: Prentice Hall.

Guettel, Charnie. 1974. *Marxism and Feminism*. Toronto: The Women's Press.

Harris, Marvin. 1977. *Cannibals and Kinds.* New York: Random House.

Hartmann, Heidi. 1976. "Capitalism, Patriarchy and Job Segregation by Sex." *Signs* 1, 3:773-6.

Humphries, Jane. 1979. "Class Struggle and the Persistence of the Working Class Family." *Cambridge Journal of Economics* 1, 3:241-58.

Kollentai, Allexandra. 1979. "The Social Basis of the Women Question." In *Selected Writings*, Allexandra Kollentai. London: Allison & Busby.

Leacock, Elinor, ed. 1979. *Women and Colonialism.* New York: Praeger.

———. 1981. *Beyond Male Dominance.* New York: Monthly Review Press.

Lenski, Gerhard, and J. Lenski. 1983. *Human Societies.* New York: McGraw-Hill.

Mackintosh, Maureen. 1977. "Reproduction and Patriarchy." *Capital Class* no 2: 119-27.

McDonough, Roisin, and R. Harrison. 1978. "Patriarchy and Relations of Production." In *Feminism and Materialism*, edited by Annette Kuhn and Ann Marie Wolpe. London: Routledge & Kegan Paul.

Meillassoux, Claude. 1975. *Femmes, greniers et capitaux.* Paris: Maspero.

Mitchell, Juliet. 1975. *Psychoanalysis and Feminism.* New York: Vintage.

Reich, Michael. 1971. "The Economics of Racism." In *Problems of Political Economy*, edited by David Gordon. Lexington, MA: D.C. Heath.

Rowntree, John, and M. Rowntree. 1970. "More on the Political Economy of Women's Liberation." *Monthly Review* 21, 8 (January):26-32.

Sacks, Karen. 1976. "Class Roots of Feminism." *Monthly Review*, February.

Szymanski, Albert. 1976. "The Socialization of Women's Oppression." *The Insurgent Sociologist* 2 (Winter):31-58.

———. 1977. "Male Gain from Sexual Discrimination." *Social Forces* 56, 2 (December):611-25.

10

Thinking About Social Class: Structure, Organization, and Consciousness

Scott G. McNall

Much time and energy has been devoted to describing the class structure of modern capitalist societies (Wright 1984, 1985; Meiksins 1986; McKenzie 1982; Oppenheimer 1985; Ehrenreich and Ehrenreich 1978). Boundary questions—about just how many classes there really are, or whether or not white collar workers occupy contradictory class locations, or whether or not members of the professional managerial classes are protocapitalists—are not significant in and of themselves. The participants in such debates are aware that such questions are directly related to political strategy and that this relationship is significant. If white collar service workers are proletarianized, then the potential for liaisons between the traditional and the new working classes is enhanced, and we should capitalize on this fact by pointing out the similarities in their positions.

Divisions have been drawn between classes with varying degrees of sophistication. Those working in a Marxist tradition have exhibited the greatest sensitivity, for they understand that the element of exploitation is key in deciding who is, and who is not, a member of each potential class formation. A class society by definition is one in which one group appropriates the surplus labor of another. Class conflict exists, and classes stand in opposition to one another because of exploitation.

However, we know that there is a great deal of diversity among those who sell their labor power. We know that people do not respond to exploitation in precisely the same way, even members of what we would think of as uniform class formations. And further-more, we are aware that many contemporary movements have been grounded in ethnicity or religion, as opposed to social class. It would seem, then, that the question we ought to ask has less to do with boundaries than with the conditions under which people recognize themselves as members of a class, and the conditions under which class movements are likely to succeed—a question that can help us arrive at a better understanding of the kind of political strategies called for. After all, our labels have little to do with how people actually define their life circumstances, or whether or not they mobilize. Classes, as Marx said, are created over time by human actors who define themselves in active opposition to other groups in the society. By implication, then, class cannot be defined in terms of occupational position or skills. Class is simultaneously structure, organization, and ideology. Let us examine in detail what this means, and its political implications.

DEFINING CLASS

How does a class become a class for itself?[1] In what is class consciousness rooted, and what role does it play in mobilizing people? We have come a long way since the days of the economic determin-ists, when class was seen as a simple reflection of one's economic position. E. P. Thompson in particular expanded our understanding of class formation. As he demonstrated in *The Making of the English Working Class*, classes are emergent.

> If we stop history at a given point, then there are no classes but simply a multitude of individuals with a multitude of experiences. But if we watch these men over an adequate period of social change, we observe patterns in their relationships, their ideas, and their institutions. Class is defined by men as they live their own history, and, in the end, this is its only definition [1963, p. 11].

A class, in Thompson's (1978, p. 295) view, is a "very loosely de-fined body of people who share the same categories of interests, social experiences, traditions, and value-systems, who have a *disposition to behave* as a class, to define themselves in their consciousness in relation to other groups of people in class ways." Class is defined in cultural terms and in opposition to other social groups. People must see and describe themselves as different. As Thompson further argues, through people's lived experiences, confrontations with the world at large and attempts to make sense out of those confrontations, classes emerge, and with them a willingness to act on the basis of class. "What we mean," he says, "is that changes take place within social beings, which give rise to changed *experience:* and this experience is *determining*, in the sense that it exerts pressures upon existent social consciousness, proposes new questions, and affords much of the material which the more elaborated intellectual exercises are about" (Thompson 1978, p. 8).

Thompson has been criticized on both empirical and theoretical grounds for his view of the process of class formation, and his idea about when the British working class came on the scene (Calhoun 1982; Hobsbawm 1984a). Two issues involved in this debate seem central for understanding class mobilization: the weight one gives to the rational class actor (agents) versus the social structure, and the extent to which one emphasizes cultural and ideological variables as opposed to economic ones.

The agency-structure debate has been pursued at length by Thompson in direct opposition to the ideas of Louis Althusser (1968, 1970) and Perry Anderson (1974, 1980). Briefly, Althusser, arguing from a structural position, rejected the notion of active human agents; people were simply the bearers of social structure. Anderson, in opposition to Thompson, said that modern history was best understood as the unfolding of the contradictions within society. If agents played a role, it was only with the rise of modern revolutionary movements. Thompson, in a pointed attack on the entire structuralist school, argued strongly for human agency; history *was* consciousness, *was* goal-directed actors pursuing their interests. Douglas Porpora (1985), in an attempt to resolve the debate, suggested that crises may be brought about, as Anderson claims, by structural contradictions in society, and that human agents may react to these changes, but in unpredictable ways. Although Porpora is correct in giving structure its due, it is important to consider how class conscious actors can generate within a system the very crises or contradictions that Anderson takes as given. This is one of the strengths of Thompson's position: he assumes that crises can be generated by active human agents. But even here a caveat is in order, for people's actions do not always produce the results they desired.

Craig Calhoun (1982) has also criticized Thompson for not being Marxist enough in his analysis of the formation of the British working class. He says that Thompson failed to deal with people's objective relationship to the means of production. Calhoun argues that radicalism, which Thompson attributed to the working class, was actually rooted in artisanal communities. This is not to reduce class to simple economic relations, but to argue (as I do) for an understanding of class as culture, structure, and social relationships. Calhoun's British artisans mobilized, not only because they understood that they must do so to protest the loss of a way of life, but because they belonged to true communities. To mobilize, "people must have strong emotional ties with each other, a faith in their strength, and an identification with the collectivity in which they are to act" (Calhoun 1982, p. 136). William G. Roy, in his summary of recent work on class conflict, notes how the traditional Marxian perspective has been altered in the work of such neo-Marxists as Calhoun.

> Neo-Marxists disagree with advocates of economic determinist versions of Marxism who assert that collective action is motivated by class-based interests. The historical record is too full of examples of collective action propelled by religious, ethnic, regional, nationalistic, and other cross-class relationships to sustain such an assertion. They alternatively propose that collective action is historically decisive to the extent that it is rooted in class relationships, which analytically links the causes and consequences of class action [1984, pp. 497-8].

Classes, then, can even affect the mode of production. The social relations of production (a part of the mode of production), and sometimes even the social forces of production are modified as a result of struggle. People may act to protect a way of life, a way of working and living. In organizing, in confronting the world in which they live, people develop class consciousness. Consciousness grows out of action. However, this consciousness is not created anew, but refined.

The importance of the lived experiences of people as the "material" out of which classes are constituted has been clearly demonstrated by, among others, Herbert Gutman (1973). Gutman points out that language, stories, and ideas of harmony and brotherhood make a people, and hence a class, unique. Ideology enters significantly into the formation of classes (see Sewell 1985 for a discussion of the "independent" structuring role of ideology). Ideologies are no more stagnant than any other part of social reality (Snow et al. 1986). As Ron Aminzade (1981) has shown in his study of French artisans, they, like Calhoun's English artisans, were a consistently radical force in preindustrial France precisely because of their noneconomic interests. These interests were expressed, argued over, sharpened and defined, and grew out of informal gatherings and associations. In short, worker capacity for political and economic mobilization stemmed from a way of life, embracing both economic position and ideas about such things as the work process and the nature of the family.

Now, if ideology is as central an element as material force in shaping class action, then it deserves as much attention in crafting political strategy as any other element. Moreover, we need to give our attention to those mechanisms in contemporary society that allow for the expression and mobilization of ideology, as well as those factors that inhibit it. Here I wish to emphasize the fact that in U.S. society one of the ways people have learned about the nature of their oppression and learned to articulate the values they wish to protect is through their participation in class organizations. In mobilizing, in trying to actually change the economic and political system, people create themselves as a class. Politics, broadly defined, is not secondary but central to the process of class formation in U.S. society. More specifically, political parties have often served as distinct class organizations.

Theda Skocpol (1980) has appropriately called our attention to U.S. political parties as a means through which contesting groups both express and attempt to act on the basis of class interests. She has been criticized (Levine 1985; Quadagno 1984), however, for ignoring social class and for failing to examine the means by which class contradictions become embedded in the modern state. Skocpol tends to see party and state as independent systems, and to see neither party nor state policy as the result of class struggle. I would argue that it is often via the political party that class contradictions become embedded within the state system. Class, party, and state are intimately linked. State structure and state policy are determined by the class contradictions embedded within them (Poulantzas, 1978). Among the Western industrialized countries, the political party has been, and can still be, a means for articulating and shaping class consciousness, which in turn forms the nature and structure of the modern state.

It would be foolish to suggest that U.S. political parties represent distinct social classes. Groups often compete for dominance within the party (in the case of the Democrats, unions, industrialists, and ethnic groups, to name but a few) in order to shape national or state policy. Much of the struggle between classes thus occurs as a result of their attempts to achieve hegemony within a party. The political process also masks class struggle. One could describe this process as a struggle over organizational capacities; in fact, as I will argue, the attempt of a class to create itself and to develop class consciousness is dependent in large part on its organizational capacities (Prezworski 1977). This position is not unlike that which Marx (1852/1919, p. 109) articulated in *The Eighteenth Brumaire:*

> In so far as millions of families live under economic conditions of existence that separate their mode of life, their interests, and their culture from other classes, and put them in hostile opposition to the latter, they form a class. In so far as there is merely a local interconnection among the small peasants, and the identity of their interests begets no unity, no national union, and no political organization, they do not form a class. They are consequently incapable of enforcing their class interest in their own name, whether through parliament or through convention.

A group's ability to become a class is affected by internal divisions, or structural capacities, and the overall nature of the class structure at any given historical moment. A diagram (Figure 10.1) clarifies the relationship between the variables. At any given time, the class structure of a society is made up of diverse economic locations or positions. Some people are white collar workers, some blue collar, others are managers and capitalists. Each of these groups possesses different structural capacities for mobilizing as a class, and these are intimately related to their organizational capacities. For instance, miners have traditionally had a high degree of interaction, have seen themselves as occupying a distinct position in society, and as a result have acted in concert. Many service workers, on the other hand, are widely separated from one another, do not live and work in the same communities, and tend not to act in unison. Furthermore, people's structural capacities might be affected by the fact that they are divided from one another by religion or ethnicity. Class consciousness, in turn, is determined by people's organizational and structural capacities, and their attempt to act as a class.

Class organizations loom large in this model as a factor, not only in shaping class consciousness, but in determining whether or not a class will be successful—become a class in and for itself. In this model there is no such thing as false consciousness. Structural conditions and class capacities combine in such a way as to produce strategies that may or may not be successful in shaping state policy. People may choose strategies that isolate them from other classes, mobilize powerful elites against them, or allow their movement to be defused at the ballot box by the dominant parties endorsing elements of their

Figure 10.1. Class Struggle and Class Formation

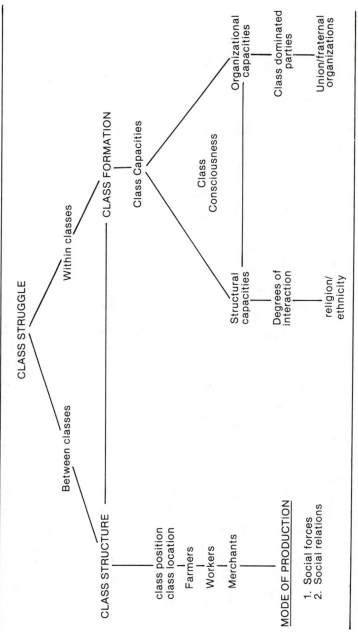

CLASS STRUGGLE

Between classes

Within classes

CLASS STRUCTURE

class position
class location
Farmers
Workers
Merchants

MODE OF PRODUCTION
1. Social forces
2. Social relations

CLASS FORMATION

Class Capacities

Structural
capacities

Class
Consciousness

Organizational
capacities

Degrees of
interaction

Class dominated
parties

religion/
ethnicity

Union/fraternal
organizations

Source: Inspired, in part, by Erik O. Wright (1978, p. 104).

platforms. In short, rational actors sometimes make strategic mistakes. (The conditions under which they might make fewer mistakes are treated below.)

Marxist class theory is an invaluable tool for understanding why class conflict exists, and for keeping our attention focused on the element of exploitation. However, traditional class theory has not helped us greatly to understand the processes by which people do or do not mobilize as classes, and why they succeed or fail to create themselves as autonomous classes. I believe that our understanding of the dynamics of class formation can be enhanced by conceptualizing class formation as a social movement.

CLASS MOVEMENTS AS SOCIAL MOVEMENTS

Sources of Solidarity and Bases of Mobilization

Something other than sheer economic distress must be invoked to account for the rise of class movements. Usually, challenges to traditional values and a sense of community cause people to take up arms. To take an example from nineteenth century U.S. history, hundreds of thousands of farmers in the North and South joined the Farmers' Alliance in an attempt to halt the growing power of corporate America over their lives. Steven Hahn (1983), in his study of those yeoman farmers from the Georgia upcountry who joined, said that it was because of changed social relations. Upcountry farmers, in Hahn's view, were reacting to a new law that would have required them, at considerable expense, to keep their livestock penned rather than roaming freely, as had been done for decades. This new law acted as a catalyst to "articulate and politicize the responses of petty producers to disruptive social change" (Hahn 1983, p. 271). The proposed changes in grazing rights led to the fear that their whole lives were being subordinated to the capitalist market system. The Farmers' Alliance, and then the Populist party which grew out of it, provided a means by which farmers could articulate threatened values and stand against challenges to their traditional ways of life. As with early nineteenth-century artisans on the continent, a threat to traditional value systems provided the impetus for mobilization.

The immediate social world of class actors plays a decisive role in determining whether they will become involved in a movement, ignore it, or abandon it at a later stage. As Mark Granovetter (1985, p. 487) has said, "Actors do not behave or decide as atoms outside a social context, nor do they adhere slavishly to a script written for them by the particular intersection of social categories they happen to occupy. Their attempts at purposive action are instead embedded in concrete, ongoing systems of relations." In the case of Hahn's Georgia yeomen, they abandoned the Farmers' Alliance because ties of kith and kin reasserted themselves when the movement foundered. It is something of a paradox, then, that although people may mobilize on the basis of traditional values and become radicalized as a result, often ties to local communities and age-old values can limit their possibilities. Sometimes people cannot transcend the localism that served to fire the original movement. In addition, as Mary Ann Clawson (1985, p. 674) has so ably demonstrated in her study of fraternal organizations at the turn of the century, a substantial number of people were and are embedded in organizations that act to "deconstruct class as a basis for organization, mobilization, and solidarity." To overcome such limiting contexts, people must be educated and must understand that they need to act as a *class*. How does this come about?

Strategy and Creative Escalation

One of the ways in which people learn to act in concert is through involvement in a social movement. The social or class movement serves several important functions. Movements help to translate grievances into a sense of injustice—a key element, as Barrington Moore (1978) noted, in sustaining mobilization. People must come to feel that traditional social rules have been violated, that injustices have been created, and that they can do something about it. A class movement, then, must possess an effective protest ideology, one that can explain past failure, current defeats, and provide hope for the future.

Though people come to a movement with definite expectations, they also develop new ones as a result of confronting the established political and economic order. Lawrence Goodwyn (1978) said that nineteenth-century U.S. farmers developed a counterideology as a result of their involvement in the Farmers' Alliance. That is, they met together, discussed their grievances, developed ideas about how to deal with their economic plight, and tried to put them into operation by forming economic cooperatives. Having formed cooperatives, they found merchants and bankers allied against them because their efforts threatened capital's control over labor power, marketing, and distribution systems. Farmers learned who their enemies were and what they were up against because they tried to change the system. In this century, coal miners who mobilized against owners and found themselves confronted with hired thugs protected by state and local governments, or even had public armies turned against them, learned that large capital and the state walked hand-in-hand.

The strategies that any given group of people use are seldom simple or limited to one technique, unless goals are very limited. For instance, a sit-down strike may be a means to achieve immediate wage concessions, but it will not be the means by which the working class comes to control the means of production. The history of groups moving toward dominance are replete with examples of first one, and then another strategy, as the group inches closer to its final purpose. In the late nineteenth century, U.S. cotton farmers found themselves facing ruin. The price of cotton had dropped to its lowest point since the Civil War, and many lived in conditions of debt peonage. Those farmers who composed the Texas Alliance first tried to work out simple trade agreements with local merchants; then, when the merchants would not cooperate, they tried to form their own stores, mills, and cotton gins. Finding themselves again challenged, they tried to market their cotton by themselves; that effort was followed by a joint-note program designed to free them from the lien system. They staged a boycott against the Jute Trust (those who produced the jute used to bag the raw cotton); and when that failed finally, they formed a political party (Barnes 1984, pp. 106-7).

There is an important relationship between strategy, creative escalation, learning, and success (Barnes 1984; McAdam 1983). Normally, it is the responsibility of the leadership of a social movement organization to promulgate an ideology that will explain failure or externalize blame (Barnes 1984, p. 98). That is, if a group is blocked in its attempts to win concessions as the result of a sit-down strike, or its withholding of rent payments or rioting, blame must be laid at the door of those the group is opposing: for example, the opposition had the support of the local police, or the "management" was negotiating in bad faith, or landlords do not care about people. If a strategy does not work, a group must move to another level to creatively escalate the battle. Doug McAdam (1983), in his analysis of the 1960s civil rights movement, described a process by which the leadership of these groups consciously adopted new strategies when morale appeared to be waning. There was a decision to stage protests in areas where the police were known for their violent behavior so that civil rights protestors and groups would gain national support, and so that they could make the implicit and explicit point that this was a racist society. The success of new strategies is highly dependent on learning, however. Members of groups must know and understand why an old strategy has failed, and why new ones must be employed.

Creative escalation has its risks; it can create schisms within an organization. In class movements, participants might not be willing to choose a revolutionary path if the struggle appears long and difficult, and if the results appear to be problematic. Without organized learning they might just as easily choose a reformist course. There is no magic formula, but one can say that strategies that are debated by the rank and file and are clearly understood by them are those likely to be supported. This is a major reason why political education has played such a prominent role among revolutionary cadres. The Vietcong, for instance, talked about the lessons to be learned from previous encounters, and these discussions served to cohere the group and boost morale.

Escalation also poses another type of threat to the organization. Escalation can cause powerful outside elites to mobilize against the group in question (Schwartz 1976). Elites, too, learn during an extended struggle (McAdam 1983). In the case of the civil rights movement, some southern law enforcement officials found that a strategy of violent response was counterproductive. Instead, they chose to adhere to the law and enforce it in a nondiscriminatory pattern. In short, they put the civil rights leaders in positions where they either acted peacefully, and hence defused the movement, or acted violently themselves and hence lost support they needed to gain concessions. A group must be in a position to choose courses of action that run the thin line between mobilizing powerful opposition groups and having their own movement die for a lack of forward movement. The importance of *both* organization and learning looms even larger when we consider the issue of the rational actor.

The Rational Class Actor:
Selective Incentives and Moral Suasion

The extreme position in the rational actor debate is taken by Mancur Olson who argued that there is little reason to expect political organizations, unions, or social movements to act on the basis of the specific interests of the individuals who make up the movement, or to have individuals act on the basis of the collective. On the contrary, "unless the number of individuals in a group is quite small, or unless there is coercion or some other specific device to make individuals act in their common interest, *rational self-interested individuals* will not act to achieve their common or group interests" (Olson 1965, p. 2). Were this true, there would be little reason to believe that people could constitute themselves and act as a class. Yet the perspective deserves examination rather than simple rejection.

Much of the controversy surrounding Olson's theory revolves around the issue of solidarity versus selective incentives (see Jenkins 1983 for a summary of the debates). Anthony Oberschall (1978), as well as John McCarthy and Mayer Zald (1973) have argued that one of the primary reasons people mobilize is to secure benefits made available to them by movement entrepreneurs, or benefits generated by the movement through political action. Bruce Fireman and William Gamson (1979, p. 10), in a spirited critique of this position, argued that although the "amount of resources at the discretion of potential constituents, the degree of previously existing organization among potential constituents . . . and—overall—the structure of the political economy constraining the mobilization and wielding of resources" are significant, the impact of these factors is often mitigated by the desire to achieve a collective good. In short, solidarity and moral vision count. Social movements, and again by implication class movements, must:

> offer the *collective incentives* of group solidarity and commitment to moral purpose. Group solidarity and purposive incentives are collective in that they entail the fusion of personal and collective interests. Movement supporters, like all socialized actors, act in terms of internalized values and sentiments as well as calculations of self-interest. The major task in mobilization, then, is to generate solidarity and moral commitment to the broad collectivities in whose name movements act [Jenkins 1983, pp. 537-8].

Bert Klandermans (1984) put the matter slightly differently. He, too, is uncomfortable with the strong version of Olson's argument. Klandermans found that people's willingness to participate in strikes depended, in large part, on their belief that other workers would participate, and that there was a reasonable chance of success. "Adequate diffusion of knowledge of the collective good is the cornerstone," said Klandermans, "of every mobilization campaign" (1984, p. 592).

John A. Hanningan (1985, p. 441), in his review of the work of Alain Touraine and Manuel Castells in social movement theory, also argued that selective incentives must "be buttressed by the collective incentives related to group solidarity and commitment to a moral purpose." More importantly, he noted that often these moral purposes, or collective agreements about means, grow out of involvement in the movement itself.

One must combine a rational-actor perspective with an understanding that people may join a movement for noninstrumental reasons, and also realize that an image of the collective good and solidarity can grow out of action. Of course there will be those who join a cause because they believe benefits will be forthcoming, and who readily exit when they are not. The longer people are in an organization and the tighter the networks that brought them together in the first place, the more probably they will come to identify with the collective and be willing to sacrifice short-term individual interests for the long-term gains of the group. People, then, can make rational decisions to participate in collective actions to produce collective goods from which they will benefit.

Yet another caveat concerning the rational-actor perspective must be introduced. Rational actions sometimes have unintended consequences, and what may be rational in the short term, whether for the individual or the class, may not be rational in the long run. Individually rational decisions may be a collective irrationality. Let us take an example to clarify the point. Calhoun (1982, p. 229), in his treatment of Marx's designation of the working class as potentially revolutionary, noted that Marx was correct to argue that only by behaving as a revolutionary class and acting in concert could working men and women achieve their goals. But, he says, Marx was wrong to assume that "class must supersede all other collectivities for the workers, and that those interests which they had in common as members of the working class must become their exclusive interests, and that, therefore, it was individually rational for each worker to participate in the collectively rational overthrow of capitalist domination by the working class." Calhoun argued that it was rational for the nineteenth-century British working class to choose options that produced immediate benefits. To the extent that workers, or any other group, had options other than engaging in pure class action—which could and did produce dire consequences—it was individually rational to pursue low-cost goals, even when the results did not advance the class as a whole (collectively irrational).

Speed of Movement Formation, Size, and Power

If mobilization for action is rapid, the organizational structures necessary for learning to occur are weak or absent. If a movement is large in size (which a class movement necessarily must be), learning is inhibited. Claus Offe (1985) has provided us with a detailed statement of the relationship between individual interests and the propensity of a group of people to mobilize and engage in prolonged action, which we will modify for our purposes. Offe developed his model on the basis of a discussion about unions, and argued that there was a contradictory relationship between the size of an organization and the power it has to affect the larger environment. That is, the greater the size of a group, the less the propensity for any given individual to be sufficiently motivated to sacrifice him/herself for the group's goals. In the case of a large union, a member might not see why it was in his/her direct interests (either economic, political, or organizational, in the sense that support would strengthen the organization and lend credibility to its demands) to act at the union's behest. For a union or any other form of class organization to be successful, people must be educated by the organization in the movement culture, and/or ideology, otherwise they are not likely to support its long-term goals and purposes. Likewise, if the time between recruitment and attempted mobilization is short, then the likelihood of a group's success is diminished because it will not have had time to develop a movement culture and/or members will not understand the organizational policies or tactics that lead to discipline. (As will be seen below in our discussion of Piven and Cloward, this means that although system crises may produce short-term gains, this very fact leads to demobilization.)

As Figure 10.2 indicates, there would be a direct and positive relationship between size and power were it not for the fact that size inevitably leads to a diversity of interests, which reduces the ability to motivate people for collective goals. (This is also true for speed of mobilization.) Here is where the boundary debates can assume importance: by isolating the common experiences of those who sell their labor power and identifying them to potential movement recruits so as to produce greater solidarity. Michael Schwartz (1976, p. 195) has recognized the paradox of size and power. "The group needs a larger membership to succeed; and at the same time, it needs success to grow." However, this process will unravel if the organization cannot solve people's grievances, and/or if it cannot educate members. Many would see the tendency toward bureaucracy or oligarchy as extraordinary and unfortunate. I see it as quite normal and potentially useful.

Figure 10.2. Bureaucratization and Mobilization in SMOS

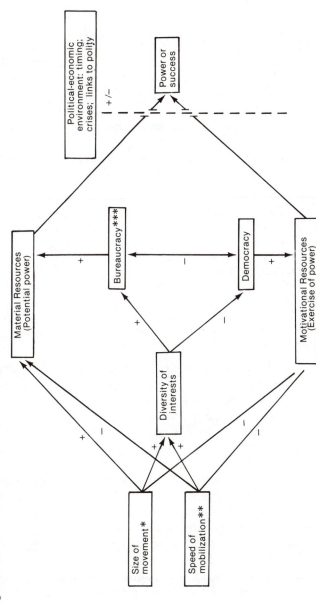

* Size of movement may result in acceptance, but is not necessarily linked to success. (Gamson, *The Strategy of Social Protest*).

** Both size and speed of mobilization contribute to the number of free riders. (Olson, *The Logic of Collective Action*).

*** Bureaucracy is not the inevitable result of size, if overall goals and values of actors are similar. (Jenkins, "Resource Mobilization Theory").

Source: Inspired in part from Claus Offe, *Disorganized Capitalism.* Cambridge: MIT Press, 1985, p. 187.

237

The Process of Bureaucratization

There has been a long-standing debate within the social movement literature between those who see bureaucratization as inevitable within a successful movement and those who do not. William Gamson (1975), for example, has suggested that groups with a well-developed division of labor and organizational structure are more capable of mobilizing constituencies with widely diverse interests. Charles Tilly and his associates (1975, 1978, 1981) have documented the shift from communally-based organizations, which engage in small-scale localized action, to those characteristic of modern industrialized societies in which centralized, formally organized movements dominate. Summarizing the position, J. Craig Jenkins has noted:

> The growth of industrial capitalism and the building of modern states destroyed the autonomy of small solidary groups and forced claimants to compete in a larger national political arena in which large numbers and bureaucratic structures were keys to success. Furthermore, urbanization and the growth of the mass media reduced the costs of large-scale mobilization, making bureaucratized associations more feasible. Finally, the institutionalization of liberal democracy, especially mass electoral participation, furnished an environment well suited to movement organizations that could mobilize large numbers of supporters [Jenkins 1983, p. 540].

Those who believe that bureaucratization is not inevitable usually point to small-scale personal growth movements, or note that the civil rights or women's movement grew without a centralized bureaucracy. But they miss an important point: even though different civil rights or women's movements pursued somewhat different specific goals and often represented different constituencies, they still shared a common set of assumptions.

As a group shifts from localized concerns—the very issues that may have drawn people into a movement—to national concerns, bureaucratization may be crucial to the group's success. If a group lacks a centralized hierarchy, or has few links between local leaders and organizations and the national unions or parties, the group's chances of success are lessened. Whether or not a group has a well-developed organizational structure from which to mount a prolonged assault strongly affects its chance of success and consequently the extent to which the organization can count on the loyalties of its members. Figure 10.3 summarizes the process by which a group achieves cohesion and outlines the processes that limit the possibility of success.

Figure 10.3. Learning, Interaction, and Success in SMOS

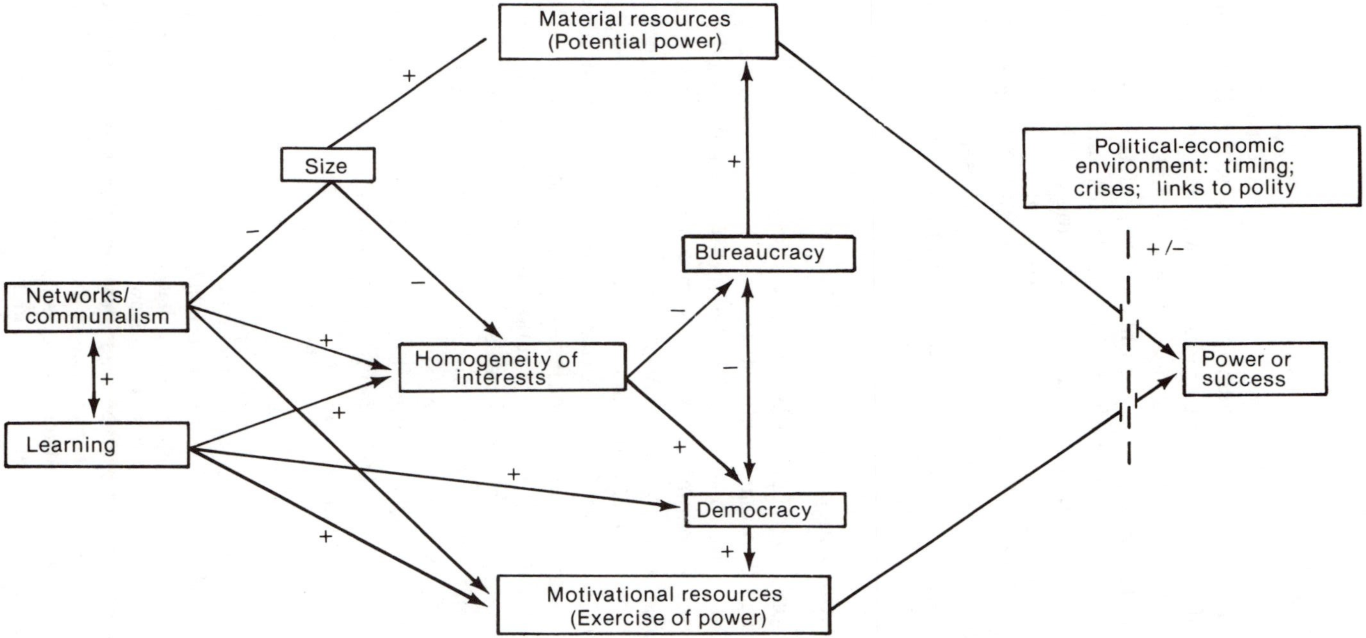

In Figure 10.2, we outlined a process whereby size leads to diversity of interests, which leads to bureaucratization (or conversely, negates full democratic decision making), which then enhances the ability of the leadership to mobilize members and gain power. In the case of a large union, this model suggests that in order to exercise or gain power, a group must command some needed material resource. Unions can threaten work stoppages, strikes, and boycotts, and their threats may be taken seriously, depending on the size of the organization and the extent to which the leadership is able to call the members out, keep them out, or prevent members from walking off the job. Individualistic interests must be suppressed in favor of an overarching goal, and this is usually accomplished through a centralized or bureaucratic organization.

Organization, Success, and System Crises

Gamson's (1975, 1980) detailed study of groups that have challenged the dominant political-economic order isolated several variables that relate to success. His dependent variable was defined as full acceptance, meaning that the social movement organization was recognized as a central political actor (it made a difference and its concerns were taken into account as, say, were the concerns of Jesse Jackson's Rainbow Coalition during the 1984 presidential campaign), and that it had actually achieved the goals and objectives laid out by the organization. First, he found that size was positively related to acceptance, though not necessarily to success. Therefore, dominant political parties will try to absorb renegade movements either by co-opting the leadership, or through the selective endorsement of the movement's less radical demands. Gamson argued that bureaucratization and centralization were central to success because most attempts to challenge a given order demand long and sustained political conflict.

> Bureaucratic organization provides a solution to the problem of combat readiness—a cadre of reliable workers with coordinated tasks. Its contribution to the management of internal dissent is minimal; bureaucratic groups are at least as likely to experience factional splits as nonbureaucratic ones. But their ability to act quickly also depends on their having solved the problem of internal division. Centralization of power is an organizational device for handling the problem of internal division and providing unity [Gamson 1975, pp. 107-8].

Gamson also found that bureaucratic organizations that narrowed their goals could offer members definite resources for participation and that were unruly during periods of political crisis were most likely to achieve success. Tilly (1978) and Skocpol (1979) have also demonstrated that a group's chances of success are substantially increased during periods of crisis, be they economic or political.

Can a class movement succeed only if it has at its core a solid organization of dedicated members ready to seize upon weaknesses in the political-economic order? Frances Fox Piven and Richard A. Cloward argue powerfully to the contrary. In their study, *Poor People's Movements* (1977), they have argued that movement organizers who concentrate on building an organization risk the very goals they hope to realize.

> During those brief periods in which people are aroused to indigna-
> tion, when they are prepared to defy the authorities to whom they
> ordinarily defer . . . those who call themselves leaders do not usually
> escalate the momentum of the people's protests. They do not be-
> cause they are preoccupied with trying to build and sustain embry-
> onic formal organizations in the sure conviction that these organiza-
> tions will enlarge and become powerful [Piven and Cloward, cited in
> Hobsbawm 1984b, p. 283].[2]

Piven and Cloward say, even more precisely, "The poor can create crises but cannot control the response to them" (cited in Hobsbawm 1984b, p. 286). According to them, poor people must seize whatever benefits the moment presents, not waste their precious time and resources building organizations that in the long run will be co-opted anyway. The U.S. political system is supposed to be particularly vulnerable to mass protests and demonstrations in which people settle for what they can get, rather than holding out for long-term "revolutionary" change. If there is a strategy for movements of the poor, it is to wait for and identify those situations in which the system is particularly vulnerable, when politicians will make concessions. (This is not a bad strategy, especially if the concessions relate to an increased share of the surplus value, which is what class conflict ultimately comes down to. It is a weak strategy if people cannot sustain continued demands.)

One of Piven and Cloward's main contributions has concerned how protest is institutionally determined and shaped—what is, and is not, permitted—and why the protest of the poor is often aimed at very specific targets rather than at what one might think of as social structures. It is aimed at specific people or companies because working men and women "do not experience monopoly capitalism" but the factory, the assembly line, the foreman, the pay packet, and the employer; the people on relief "do not experience American welfare policy," but shabby waiting rooms, overseers, case workers, and the dole (cited in Hobsbawm 1984b, p. 290). This is exactly why education through action, guided by an organization, is so important.

As Eric Hobsbawm (1984b) has pointed out in his masterful summary and critique of Piven and Cloward that what "the situation permits protestors to do depends on how the protesting groups have organized their everyday lives and labor" (1984b, p. 290). The unorganized poor *can* withhold their support from the system, refuse collaboration, and rebel "against the rules and authorities associated with everyday activities" (p. 290). According to Piven and Cloward, this localized protest is the most effective. But as Hobsbawm correctly emphasizes, mass protest cannot be an end in itself. Labor unionization or organization in the United States developed *out of* the mass protests and mobilizations of relatively unorganized workers. Piven and Cloward are right to criticize organizing efforts that get in the way of mobilization, but they are mistaken in arguing that lasting gains can be achieved without organization. If unionization occurred because of mass protests, workers made gains in the years that followed, not because they disbanded, but because there were organizations that represented their interests. Organizations sustain people's efforts to change their lives.

I agree with Hobsbawm that the poor, "indeed, any subaltern group, become a subject rather than an object of history only through formalized collectivities" (1984b, p. 293). Change does not occur through blind reaction—challenging the system to see how elites respond—but through organized efforts (see Traugott 1985 for a discussion of the importance of organizations in crystallizing and mobilizing class sentiment). Organizations grounded in people's own experiences, that represent peoples' interests, have the greatest likelihood of wringing concessions from the state and winning control of the political and economic system. Organized groups, whether of the poor or the middle classes, have always posed the greatest threat to state power. It is organized protest, today as in the past, that authorities seek to prevent.

POLITICAL IMPLICATIONS

I have said that class must be conceptualized as structure, ideology, and organization. Ideology is an essential element out of which class is created. It is just as important as structure or economic position. For a class to realize itself as a class, it must organize, and the struggle between classes begins at this level. If we see class and class struggle as a dynamic process involving these central elements, we can see that the battle for class hegemony must take place on several fronts simultaneously. A class must come to be possessed of a unique ideology and an autonomous organization.

The issue of structure, of whether or not a class can be composed of those occupying unique or very diverse positions in the division of labor, is a more thorny problem. Clearly the dividing line between exploiters and exploited is an important one, but the fact remains that those who sell their labor power, whether factory workers, teachers, or members of a professional managerial class, experience and react very differently to the capitalist system. We might argue that their interests are basically the same, but it remains for people to act in concert before they become a class.

Class, as I have argued, is not static; it grows out of a confrontation with other classes, with "the system." One of the ways in which those who occupy different economic positions in the class structure can become members of a similar class is by developing a comparable ideology and by forging organizational alliances that act in the interests of all wage laborers. This does not happen by magic and it does not happened overnight. If we see the formation of a class as similar to the formation and development of a social movement, we see that a uniform ideology develops from a sustained attempt at change, and that people come to act in the name of the collective rather than for themselves *through the movement.* People must learn to speak and act as one, and this comes about by creatively escalating the battle. Here, class organizations loom large: they are the means by which information is exchanged and new strategies are developed. A centralized, bureaucratic organization is essential for accomplishing these purposes. Ideally, the centralized bureaucracy will be composed of "organic" intellectuals who act in the name of the class and who have well-developed mechanisms for continuing the education of the class.

NOTES

1. Portions of the following discussion on social class formation come from Scott G. McNall, *The Road to Rebellion* (Chicago: University of Chicago Press, forthcoming). See, in particular, chapter 1.

2. My analysis of Piven and Cloward's argument follows that of Hobsbawm (1984b).

REFERENCES

Althusser, Louis. 1970. *For Marx*. New York: Vintage.

Althusser, Louis, and Etienne Balibar. 1968. *Rading Capital*. London: New Left Books.

Aminzade, Ron. 1981. *Class, Politics, and Early Industrial Capitalism: A Study of Mid-Nineteenth Century Toulouse, France*. Albany: State University of New York Press.

Anderson, Perry. 1974. *Passages from Antiquity to Feudalism*. London: New Left Books.

————. 1980. *Arguments within English Marxism*. London: New Left Books.

Barnes, Donna. 1984. *Farmers in Rebellion: The Rise and Fall of the Southern Farmers' Alliance and People's Party in Texas*. Austin: University of Texas Press.

Calhoun, Craig. 1982. *The Question of Class Struggle: Social Foundations of Popular Radicalism during the Industrial Revolution*. Chicago: University of Chicago Press.

Clawson, Mary Ann. 1985. "Fraternal Orders and Class Formation in the Nineteenth-Century United States." *Comparative Studies in Society and History* 27:672-95.

Ehrenreich, John, and Barbara Ehrenreich. 1978. "The Professional Managerial Class." In *Between Labour and Capital*, edited by Pat Walker, pp. 5-45. Montreal: Black Rose Books.

Fireman, Bruce, and William Gamson. 1979. "Utilitarian Logic in the Resource Mobilization Perspective." In *The Dynamics of Social Movements*, edited by John D. McCarthy and Mayer N. Zald, pp. 8-44. Cambridge: Winthrop.

Gamson, William. 1975. *The Strategy of Social Protest*. Homewood, IL: Dorsey.

————. 1980. "Understanding the Careers of Challenging Groups: A Comment on Goldstone." *American Journal of Sociology* 85:1043-60.

Goodwyn, Lawrence. 1978. *The Populist Moment*. New York: Oxford University Press.

Granovetter, Mark. 1985. "Economic Action and Social Structure: The Problem of Embeddedness." *American Journal of Sociology* 91:481-510.

Gutman, Herbert. 1973. "Work, Culture, and Society in Industrializing America, 1815-1919." *American Historical Review* 78:531-88.

Hahn, Steven. 1983. *The Roots of Southern Populism: Yeoman Farmers and Transformation of the Georgia Upcountry, 1850-1890*. New York: Oxford University Press.

Hannigan, John A. 1985. "Alain Touraine, Manuel Castells and Social Movement Theory: A Critical Appraisal." *The Sociological Quarterly* 26:435-54.

Hobsbawm, Eric. 1984a. "The Making of the Working Class, 1870-1914." In *Workers: Worlds of Labor*, Hobsbawm, pp. 194-213. New York: Pantheon.

————. 1984b. "Should Poor People Organize." In *Workers: Worlds of Labor*, Hobsbawm, pp. 282-96. New York: Pantheon.

Jenkins, J. Craig. 1983. "Resource Mobilization Theory and the Study of Social Movements." *Annual Review of Sociology* 4:527-53.

Klandermans, Bert. 1984. "Social-Psychological Expansions of Resource Mobilization Theory." *American Sociological Review* 48:735-53.

Levine, Rhonda. 1985. "Marxism, Sociology, and Neo-Marxist Theories of the State." *Current Perspectives in Social Theory* 6:149-68.

Marx, Karl. 1852/1919. *The Eighteenth Brumaire of Louis Bonaparte.* Chicago: Charles Kerr.

McAdam, Doug. 1983. "Tactical Innovation and the Pace of Insurgency." *American Sociological Review* 48:735-53.

McCarthy, John D., and Mayer N. Zald. 1973. *The Trend of Social Movements.* New York: General Learning.

McKenzie, Gavin. 1982. "Class Boundaries and the Labour Process." In *Social Class and the Division of Labour,* edited by Anthony Giddens and Gavin McKenzie. New York: Cambridge University Press.

Meiksins, Peter. 1986. "Beyond the Boundary Question." *New Left Review* 157: 101-20.

Moore, Barrington. 1978. *Injustice: The Social Basis of Obedience and Revolt.* White Plains, NY: Sharpe.

Oberschall, Anthony. 1978. "Theories of Social Conflict." *Annual Review of Sociology* 4:291-315.

Offe, Claus. 1985. *Disorganized Capitalism.* Cambridge: Massachusetts Institute of Technology Press.

Olson, Mancur. 1965. *The Logic of Collective Action: Public Goods and the Theory of Groups.* Cambridge, MA: Harvard University Press.

Oppenheimer, Martin. 1985. *White Collar Proletariat.* New York: Monthly Review Press.

Piven, Frances Fox, and Richard A. Cloward. 1977. *Poor People's Movements: Why They Succeed, How They Fail.* New York: Pantheon.

Porpora, Douglas V. 1985. "The Role of Agency in History: The Althusser-Thompson-Anderson Debate." *Current Perspectives in Social Theory* 6: 219-41.

Prezworski, Adam. 1977. "The Process of Class Formation from Karl Kautsky's *The Class Struggle* to Recent Debates." *Politics and Society* 7:64-85.

Quadagno, Jill. 1984. "Welfare Capitalism and the Social Security Act of 1935." *American Sociological Review* 49:632-47.

Roy, William G. 1984. "Class Conflict and Social Change in Historical Perspective." *Annual Review of Sociology* 10:483-506.

Schwartz, Michael. 1976. *Radical Protest and Social Structure: The Southern Farmers' Alliance and Cotton Tenancy, 1880-1890.* New York: Academic.

Sewell, William H., Jr. 1985. "Ideologies and Social Revolutions: Reflections on the French Case." *The Journal of Modern History* 57:57-85.

Skocpol, Theda. 1979. *States and Revolutions.* New York: Cambridge University Press.

———. 1980. "Political Response to Capitalist Crisis: Neo-Marxist Theories of the State and the Case of the New Deal." *Politics and Society* 10:155-202.

Snow, David, E. Burke Rochford, Jr., Steven K. Worden, and Robert D. Benford. 1986. "Frame Alignment and Mobilization." *American Sociological Review* 48:735-53.

Thompson, E. P. 1963. *The Making of the English Working Class.* New York: Vintage.

———. 1978. *The Poverty of Theory.* New York: Monthly Review Press.

Tilly, Charles. 1978. *From Mobilization to Revolution.* Reading, MA: Addison-Wesley.

Tilly, Charles, and Louise Tilly. 1981. *Collective Action and Class Conflict.* Beverly Hills: Sage.

Tilly, Charles, Louise Tilly, and R. Tilly. 1975. *The Rebellious Century*. Cambridge, MA: Harvard University Press.

Wright, Erik O. 1978. *Class, Crisis and the State*. London: New Left Books.

———. 1984. "A General Framework for the Analysis of Class Structure." *Politics and Society* 13:383-423.

———. 1985. *Classes*. London: Verso Books.

Selected Bibliography

Abercrombie, Nicholas and John Urry. 1983. *Capital, Labor, and the Middle Classes.* London: Allen and Unwin.

Aminzade, Ron. 1981. *Class, Politics, and Early Industrial Capitalism.* Albany: State University of New York Press.

Anderson, Perry. 1976. *Considerations on Western Marxism.* London: New Left Books.

Bluestone, Barry, and Bennett Harrison. 1982. *The Deindustrialization of America.* New York: Basic Books.

Braverman, Harry. 1974. *Labor and Monopoly Capital.* New York: Monthly Review Press.

Calhoun, Craig. 1982. *The Question of Class Struggle.* Chicago: University of Chicago Press.

Carchedi, Guglielmo. 1977. *On the Economic Identification of Social Classes.* London: Routledge & Kegan Paul.

Chase-Dunn, Christopher, ed. 1982. *Socialist States in the World-Economy.* Beverly Hills: Sage.

Eisenstein, Zillah, ed. 1979. *Capitalist Patriarchy and the Case of Socialist Feminism.* New York: Monthly Review Press.

Evans, Peter, Dietrich Rueschemeyer, and Theda Skocpol, eds. 1985. *Bringing the State Back In.* New York: Cambridge University Press.

Geschwender, James A. 1978. *Racial Stratification in America.* Dubuque, IA: William C. Brown.

Gorz, André. 1980. *Farewell to the Working Class.* Boston: South End.

Hall, Peter, and Ann Markusen, eds. 1985. *Silicon Landscapes.* Boston: Allen and Unwin.

Harvey, David. 1982. *The Limits of Capital.* Chicago: University of Chicago Press.

Hopkins, Terrence K., Immanuel Wallerstein, and associates. 1982. *World System Analysis: Theory and Methodology.* Beverly Hills: Sage.

Jessop, Bob, 1982. *The Capitalist State.* New York: New York University Press.

Leacock, Elinor. 1981. *Beyond Male Dominance.* New York: Monthly Review Press.

Lembcke, Jerry, and William Tattam. 1984. *One Union in Wood.* New York: International Publishers.

Miliband, Ralph. 1973. *The State in Capitalist Society.* London: Quartet Books.

Offe, Claus. 1985. *Disorganized Capitalism.* Cambridge: Massachusetts Institute of Technology Press.

Oppenheimer, Martin. 1985. *White Collar Proletariat.* New York: Monthly Review Press.

Peet, Richard. 1977. *Radical Geography*. Chicago: Maaroufa.

Poulantzas, Nicos. 1973. *Classes in Contemporary Capitalism*. London: New Left Books.

————. 1978. *State, Power, Socialism*. London: New Left Books.

Roemer, John. *A General Theory of Exploitation and Class*. Cambridge: Harvard University Press.

Szymanski, Al. 1978. *The Capitalist State and the Politics of Class*. Cambridge: Winthrop Publishers.

Wallerstein, Immanuel. 1979. *The Capitalist World-Economy*. Cambridge: Cambridge University Press.

————. 1983. *Historical Capitalism*. London: New Left Books.

Wood, Ellen Meiksins. 1986. *The Retreat From Class*. London: Verso Books.

Wright, Erik Olin. 1985. *Classes*. London: Verso Books.

Index

List of Contributors

Alex Dupuy is associate professor of sociology and Afro-American studies and chair of the Afro-American Studies Program at Wesleyan University.

James A. Geschwender is professor of sociology and chair of the Sociology Department at the State University of New York at Binghamton.

Jerry Lembcke is assistant professor of sociology at Lawrence University.

Rhonda F. Levine is assistant professor of sociology at Colgate University.

Scott G. McNall is professor of sociology at the University of Kansas.

Peter Meiksins is assistant professor of sociology at the State University of New York at Geneseo.

Richard Peet is professor of geography at the Graduate School of Geography, Clark University.

Peter Seybold is administrative associate in the Labor Studies Division, Indiana University.

Albert Szymanski was professor of sociology at the University of Oregon, 1973–85.

Barry Truchil is associate professor of sociology at Rider College.